TRANSACTIONS

of the

American Philosophical Society

Held at Philadelphia for Promoting Useful Knowledge

VOLUME 79, Part 4

Octavian's Campsite Memorial for the Actian War

William M. Murray
and
Photios M. Petsas

THE AMERICAN PHILOSOPHICAL SOCIETY

Independence Square, Philadelphia

1989

Library of Congress Catalog
Card Number 89-84932
International Standard Book Number 0-87169-794-7
US ISSN 0065-9746

TABLE OF CONTENTS

List of Tables v

List of Figures v

Preface ix

I: Introduction (William M. Murray)................................. 1

II: Octavian's Campsite Memorial for the Actian War
  (William M. Murray and Photios M. Petsas)
1. The Ancient Testimonia... 9
2. The Rediscovery of the Monument 12
3. The Survey of 1986 22
  a. The Sockets and Their Importance 34
  b. The Sockets: Methodology of Measurement................... 42
  c. The Sockets: Catalog of Dimensions......................... 45
    1.) Remarks on the Catalog of Dimensions ,................. 49
  d. The Profiles of the Sockets 51
  e. The Original Number of Rams on the Campsite
    Memorial.. 55
  f. The Sequence of Construction 57
  g. The Photo Mosaic 60
  h. The Dedicatory Inscription 62
    1.) The Dedication Text from Octavian's Campsite
      Memorial 76
4. The Stoa 77
5. A Reconsideration of the Campsite Memorial.................... 85

III: The Relative Sizes of Ancient Warship Bows
  (William M. Murray)
1. The Problem of Ancient Ship Classes........................... 95
2. The Ship Classes of the Sockets 99
  a. The Significance of the Profiles 100
  b. The Weight of the Athlit Ram............................... 103
  c. The *Anaglypha Traiani* and the Sizes of Suspended Rams   105

　　　1.) The Rams of the Roman Rostra 109
　　　2.) The Sizes of Suspended Rams........................... 110
　　d. A Tentative Sequence of Ship Classes...................... 113

IV: The Significance of the Campsite Memorial's Design
(William M. Murray).. 115
　1. The Successive Phases of the Rostra........................... 117
　2. Octavian's Own Rostra Displays 121

V: Nikopolis, the First *Aktia* and the Dedication of the
　　Campsite Memorial (William M. Murray) 125

VI: New Light on the Battle of Actium (William M. Murray)
　1. The Kromayer-Tarn Debate 131
　　　a. Antony's Battle Strategy..................................... 132
　　　b. Numbers of Combatants..................................... 133
　　　c. The Use of Fire 134
　　　d. Degree of Destruction.. 135
　　　e. Military Significance of the Battle........................... 136
　2. The Evidence from the Campsite Memorial..................... 137
　　　a. The Numbers of Captured and Destroyed Ships........... 137
　　　b. The Composition of Antony's and Cleopatra's Fleet....... 142
　　　c. The "Heavy Fleet vs. Light Fleet" Tradition of the Battle 143

VII: Conclusion (William M. Murray) 153

Bibliography 157

Indices
　Index of Modern Authors... 163
　General Index 165
　Index of Ancient Citations 170

LIST OF TABLES

Table 1: Measurement Definitions 41
Table 2: Measurement Procedures 43
Table 3: "y to y" Measurements 57
Table 4: The Fragments as Numbered by Gagé 62
Table 5: Sizes and Locations of Fragments 73
Table 6: Blocks Reported by Rhomaios in 1922 75

LIST OF FIGURES

Fig. 1: Map showing Actium and Nikopolis. xi
Fig. 2: View toward Michalitsi from the south. 13
Fig. 3: 1913 view of Philadelpheus' "temple."
After PHILADELPHEUS 1913, p. 88. 13
Fig. 4: Corinthian capital found in the 1913 excavations. After
PHILADELPHEUS 1913, p. 89. 14
Fig. 5: Rostral monument(?) depicted on a denarius minted in 16
B.C. by C. Antistius Vetus (cf. SUTHERLAND 1984, #365–66,
Plate 7). Photo courtesy of the Staatliche Münzsammlun-
gen, Munich. 17
Fig. 6: Stylobate of the stoa from the west. 20
Fig. 7: Stylobate of the stoa from the east. 20
Fig. 8a, b: Cuttings in the stylobate's surface. 22
Fig. 9: Site plan of the Campsite Memorial. 24
Fig. 10: Site from the east. 26
Fig. 11: Site from the west. 27
Fig. 12: Western retaining wall. 27
Fig. 13: Southern retaining wall from the east. 28
Fig. 14: Concrete bedding beneath the western retaining wall. ... 28
Fig. 15: Concrete bedding at the east end of the southern retaining
wall. 30
Fig. 16: Concrete bedding behind the southern retaining wall at
the southwest corner; view from the southwest. 30

Fig. 17: Photo mosaic; sockets [1] to [7]............................... 31
Fig. 18: Photo mosaic; sockets [8] to [17]. 32
Fig. 19: Photo mosaic; sockets [18] to [E]. 33
Fig. 20: Drawings of sockets [1] to [8]............................... 35
Fig. 21: Drawings of sockets [9] to [16]. 36
Fig. 22: Drawings of sockets [17] to [E] plus hypothetical sockets
         for the Athlit, *Olympias* (trireme replica), and Bremerhaven
         rams (Rams 1–3). 37
Fig. 23: Cross-section of the Athlit ram, looking aft; taken along
         the "A" line (cf. Fig. 25). 38
Fig. 24: Measurements and profiles taken on an average socket .. 39
Fig. 25: The Athlit ram; top and side views. 40
Fig. 26: The "Measuring Device" in use. 45
Fig. 27: Profiles of sockets [2] to [8]. 52
Fig. 28: Profiles of sockets [9] to [18]. 53
Fig. 29: Profiles of sockets [A] to [E]. 54
Fig. 30: Clamp cutting in the stem block of socket [B]. 59
Fig. 31: Laying out the camera points with the string triangle. ... 60
Fig. 32: Rhomaios' drawing of the inscription blocks. After
         RHOMAIOS 1922, Fig. 1 (p. 1)................................. 63
Fig. 33: Inscription block #G27 (uninscribed block). 63
Fig. 34: Inscription block #G2 (F·VICT). 65
Fig. 35: Inscription block #G11 (O·Q)............................... 65
Fig. 36: Inscription block #G15 (BLIC). 66
Fig. 37: Inscription block #19 (T·IN·HAC)........................... 66
Fig. 38: Inscription block #G17 (TA·C). 67
Fig. 39: Inscription block #G13 (C·REGI). 67
Fig. 40: Inscription block #G6 (VM·PA). 68
Fig. 41: Inscription block #G22 (QVIBV). 68
Fig. 42: Inscription block #G20 (TVNO). 69
Fig. 43: Inscription block #G28 (E[·]P)............................. 69
Fig. 44: Inscription block #G21 (ASTRA). 70
Fig. 45: Inscription block #G24 (RT). 70
Fig. 46: Inscription block #G23 (SEQ)............................... 71
Fig. 47: Column drum showing stucco and flutes. 79
Fig. 48: Column drum showing no flutes............................. 79
Fig. 49: Column base. 80
Fig. 50: Fragment of a lion's head water spout from the roof. 81
Fig. 51: Marble moldings from the stoa............................... 81
Fig. 52: Blocks of the stoa's stylobate uncovered in 1974; restored
         view. 82
Fig. 53: View from Octavian's campsite looking toward the
         southeast. 87
Fig. 54: Restored general view of the monument from the southeast
         (drawing by Richard A. Scott). 88

Fig. 55: Restored view of the monument from the gap between
         sockets [18] and [A] (drawing by Richard A. Scott).   89
Fig. 56: Naval equipment depicted on the triumphal arch at
         Orange (France); northeast panel. Adapted from AMY
         1967, Pl. 24.   94
Fig. 57: Rams depicted on the triumphal arch at Orange (France).
         Adapted from AMY 1967, Pl. 50.   102
Fig. 58: The Bremerhaven ram. Photo courtesy of the Deutsches
         Schiffahrtsmuseum, Bremerhaven.   104
Fig. 59: *Anaglypha Traiani* relief, right panel (bottom), left panel
         (top). After THÉDENAT 1896, Figs. 3261 (p. 1298) and 3267
         (p. 1305).   106
Fig. 60: The *Rostra Augusti* on the *Anaglypha Traiani* (right panel).
         Photo courtesy of the German Archaeological Institute in
         Rome.   107
Fig. 61: The *Rostra Aedis Divi Iulii* on the *Anaglypha Traiani* (left
         panel). Photo courtesy of the German Archaeological In-
         stitute in Rome.   108
Fig. 62: Hadrianic coin (cf. MATTINGLY 1936, p. 433, #1309–10, and
         Plate 81, 10) showing the *Rostra Aedis Divi Iulii*. After THÉD-
         ENAT 1896, Fig. 3266 (p. 1305).   110
Fig. 63: The *columna rostrata* of Octavian depicted on a denarius,
         29–27 B.C. (cf. SUTHERLAND 1984, p. 60, #271, and Plate
         5). Photo courtesy of the American Numismatic Society,
         New York.   112
Fig. 64: The equestrian statue of Octavian (?) *in rostris* depicted on
         a denarius minted by Cossus Cornelius Lentulus in 12 B.C.
         (cf. SUTHERLAND 1984, p. 73, #412, and Plate 7). Photo
         courtesy of the American Numismatic Society, New
         York.   112
Fig. 65: The "Antonian Rostra" depicted on a denarius minted by
         Lollius Palicanus in 45 B.C. (cf. CRAWFORD 1974, Vol. I, pp.
         482–83, #473/1). Photo courtesy of the American Numis-
         matic Society, New York.   112
Fig. 66: The *Rostra Augusti* depicted on a denarius minted by C.
         Sulpicius Platorinus in 13 B.C. (cf. SUTHERLAND 1984, p.
         73, #406–407). After ZANKER 1988, Fig. 168b (p. 216).   123

For
Suzanne
and
Katie

PREFACE

On October 8, 1980, Mr. Dionysios Livanos (then Secretary General of the Greek Ministry of Transport and Communications) reported that shipwrecks from the Battle of Actium had been located at Actium near the entrance to the Ambracian Gulf. Understandably, the news spread quickly throughout the Greek press and was reported the following day by Paul Anastasi in the *New York Times*.[1] Such was the enthusiasm in Greece which greeted this announcement that Prime Minister Georgios Rallis pledged his government's support for a joint Greek-American project to salvage the vessels. Although the story eventually turned out to be false, the degree of interest stirred up by the announcement is remarkable and reveals the abiding notoriety of Antony, Cleopatra and the Battle of Actium.

This book presents what could not be produced in 1980—tangible evidence from warships that participated in the Battle of Actium. Although, this time, we do not claim to have found any actual ships, we have recovered direct evidence from the bows of Antony's largest ships. This evidence is preserved in one of the most important monuments of the Augustan Age—a memorial built on the site of Octavian's personal camp to commemorate the victory over Antony and Cleopatra in the Actian War. It is our hope that the implications of this monument and the information that it preserves will be carefully debated in the years to come.

For this reason, we have chosen to err on the side of expediency rather than caution in presenting our results. Considering the long history of this monument (which was originally discovered in 1913), and the fact

---

[1] Paul Anastasi, "Greece Reports Finding Wrecks of Roman Ships," *The New York Times,* 9 October 1980, p. 7, cols. 1–3. The report was extremely definite concerning the magnitude of the discovery: According to Mr. Livanos (col. 1), "Any diver with a mask can see the shipwrecks. . . Some are in very good condition." He also added that Cleopatra's treasure galley has been found and concluded (col. 2): "Therefore, the find is not only of historic, archaeological and romantic value, but also literally a treasure." The authors thank Michael Katsev for sending them a copy of this article as well as copies of the following ones, appearing shortly after the *New York Times* piece, which document the announcement of this supposed "discovery": "Ancient Roman ships to be raised," *Athens News,* 10 October 1980; "Antonios kai Kleopatra enantion Oktaviou meta 2,000 chronia," ("Antony and Cleopatra against Octavian after 2,000 years") *To Bema,* 15 November 1980, p. 9, cols. 1–5; "Nauagia apo te naumachia tou Aktiou," ("Shipwrecks from the Battle of Actium") *Nautike Epitheoresis,* November-December (1980) p. 437, cols. 1–2.

that few scholars know of its existence, we believe it important to publish the results of our investigations quickly. This seemed preferable to a comprehensive consideration of the monument in light of every study dealing with Augustus, Augustan architecture or the Battle of Actium. Since the literature on these subjects is vast, complex and growing at a fast pace, we thought it best to publish our results quickly so that others might debate the evidence. We therefore offer this report in a spirit of humility, understanding that we are just initiating the long process of analysis rather than composing the definitive work on the subject.

Over the years that we have worked singly or together at the site, our work has received the generous support of the Athens Archaeological Society, the American Philosophical Society, the University of South Florida, the Demos of Preveza, and the American School of Classical Studies at Athens.[2] This book would not have been possible without their help. We express here our sincere thanks to the Greek Archaeological Service for permission to work at the site; to E. Linder and J. Ringel for permission to study the Athlit ram; to J.S. Morrison and J.F. Coates for providing us with specific details about the trireme replica *Olympias*; to D. Ellmers for providing photos, measurements and a cross-section of the Bremerhaven ram; and to J.R. Steffy for the original pencil drawings behind our Figs. 23 and 25. We also record our sincere thanks and appreciation to all those, too numerous to mention here, who have facilitated our research in Greece and America.

During the process of composition, certain friends and colleagues have helped by commenting on various drafts of this book. We especially thank J.R. Steffy, L. Casson, F.S. Kleiner, R.S. Carter, and an anonymous reader who reviewed the manuscript for J.S. Brill. Although we obviously take full responsibility for those errors that remain in the text, it is certain that many errors have been avoided by their thoughtful comments. One must not construe this help, however, as an indication of their support for every opinion that appears in this book. All errors in judgment and method remain the responsibility of the authors.

And last, but not least, we thank our wives, without whose support and understanding, neither the research nor the book would ever have been completed. At various times, they endured our long days in the field and tolerated our lengthy discussions about the site during the hot summers of 1986, 1987 and 1988. They also tolerated our absence (both mental and physical) while the manuscript was being written, the plans drawn and the photos printed. For numerous reasons known best to each one of us, we dedicate this book with love and affection to our wives.

――――――
[2]The bulk of the portion written by W.M. Murray was initially completed during a semester of reduced teaching load provided by the Department of History at the University of South Florida. Grants to help defray the cost of illustrating this work were provided by the Department of History, the Dean of the College of Social and Behavioral Sciences and the Division of Sponsored Research at the University of South Florida.

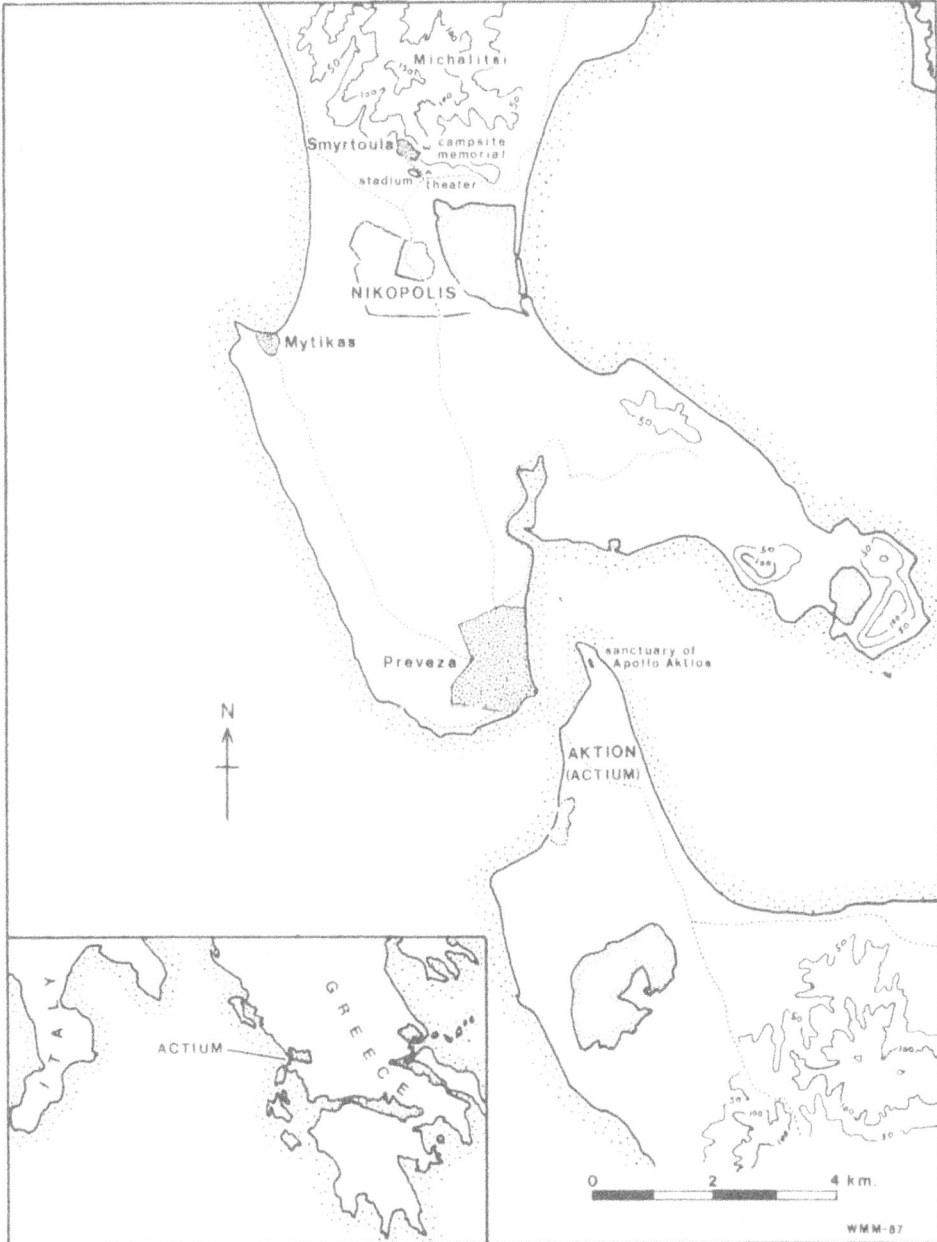

Fig. 1.

I: Introduction (cf. Fig. 1)

O n September 2, 31 B.C., East met West in the last major naval battle of antiquity. Mark Antony, Cleopatra and Octavian played the pivotal roles in a drama that has been retold countless times by historians, playwrights and poets.[1] Although the precise details of the battle fought off Cape Actium are open to debate, there is no doubt about the battle's effect on the subsequent course of Western history. In the succeeding years, Actium's victor, Octavian, evolved from a revolutionary leader into a masterly statesman—one who was actually able to rejuvenate and reform the shattered Roman state. His numerous successes earned him the name Augustus, the praise of his contemporaries, and the admiration of future generations for whom he was the first in a long line of Roman emperors.[2] Because of the importance accorded to the Actian War by every account that chronicles this period, it seems likely that Augustus considered this to be the crucial event in his final rise to power. As Dio observed at the beginning of his fifty-first book, Octavian's monarchy began after his victory at Actium.[3]

Partly because of Actium's importance to Augustus, partly because of the high drama involved, and partly because it represents the last major ancient sea battle, historians have tried for a century to reconstruct what "really happened." Their efforts, unfortunately, have been hampered by the nature of our sources of information. In the years immediately following the battle, Augustus and his followers uniformly described the conflict to their advantage as a heroic struggle between forces of unequal size, patriotism and resolve. And although there is undoubtedly some truth to these accounts, many of the elaborate details are so obviously false that doubt is cast on the straightforward portions of the narrative. Some scholars have even argued that our most detailed accounts should be rejected altogether.[4] For this reason, historians must

---

[1] The intertwining stories of Antony, Octavian and Cleopatra have captured the fascination of modern men and women since the time of the Renaissance. For the period between 1540 and 1905, it has been calculated that Cleopatra was the subject of 77 plays, 45 operas and 5 ballets (cf. G.H. Möller's work cited in VOLKMANN 1958, p. 228). This enduring story was brought to the twentieth century by Bernard Shaw's *Caesar and Cleopatra* (written in 1898); this drama, in turn, captured the attention of the next two generations in the form of two memorable films—one starring Claudette Colbert, and the other, Elizabeth Taylor.

[2] The literature dealing with Augustus and his accomplishments is vast. See, for example, the bibliography in KIENAST 1982.

[3] For the important role played by Actium in the propaganda of Augustus, see JOHNSON 1976, pp. 21–110. The central role of Actium in the imagery of the Augustan Age is described by HÖLSCHER 1984 and 1985; cf. also ZANKER 1988, pp. 82–85.

[4] For the most part, the evidence contemporary with the battle provides no connected narrative, and the facts preserved by this evidence are open to interpretation: Hor. *Epod.*

1

resort to non-literary evidence to supplement and modify the surviving written accounts.[5]

It is in this particular context that we offer a "new" piece of evidence concerning the Battle of Actium. Near the site of the final battle, at the exact place where he had placed his command post, Octavian constructed a war memorial to commemorate his victory. Vestiges of the monument survive to this day near Smyrtoula, a small suburb of modern Preveza. Though few scholars know of the site's existence, and even fewer of its full significance, here, preserved in stone, lie amazing new clues from a battle that redirected the course of Western history. In order to appreciate fully the monument's intended purpose, and to understand the impact of the new evidence it preserves, we should begin our analysis with the surviving historical tradition (whether it is faulty or not) concerning the battle and its aftermath.[6]

By the end of summer, 32 B.C., Antony had moved his large army and navy into Greece, establishing bases along the western coast of the mainland and Peloponnesus.[7] He decided to forego an invasion of Italy, and thereby forced Octavian to fight for control of the Roman world in Greece. In retrospect, we might agree with Plutarch (*Ant*. 58.2) that this defensive posture cost him dearly. During the late winter and spring that followed, M. Agrippa, Octavian's most successful general and naval commander, methodically expelled Antony's western Greek bases and began to harass his food convoys.[8] At roughly the same time, Octavian

---

9; *Carm*. 1.37; a fragment of Augustus' *Memoirs* (PETER 1906, p. 62, #15 = MALCOVATI 1969, p. 95, #17 = Plut. *Ant*. 68.1); a series of *denarii* issued by Octavian after the battle (cf. TRILLMICH 1988; pp. 483–85, 506–10; and ZANKER 1988, pp. 53–57, who accepts an alternate view that the series was minted before the final battle was fought); and the inscription placed on the victory monument at Nikopolis (see infra Chapter II, Section 3.h). The two most detailed narratives of the battle and its immediate aftermath (Dio 50.11.1–51.15.5 and Plut *Ant*. 61–68) fail to agree concerning Antony's overall strategy and conflict in some of their details of the actual battle. Other secondary accounts (Vell. 2.84–85, Florus 2.21 and Orosius 6.19.5–12) fail to resolve these basic differences. In addition to the purely historical accounts, a few poems of Propertius (3.11 and 4.6) and Virgil's *Aeneid* (8.671–713) also refer to the battle, but provide only a few details which are unrecorded elsewhere (for a discussion of the poetic tradition of the battle, see PALADINI 1958 and LEROUX 1968, pp. 37–47, 55–61). The conflicting nature of this evidence has resulted in a spirited debate among modern historians concerning "what really happened" at the Battle of Actium. Two basic points of view have emerged. One side (FERRABINO 1924; and TARN 1931, 1934, 1938; cf. also SYME 1939, p. 297) argues that the true story of the battle can never be recovered because of the obvious distortions that exist in the preserved accounts; they argue, therefore, that most of what we learn from the secondary sources concerning the heroic struggle of the combatants and the glory of the final victory must be discounted. The other side (cf. KROMAYER 1899, 1931, 1933; RICHARDSON 1937; PALADINI 1958; LEROUX 1968; CARTER 1970, pp. 200–27; JOHNSON 1976, pp. 21 110; and HARRINGTON 1984) argues that, although the secondary accounts may be guilty of rhetorical flourishes and colorful distortions, the tradition of a major naval battle at Actium is corroborated by the contemporary evidence and is essentially correct.

[5] See GAGÉ 1936 as an excellent example of this kind of approach.

[6] In the following synopsis of events leading up to and including the Battle of Actium, references to the major accounts, only, are provided. For further details, the reader is urged to consult the studies cited in n. 4, supra.

[7] Plut. *Ant*. 57.1, 58.1; Dio 50.9.2–3.

[8] Dio 50.11.3; Vell. 2.84.2; Orosius 6.19.6.

crossed his army to Epirus and seized Antony's base at Corcyra.[9] He
next moved southward to the northern shores of the Ambracian Gulf
and, in response, Antony moved the bulk of his forces to Actium.[10] By
early summer of 31 B.C., two hostile forces occupied both sides of the
Actian straits.

As the summer wore on, we are told that Antony was driven to
desperation by a number of defeats, by Agrippa's continued success in
intercepting his food convoys, and by the unhealthy position of his camp
within the entrance to the Ambracian Gulf.[11] In addition to these logistical factors, Octavian ridiculed Antony's alliance with Cleopatra and
offered it as proof that Antony was no longer truly Roman—propaganda
which seems to have had an effect on some of Antony's officers.[12] In a
desperate move on September 2, we are told that Antony manned his
largest ships, put aboard his masts and sails, and burned every hull he
was unable through desertion or disease to fill with crews.[13] By mid-
morning, each fleet lay off the entrance to the gulf waiting for the other
side to make the first move. Sometime soon after midday, the fleets
finally engaged.[14] Arrows, sling bullets and catapult shots filled the air
as ships from each side prepared to ram, board or grapple their oppo-
nents' vessels.[15]

According to most of the detailed accounts, Antony's warships were
too large to use their rams effectively and, as a result, Octavian's smaller,
more maneuverable vessels won the day. We are told they coordinated
their attacks against the larger ships by darting in to deliver their blows,
and then retreating to a safe distance to allow others to carry out their
own strikes. The largest vessels, whose timbers were too heavy to be
damaged by ramming, were set upon by two or three smaller ships
which landed their marines on the enemy's decks.[16] At some critical
moment, we are told, Cleopatra took fright, broke through the front line
from the rear with her squadron of 60 ships, hoisted sail, and fled
southward. When Antony saw the queen's flight, he broke off his own
attacks, followed in her wake and left behind the rest of his undefeated
navy and entire army to fend for themselves.[17]

Unaware of Antony's departure, his navy fought on and only began
to surrender after a long, drawn-out, heroic struggle in which most of
their ships were destroyed.[18] According to one colorful account, the sea,
choked with wreckage from the Asiatic vessels, was flecked with purple

[9] Dio 50.12.1–2; Orosius 6.19.7.
[10] Dio 50.12.2–4, 13.1–2.
[11] Dio 50.12.8, 13.5, 30.1; Vell. 2.84.2; Florus 2.21.4; Orosius 6.19.7.
[12] Dio 50.13.6–8, 23.1; Vell. 2.84.1–2.
[13] Plut. Ant. 64.1–2; Dio 50.15.3–4; Vell. 2.84.1; Orosius 6.19.5,9.
[14] Plut. Ant. 65.3–5; Dio 50.31.4–6; Orosius 6.19.10.
[15] Plut. Ant. 66.1–2; Dio 50.32.
[16] For a reevaluation of this tradition, including the appropriate references to the ancient
sources, see Chapter VI.
[17] Plut. Ant. 66.3–5; Dio 50.33.1–3; Vell. 2.85.3.
[18] On this particular matter see Chapter VI.

and gold ornaments.[19] Dio says (50.34–35) that fire was brought from the Roman camp to set ablaze the remainder of the enemy fleet as a grand finale. Such versions obscure the fact that a final victory was not achieved until a week later, when Antony's army of 19 legions surrendered after negotiating generous terms.[20] Only after these matters were settled was Octavian's victory complete. Although we might reasonably doubt the veracity of the battle's more colorful accounts, subsequent events revealed the full magnitude of the victory won at Actium. In less than a year, Antony and Cleopatra were dead and Octavian was left alone to heal the wounds of war and reform the shattered Republic into the Roman Principate.

Immediately following the battle, however, all this was far from clear. During the ensuing winter, for example, the veterans who had been discharged following the Actian War's conclusion rioted and demanded payment of their promised bonuses and grants of land. Although this short-term crisis was quickly defused by limited grants of land and further promises, the recent riots represented a far greater problem than could be solved by veteran land grants.[21] Years of war and piracy had eroded commercial confidence and paralysed trade and commerce. A full recovery could only be achieved through the reestablishment of secure trading routes and a general revitalization of Greece and the East.

As part of a general solution to this widespread economic crisis, a new city was planned for the site of the army's former camp in southern Epirus; it was intended to serve as the major city on the west coast of Greece.[22] Its name Nikopolis, or "Victory City," reveals another reason for its founding. In a Greek tradition stretching back to Alexander, great generals had established "Victory Cities" near the sites of major battles.[23] Although called a "colony" by Pliny and Tacitus, Octavian's Nikopolis seems to have been a purely Greek foundation which held the rights of a "free city" like Athens and Sparta.[24] The surrounding communities

---

[19] Florus 2.21.7–8.

[20] Plut. *Ant.* 68.3; Dio 51.1.4–5, 3.1.

[21] Dio 51.3.4., 4.2–5.1; Suet. *Aug.* 17.3.

[22] This economic interpretation of Nikopolis' foundation is expressed by HOEPFNER 1987, pp. 129–30.

[23] Examples of other "Victory Cities" are provided by JONES 1987, pp. 106–108.

[24] Cf. Pliny *HN* 4.5; Tac. *Ann.* 5.10; and MOMMSEN 1887, pp. 320–22. Octavian appears as the *oikistes* or "founder" of Nikopolis on some of the coins minted at the city. For the coinage of Nikopolis, cf. OIKONOMIDOU 1975, and KRAAY 1976. Despite the fact it was not a Roman colony, the city was a personal foundation of Octavian and accordingly given power and prestige commensurate with its patron. MOMMSEN 1887, p. 322, suggests that Octavian may have experimented with a new type of Roman foundation which he later abandoned when Patras was settled as a Roman colony. Whatever the truth, Nikopolis was clearly intended to be an important city. For this reason it received six votes (out of 30) in the Delphic Amphictyony as reorganized by Augustus (Paus. 10.8.3). This number is the highest total accorded to any one city and was equaled only by Macedonia and Thessaly. Most cities on the council, such as Athens or Corinth, received but one vote. Moreover, Nikopolis delivered her six votes on each occasion (as did Delphi with its two votes and Athens with its one), whereas the votes of other members alternated; e.g., the one vote of the Peloponnesian Dorians alternated between Argos, Sikyon, Corinth and

were encouraged to migrate there by an officially sponsored synoecism (another old Greek tradition), and this in turn provided the population necessary for the city's development.[25] Though the full details of this growing process are not recorded, the plan was a success, the population grew and the city prospered.[26]

In addition to being the region's major administrative center, Nikopolis also served as a living monument to Octavian's final victory, a role clearly stressed by at least two of the city's first building projects. According to Strabo, who wrote his account before A.D. 21 (and probably before 7 B.C.) a *temenos* sacred to Apollo occupied a suburb of the city.[27] Containing a sacred grove, stadium and gymnasium, this *temenos* was clearly built for the newly revived *Aktia* or Actian Games. Originally, this festival had been hosted by the people of Anaktorion across the gulf at the sanctuary of Apollo Aktios. It was now reestablished as a quadrennial celebration, moved to Nikopolis and placed on a par with the four traditional Panhellenic festivals. The games, most likely held on the anniversary of the battle, served to commemorate the birth of the emerging Augustan Age.[28]

To memorialize the naval victory and emphasize the peace that resulted from it, Octavian planned and executed two war memorials in the city's environs. One, a sort of naval museum, was built across the straits of Cape Actium near the ancient grove and newly refurbished

---

Megara (cf. MOMMSEN 1887, p. 275 with n. 1). This favored position of Nikopolis may help to explain the apparent confusion of Pliny and Tacitus concerning the precise legal status of the city. If it was not strictly a Roman colony, it seems to have been easy enough to confuse it with one. For additional views on this complex matter, see most recently PURCELL 1987 and JONES 1987.

[25] A curious passage in Pausanias (7.18.9) allows us to see one of the ways the *synoikismos* was promoted: many Akarnanian and Aetolian cult images were transferred to Nikopolis by Octavian from their ancient shrines in order to encourage migration to the new city. Surviving sources list the Ambracians, Leukadians, Akarnanians, Amphilochian Argives and the Aetolians as taking part in the city's foundation. Our sources for the foundation include: Dio 51.1.3; Strabo 7.7.6; 10.2.2; Paus. 5.23.3; 7.18.8; 8.24.11; 10.38.4; Zonaras 10.30; Suet. *Aug.* 18.2; Serv. *Verg. Aen.* 3.276; Mamertinus in *Paneg. Lat.* 11.9; and Antipatros in *Anth. Pal.* 9.553); cf. also SCHOBER 1936, p. 516. According to Strabo (10.2.2), communities which remained inhabited under the administrative control of Nikopolis (i.e., as *perioikides*) included Palairos, Alyzeia, Leukas, Amphilochian Argos and Ambracia; most likely there were others. HOEPFNER 1987, pp. 131–32, also believes that Augustus deliberately destroyed city circuits in Epirus, Aetolia and Akarnania to discourage the return of peoples to their ancestral homes.

[26] Cf. Strabo 7.7.6: "Nikopolis is populous, and its numbers are increasing daily . . ." On the history of Nikopolis, see SCHOBER 1936, pp. 516–18. In 1984, the First International Symposium on Nikopolis was held in Preveza, Greece. The published proceedings of this conference (NICOPOLIS 1987) present a wealth of detail concerning different aspects of the city's archaeology and historical development conveniently collected into one volume.

[27] Strabo lived at least until A.D. 21, but may have written the major portions of his *Geography* by 7 B.C.; cf. JONES 1931, pp. xxi–xxvi.

[28] For the original games held by the Akarnanians at Actium, see HABICHT 1957, pp. 102–109. For the nature of the reinstituted games, see REISCH 1894, cols. 1213–14; GAGÉ 1936, pp. 92–97; and SARIKAKIS 1965, pp. 145–62. The games are referred to as "ludos. . . quinquennales" by Suetonius (*Aug.* 18.2) and others. Counting inclusively, this means they were held every four years.

temple of Apollo Aktios.[29] The other he placed on the hillside where his command post and tent had stood before the battle, overlooking the straits, the growing new city, and the grove where the *Aktia* were now celebrated. As the official war memorial of Nikopolis, a city which was itself a "living" victory monument, this building may have been the most important structure built by Octavian outside of Italy. It was certainly the most important monument associated with the new city.

Amazingly, Octavian's Campsite Memorial still exists. And equally amazing is the fact that few people know of its existence (though it was discovered 75 years ago) and almost no one realizes its rich historical significance.[30] But it is only here, high on a hillside at the site of Octavian's tent, that one can physically see the immense sizes of Antony's ships and begin to appreciate Octavian's early grasp of Actium as political propaganda. Here is also to be found Octavian's first official statement on the Actian War in an important inscription that has yet to be properly published. Long before the Augustan historians and poets completed their versions of the battle in the straits, this monument was built to deliver the message of the New Order. The message is propaganda, to be sure, but it comes directly from the mind of Octavian shortly after he found himself alone in power. As such, it stands among the earliest sources we possess for the Actian War, and represents a find as important as a fragment from Augustus' lost memoirs.

We begin, therefore, with Octavian's Campsite Memorial at Nikopolis. After determining as much of its original appearance as its surviving remains allow, we consider the evidence it preserves for the immense ships that fought in the Battle of Actium. We then examine the design of the monument in an attempt to discover the messages (both blatant and subtle) that it was intended to convey. And last, but not least, we use the monument and the evidence it preserves to reassess some important historical problems associated with the battle and the foundation of Nikopolis. Above all, however, our primary goal is to make known an important Augustan monument and begin the discussion of the com-

---

[29] This memorial had burned to the ground by the time Strabo composed his account of the region (7.7.6; the text comes from JONES 1924): . . . καὶ ἱερὸν τοῦ Ἀκτίου Ἀπόλλωνος ἐνταῦθα ἐστι πλησίον τοῦ στόματος, λόφος τις, ἐφ' ᾧ ὁ νεώς, καὶ ὑπ' αὐτῷ πεδίον ἄλσος ἔχον καὶ νεώρια, ἐν οἷς ἀνέθηκε Καῖσαρ τὴν δεκαναΐαν ἀκροθίνιον, ἀπὸ μονοκρότου μέχρι δεκήρους· ὑπὸ πύρος δ' ἠφανίσθαι καὶ οἱ νεώσοικοι λέγονται καὶ τὰ πλοῖα. "Here too, near the mouth [of the Ambracian Gulf], is the sacred precinct of Actian Apollo a hill on which the temple stands; and at the foot of the hill is a plain which contains a sacred grove and a naval station, the naval station where Caesar dedicated as first fruits of his victory the squadron of ten ships— from a warship called a 'one' up to a warship called a 'ten.' It is said, however, that not only the boats but also the boathouses have been wiped out by fire." Note that Strabo relied on the reports of others concerning the fire which damaged the *neoria*. Concerning the date of Strabo's account, cf. supra n. 27. For Octavian's refurbishing of Apollo's sanctuary on the Actian promontory, cf. Suet. *Aug.* 18.2, and infra Chapter II, n. 8.

[30] In the proceedings of a recent international symposium concerning ancient Nikopolis, the monument is mentioned only a few times, and only once in any detail; cf. NICOPOLIS 1987 and SOULE 1987, pp. 171–73.

plex clues it preserves concerning the monstrous ships in Antony's and Cleopatra's fleet. We do not intend to resolve all the problems raised by the Campsite Memorial, but if we, at long last, stir up interest in a monument too long neglected, then our study will have fulfilled its intended purpose.

II: Octavian's Campsite Memorial for the Actian War

1. *The Ancient* Testimonia

During the generations of peace that followed the victory at Actium, many visitors paid homage to the region officially proclaimed the birthplace of the New Order. Midway along the coastal route from Greece to Italy, Nikopolis provided a welcome break for travelers on their way to the West. The entrance to the gulf offered excellent anchorages and there was plenty for tourists to see on both sides of the straits. To the south lay the old temple of Apollo Aktios, newly refurbished after the capture of Egypt. A whole set of warships had been dedicated there by Octavian (but they and their boathouses had burned to the ground within a generation of their dedication). Other sights could be found in the new city to the north of the straits. Of all the new buildings, the theater, gymnasium and shrines, the memorial most closely associated with the founder and architect of the Principate could be found where his tent had stood during those fateful summer days of 31 B.C.

Large and impressive, it sat on a hill to the north of the city and was clearly intended to serve as the premiere memorial of the founder's "Victory City." It should surprise no one that more ancient references to it have survived than to any other building in Nikopolis. Unfortunately, these *testimonia* confuse as much as they enlighten. Nevertheless, we must start with these observations if we ever hope to reveal the true nature or to reconstruct the intended impact of Octavian's monument.

1. Dio Cassius 51.1.3: τό τε χωρίον ἐν ᾧ ἐσκήνησε, λίθοις τε τετραπέδοις ἐκρηπίδωσε καὶ τοῖς ἁλοῦσιν ἐμβόλοις ἐκόσμησεν, ἕδος τι ἐν αὐτῷ τοῦ Ἀπόλλωνος ὑπαίθριον ἱδρυσάμενος.[1]

   On the spot where he had pitched his tent, he laid a foundation of square stones, adorned it with the captured ships' rams, and established on it a kind of open-air place, sacred to Apollo.

2. Suet. *Aug* 18.2: Quoque Actiacae victoriae memoria celebratior et in posterum esset, urbem Nicopolim apud Actium condidit ludosque illic quinquennales constituit et ampliato vetere Apollinis templo locum castrorum, quibus fuerat usus, exornatum navalibus spoliis Neptuno ac Marti consecravit.[2]

   To extend the fame of his victory at Actium and perpetuate its memory, he founded a city called Nikopolis near Actium, and provided for the

---

[1] The text comes from the Loeb edition of CARY 1917; cf. also n. 7, infra.

[2] The text comes from the Loeb edition of ROLFE 1951.

celebration of games there every four years; enlarged the ancient temple of Apollo; and consecrated the site of the camp that he had used to Neptune and Mars, after adorning it with naval spoils.

3. Suet. *Aug.* 96.2: Apud Actium descendenti in aciem asellus cum asinario occurrit: homini Eutychus, bestiae Nicon erat nomen; utriusque simulacrum aeneum victor posuit in templo, in quod castrorum suorum locum vertit.[3]

At Actium as Octavian was going down to begin the battle, he met an ass with his driver, the man having the name Eutychos [Lucky] and the beast that of Nikon [Victor]; and after the victory he set up bronze images of the two in the sacred enclosure into which he converted the site of his camp.

4. Plut. *Ant.* 65.3: Καίσαρι δὲ λέγεται μὲν ἔτι σκότους ἀπὸ τῆς σκηνῆς κύκλῳ περιϊόντι πρὸς τὰς ναῦς ἄνθρωπος ἐλαύνων ὄνον ἀπαντῆσαι, πυθομένῳ δὲ τοὔνομα γνωρίσας αὐτὸν εἰπεῖν. "Ἐμοὶ μὲν Εὔτυχος ὄνομα, τῷ δὲ ὄνῳ Νίκων." διὸ καὶ τοῖς ἐμβόλοις τὸν τόπον κοσμῶν ὕστερον ἔστησε χαλκοῦν ὄνον καὶ ἄνθρωπον.[4]

Caesar, we are told, who had left his tent while it was yet dark and was going around to visit his ships, was met by a man driving an ass. Caesar asked the man his name, and he, recognizing Caesar, replied: "My name is Lucky, and my ass's name is Victor." Therefore, when Caesar afterwards decorated the place with the rams from the ships, he set up bronze figures of an ass and a man.

5. Philippus in *Anth. Pal.* 6.236:

'Ἔμβολα χαλκογένεια, φιλόπλοα τεύχεα νηῶν,
  Ἀκτιακοῦ πολέμου κείμεθα μαρτύρια·
ἠνίδε σιμβλεύει κηρότροφα δῶρα μελισσῶν
  ἐσμῷ βομβητῇ κυκλόσε βριθόμενα.
Καίσαρος εὐνομίης χρηστὴ χάρις· ὅπλα γὰρ ἐχθρῶν
  καρποὺς εἰρήνης ἀντεδίδαξε τρέφειν.[5]

Bronze jaw-beaks, ships' voyage-loving armor, we lie here as witnesses to the Actian War. Behold, the bees' wax-fed gifts are hived in us, weighted all round by a humming swarm. So good is the grace of Caesar's law and order; he has taught the enemy's weapons to bear the fruits of peace instead.

6. Strabo 7.7.6: ἡ μὲν οὖν Νικόπολις εὐανδρεῖ καὶ λαμβάνει καθ' ἡμέραν ἐπίδοσιν, χώραν τε ἔχουσα πολλὴν καὶ τὸν ἐκ τῶν λαφύρων κόσμον, τό τε κατασκευασθὲν τέμενος ἐν τῷ προαστείῳ τὸ μὲν εἰς τὸν ἀγῶνα τὸν πεντετηρικὸν ἐν ἄλσει ἔχοντι γυμνάσιόν τε καὶ στάδιον, τὸ δ' ἐν τῷ ὑπερκειμένῳ τοῦ ἄλσους ἱερῷ λόφῳ τοῦ Ἀπόλλωνος·[6]

Nikopolis is populous, and its numbers are increasing daily, since it has not only a considerable territory and the adornment taken from the spoils of the battle, but it also has in its suburbs the thoroughly equipped sacred

---

[3] The text comes from the Loeb edition of ROLFE 1951.
[4] The text comes from the Loeb edition of PERRIN 1920. Zonaras 10.30 (p. I 526 D) repeats this same story and adds that the two statues were later carried off to Byzantion and set up in the hippodrome.
[5] The text comes from GOW-PAGE 1968, Vol. I, pp. 298–99 (cf. also the commentary in Vol. II, p. 331).
[6] The text comes from the Loeb edition of JONES 1924.

precinct—one part of it being in a sacred grove that contains a gymnasium and a stadium for the celebration of the quadrennial games, the other part lying above the grove on the hill that is sacred to Apollo.

According to Dio, Octavian set up a foundation or podium decorated with warship rams, and on top established some sort of open-air shrine that was sacred to Apollo; his description of this "open-air place" is not very exact.[7] Suetonius, on the other hand, mentions no shrine and implies that the memorial consisted largely of a display of naval spoils. According to him, the site of the camp was turned into a "templum" or sacred enclosure and everything, including the spoils and two votive statues, was dedicated to Neptune and Mars; he makes no reference at all to Apollo.[8] Strabo, on the other hand, seems to imply that the Campsite Memorial was part of a large complex sacred to Apollo. He says that one part of "the thoroughly equipped sacred precinct" was located on a hill, itself sacred to Apollo, above the grove. Since the other part of the precinct (containing a grove, stadium and gymnasium) was clearly sacred to Apollo, was he not implying that the part on the hill was sacred to Apollo as well?[9] Although the Greek text states simply that the hill,

---

[7] The word Dio uses to describe this shrine, *hedos*, is a vague one used elsewhere by the same author to describe both a statue and perhaps a statue base (cf. 48.14.5–6, and 59.28.4). Presumably from examples like these GAGÉ 1936, p. 55, has taken the Greek words *hedos ti . . . tou Apollonos hypaithrion* to mean that Octavian set up not a shrine, but rather a statue of Apollo. "Statue," however, is not the only meaning of the word. The earliest and simplest sense of *hedos* is "seat" or "abode," and in later times it was used to indicate the seat of a deity or its temple. From an entry in the *Lexicon* of Timaeus Grammaticus, we find that the word could be used for both the statue and the place where the statue stood: "ἕδος· τὸ ἄγαλμα, καὶ ὁ τόπος ἐν ᾧ ἵδρυται"; cf. *LSJ* s.v. "ἕδος (3)". Primarily because of the physical remains of the monument, which are discussed below, we do not believe it necessary to restore a statue of Apollo as the central feature of the shrine.

[8] Because Suetonius lumps a number of Octavian's acts into one sentence, PICARD 1928, p. 221 n. 6, has placed the "ancient temple" of Apollo at Nikopolis, and identifies it with the site of the victory monument. This interpretation is clearly impossible and has rightly received little attention, although it has made it into at least one handbook in a slightly altered form; cf. KIRSTEN-KRAIKER 1967, Vol. II, p. 753 and infra nn. 12 and 14. The "ancient temple" referred to by Suetonius is simply the old Akarnanian cult place of Apollo Aktios located on Cape Actium. Since it was ravaged by years of war and piracy, Octavian apparently saw to its renovation and repair when he built his naval museum there. For the site of the sanctuary, largely obliterated by a nineteenth century fortification of Ali Pasha, see MURRAY 1982, pp. 266–71.

[9] GAGÉ 1936, pp. 53–55, interprets the Greek to mean that two *temene* of Apollo existed in this suburb. He says (n. 1, p. 54) that the singular *to . . . temenos* followed by the parallel construction *to men . . . , to de . . . ,* is somewhat odd, and that one should expect the dual form here: *to temene*. He further argued (GAGÉ 1955, p. 510) that the rostra display was located in the *temenos* containing the gymnasium and the stadium, while the second *temenos* was probably to be identified with "hill 158" of Mt. Michalitsi (cf. his map, GAGÉ 1936, p. 43 and 1955, p. 501). He believed (GAGÉ 1955, p. 510) that the *temenos* might be on the summit of the hill. Strabo's text makes it certain that the *temenos* is not on the hill (as Gagé thinks is possible, cf. GAGÉ 1936, p. 55), but rather, *is* the hill. The adjective *hiero*, "sacred," agrees with *lopho* "hill" and makes it certain that Strabo intended the hill to be sacred to Apollo. Although it seems natural to conclude that everything in this region of the city (e.g., hill, grove and associated shrines) were sacred to the same deity or deities, this may not have been the case (see infra). And strictly speaking, Strabo makes no comment on the matter.

and not necessarily the memorial, was sacred to Apollo, one is left to ponder the suitability of a monument for Neptune and Mars on a hill sacred to Apollo.[10]

Our sources are not fully consistent with one another, and thus present us with the following problem. Although we know that a memorial was built on the site of Octavian's camp to commemorate his victory at Actium, we are not sure to whom it was dedicated, nor do we know the precise nature of its original construction.[11] Clearly, a definite solution requires more evidence than that of the ancient texts. For this, we must carefully examine the monument itself, discovered almost 75 years ago but never extensively published. As a result, the existence of this important monument remains unknown to most scholars of the Augustan period, while those who do know of it are faced with conflicting and incorrect descriptions of the remains.[12] In order to appreciate fully what Octavian built at his campsite, why it has been so poorly understood, and the wealth of information it preserves, we must begin with the rediscovery of the monument in the nineteenth century.

2. The Rediscovery of the Monument (cf. Fig. 1)

In June 1805, Col. W.M. Leake paid a visit to southern Epirus and correctly identified the ruins near Preveza with ancient Nikopolis. He also located the region of the sacred grove for the *Aktia*, which was clearly indicated by the ruins of a stadium and a large theater, at the foot of a hill called Michalitsi (Fig. 2).[13] As for the Campsite Memorial, Leake thought the best place for Octavian's command post (and thus

---

[10] There are good reasons, however, to assume that this was precisely the case; see infra Section 5.

[11] These are essentially the questions posed by GAGÉ 1936, p. 53: "En fait, s'agit-il bien d'un 'temple'? Et, temple ou non, quels dieux devons-nous retenir?"

[12] Cf. for example: GAGÉ 1955, p. 510, who implies that the campsite is in the *temenos* with the grove, gymnasium and stadium at the base of the hill, although he knows that the fragments of the inscription were found on Michalitsi; KIRSTEN-KRAIKER 1967, Vol. II, p. 753, who incorrectly locate both a temple of Neptune and a temple of Apollo Aktios on Mt. Michalitsi; WEIS 1976, p. 626, who judiciously interprets the remains on Michalitsi as a structure of unknown form with an inscription referring to Neptune; and CARTER 1970, p. 235, who correctly attributes the monument to Neptune and Mars, but incorrectly places the shrine in front of the ram display rather than on the terrace above it. As he visited the site in 1967, seven years before the excavations of 1974, he had no way of knowing that the "open-air shrine" was set on top of the podium; cf. CARTER 1977, p. 228. Most recently, OIKONOMIDOU 1975, pp. 56–58, argues on the evidence of four coins that a temple was built at the site during the reign of Septimius Severus; before that time there had been simply an open-air shrine as described by the ancient authors. Her view has been restated recently by SOULE 1987, pp. 171–73.

[13] The theater (built for the music contests which formed a part of the *Aktia*; cf. SARIKAKIS 1965, p. 152) was presumably constructed sometime after Strabo published his *Geography* (see Chapter I, n. 27) since he does not mention it in his account of the region. HOEPFNER 1987, p. 133, with Plate 11 (p. 454), believes that the first phase of the theater dates to the original foundation of the city.

Fig. 2.

Fig. 3.

the monument) was on top of Michalitsi behind the grove.[14] The true site of this post went undetected until 1913, when, after an exhaustive search on the southern flank of the hill, Alexander Philadelpheus located and partially excavated what he identified as a large temple of the Corinthian order (Fig. 3). According to the first report, the temple was preserved only in its foundations which measured some 56 by 23 meters. Later, after further excavation of the site in 1921, Philadelpheus estimated its size as 62 by 45 meters.[15]

During the course of the 1913 excavation, Philadelpheus unearthed a Corinthian capital (Fig. 4), column drums of local limestone, fragments

Fig. 4.

[14] LEAKE 1835, pp. 193–94. Curiously, KIRSTEN-KRAIKER 1967, Vol. II, p. 753, apparently following the idea first expressed by PICARD 1928, p. 221, n. 6, that a temple of Apollo Aktios was placed at Octavian's campsite, locate this site, with Leake, on the top of Michalitsi. Although Leake clearly indicates that this is where one ought to expect Octavian's campsite, he never claims to have found such a site. In fact, no such site, either temple or campsite, has ever been found on the summit of the hill.

[15] PHILADELPHEUS 1913, pp. 83–112. He says (p. 90) that the precise dimensions of the temple were difficult to obtain because of the large numbers of disturbed foundation blocks. Philadelpheus returned to the site in 1921 to continue his excavation of the "temple." He reports only that the foundations were uncovered from west to east, and that numerous architectural fragments were found along with more large pieces of the inscription (PHILADELPHEUS 1921, p. 42). Many years later, he told J. Gagé that the dimensions of the "temple" were at least 62 by 45 meters (GAGÉ 1936, p. 57, n. 1). These figures correspond well to the length of the podium's southern retaining wall and the distance from this wall to the stoa's north foundation; see infra Section 4. Did Philadelpheus find the northern stylobate of the stoa, uncovered by Ph. Petsas in 1974?

of a cornice, and rooftiles of both Laconian and Corinthian type.[16] In addition, nine fragments from the monument's large dedicatory inscription were found, which alluded, he felt, to the donor, the victory, and the god to whom the temple was dedicated. The text, he believed, was originally carved on a frieze course supported by the temple's columns.[17] Satisfied that he had found Octavian's Campsite Memorial, but disappointed by the lack of spectacular finds, Philadelpheus turned his attention elsewhere. Hereafter, no one doubted that this important monument had been found, but the correct interpretation of its original appearance awaited further examination of the remains.

Not everyone who discussed the monument after its discovery agreed with Philadelpheus that a temple had been built at the site. Such a structure simply failed to conform with the ancient descriptions of Octavian's campsite. K.A. Rhomaios, a former student of Philadelpheus who studied the dedicatory inscription in the early 1920s, preferred the testimony of Dio to Suetonius. To explain the disagreement concerning the divine recipient(s) of the dedication, Rhomaios proposed the following three-step solution: 1) Suetonius' source was a list of the spoils placed in the sanctuary of Apollo from the Battle of Actium. 2) Among the items on this list was the famous selection of rams, and these alone were dedicated to Neptune and Mars. 3) Suetonius mistakenly generalized the recipients of this dedication to the whole memorial. Rhomaios also proposed that the original form of the monument was a simple enclosure or *temenos* containing an unroofed podium, the ram display, and at least two statues. According to him, the architectural fragments found at the site came from some unrecorded temple built at a later date. The inscription he felt was placed along the face of the ram display.[18]

In 1936, two articles appeared which discussed the monument and its inscription. One, by F. Schober, was a general treatment of Nikopolis for Pauly Wissowa's *Real Encyclopaedie*; the other, by J. Gagé, was a considerable piece of original scholarship which is discussed more fully below. By this time, 25 fragments of the large inscription had turned up and one block clearly bore the last four letters of the name Neptune.[19]

---

[16] PHILADELPHEUS 1913, p. 87. The column drums were originally plastered with stucco and bore "the canonical number of flutes"—presumably 24. If we work from what Philadelpheus says, i.e., that the circumference of the column measured 1.75 m. and that its flutes were carved about 0.08 m. apart from one another, we arrive at a total of 22 flutes; we presume that one of his measurements is in error.

[17] The precise number of fragments can be reconstructed from the text of the inscription presented by PHILADELPHEUS 1913, p. 90, and from the comments of RHOMAIOS 1925, p. 1. As more pieces of the inscription were found in the years subsequent to 1913, Philadelpheus revised his views slightly on the inscription's text; cf. PHILADELPHEUS 1927, p. 225—this same text was also presented in PHILADELPHEUS 1938, p. 16. See PHILADELPHEUS 1913, p. 87, for the inscription's placement on the "temple." On the inscription in general, see infra Section 3.h.

[18] RHOMAIOS 1925, pp. 2–3.

[19] The block reads "TVNO"; cf. PHILADELPHEUS 1927, p. 225. Although SCHOBER 1936, col. 515, reported that only 24 blocks were known by the time he wrote, GAGÉ 1936, pp. 98–100, presented 25.

Since the sea god was obviously one of the deities honored here, Schober simply concluded that the memorial was a large temple of Neptune inside which were placed, among other items, the two statues of Eutychos and Nikon.[20]

Gagé's views on the monument were contained in a detailed study of the ex-votos and trophies resulting from the Actian War.[21] Although he discussed the Campsite Memorial in depth, Gagé seems never to have visited the site. He drew his information entirely from the accounts (both published and unpublished) of Philadelpheus and Rhomaios and from communications, through intermediaries, with Philadelpheus and I. Miliadis, a subsequent ephor of Epirus who had worked briefly at the site in 1926.[22] Gagé's remarks, even without his personal examination of the site, still constitute the most complete analysis of the monument in print.

Arguing mainly from the ancient texts, Gagé concluded that a *temenos*, not a temple, existed here and that it was sacred to Apollo. He argued that Suetonius called the site a *templum* or sacred enclosure, that Dio described a podium built of squared blocks surmounted by a large statue of Apollo, and that Strabo equated the place with the *temenos* at the base of the hill, also sacred to Apollo.[23] Gagé believed the texts were not contradictory, if viewed in the correct way, because the monument was dedicated in a sense to all three deities. He even thought it possible that all three were mentioned in the dedicatory inscription.[24]

Gagé also concluded that the remains found by Philadelpheus were most appropriate to a portico (or stoa) and not a temple. "We ought, following these facts, to restore a monument completely at ground level, without elevation (unless there was some sort of portico), a sort of peribolos decorated with rams, probably on its sides. And in the middle, in the place normally occupied by the *naos*, were statues."[25] According to Gagé, Apollo's would have been the most considerable, but there would have been others, such as those of Eutychos and Nikon. Furthermore, a large cult statue of Apollo (which he thought was attested by the account of Dio; cf. n. 7) would have looked over and protected the transplanted games of Actian Apollo.

Finally, the monumental size and considerable length of the inscription led Gagé to follow Rhomaios' suggestion and envision the text on the primary facade of the monument, not around the sides of some

---

[20] SCHOBER 1936, col. 515.

[21] GAGÉ 1936, pp. 37–100; cf. especially p. 39.

[22] GAGÉ 1936, p. 52, n. 1. After Rhomaios' work on the inscription was published in 1922 and 1925, Miliadis carried out excavations at the site in 1926 and found a few more of the large inscribed blocks; cf. CHRONIQUE 1926, p. 561. Years later, when Gagé published his study of Roman Apollo (infra n. 27), he revealed that he still had not visited the site when he fails to describe correctly the exact placement of the monument's remains (cf. supra n. 12).

[23] Cf. supra nn. 7 and 9.

[24] GAGÉ 1936, pp. 70–71.

[25] GAGÉ 1936, pp. 55–56.

temple. Thus, for Gagé, the monument had a form somewhere between a monumental trophy of massive cylindrical shape and a *temenos* or religious enclosure inhabited by a divinity. In this hybrid form, therefore, Octavian would have combined the traditional Roman trophy with the great commemorative monuments of the Greek world.[26]

In 1955, Gagé restated his interpretation of the monument when he published his study of Roman Apollo.[27] Three years later, G. Ch. Picard published a study of Roman trophy architecture and included a description of the Campsite Memorial based in part on Gagé's observations.[28] He argued that this type of monument was depicted on a series of denarii minted by C. Antistius Vetus in 16 B.C. (Fig. 5).[29] It was not exactly the same, however, because its statue group was more complex than the single deity shown on the coin. An example of such a group could be found, Picard thought, in a composite trophy-group of Augustan date at St. Bertrand (in France). From this example, Picard concluded that the statues of Neptune, Mars and Apollo were arrayed in a manner similar to the St. Bertrand group, but were set up on a rectangular base whose sides were decorated with warship rams.[30]

Aside from Picard, who demonstrates the danger of concluding too much from a site that has been improperly published, scholars have generally ignored the arguments of Rhomaios and Gagé concerning the monument. This includes the scholarly community outside Greece, the

Fig. 5.

---

[26] GAGÉ 1936, pp. 57–58. He later altered his view; cf. infra n. 27.

[27] GAGÉ 1955, pp. 509–10. At this time he had changed his view slightly concerning the nature of the monument's design: cf. GAGÉ 1955, p. 511: "C'était, on le voit, un trophée qui, quel que fût son style architectural, était de strict tradition romaine par l'exactitude de l'emplacement comme par le choix des dieux."

[28] PICARD 1957, pp. 260–62.

[29] PICARD 1957, p. 261.

[30] PICARD 1957, p. 262; for the monument at St. Bertrand, see his pp. 270–73; a drawing of the group is found between pp. 272 and 273.

subsequent editors of the monument's inscription, and the educated members of the local community.[31] A small sign was placed years ago near the junction of the town's main street with the Preveza-Arta highway reading ΠΡΟΣ ΤΟΝ ΝΑΟΝ ΤΟΥ ΑΠΟΛΛΩΝΟΣ ("To the Temple of Apollo"). It was replaced a few years ago with a large blue and yellow road sign which points an arrow to the town's main street and reads "Temple of Apollo." Old ideas die hard.

Eugene Vanderpool, who visited the site every few years while professor of archaeology at the American School of Classical Studies, seems to have been the first to draw attention to the cuttings in the face of the preserved podium. Though unable to explain exactly how they worked, he recognized that a series of complex holes "shaped like enormous bass-viols" somehow served to attach the rams originally displayed at the site.[32] And this is where the matter rested until 1974 when a complete reinvestigation of the monument was begun by Ph. Petsas and the Athens Archaeological Society.

Petsas was interested in this monument for a number of reasons. First, there was its unique importance as the official memorial of the Battle of Actium, one of the major events of world history according to ancient and modern opinion.[33] Second, the monument's known date (29 B.C.) was expected to provide a useful fixed point in the local chronology of Roman Nikopolis. This, in turn, was intended to aid research on other Roman monuments at Nikopolis, particularly those from the period of the city's founding. And finally, though the Campsite Memorial was partially excavated 61 years prior to 1974, it really remained unpublished. Except for Philadelpheus and Gagé, scholars had focused their attention exclusively on the dedicatory inscription. As a result, a full description of the site, illustrated with plans and photographs, had never been published. In addition, the podium's surface had never been systematically excavated.

Unfortunately, the hopes of a comprehensive study were cut short by the military events afflicting Cyprus in 1974. Work at the site was terminated by a general mobilization of the Greek armed forces on July 20, and the project was never renewed. To make matters worse, there had

---

[31] Two recent treatments of Nikopolis, KIRSTEN-KRAIKER 1967, Vol. II, pp. 751–55, and WEIS 1976, seem to be entirely unaware of Gagé's important article, while CARTER 1977, pp. 227–28, ignores the fact that Gagé did anything more than publish 25 fragments of the inscription. The first scholar to reconstruct a reasonable text from the 25 fragments, J.H. Oliver, studiously avoids discussing the monument at all; cf. OLIVER 1969, pp. 178–82. Of all those who mention the monument and its inscription, only JUCKER 1982 seems to use the other arguments put forth by Gagé. In 1982, when a local newspaper (The Topographike Phone) published an interview with us concerning our work at the monument, the editor referred to it throughout his text as the "Naos tou Apollonos," even though we repeatedly urged him to call it Octavian's Campsite Memorial.

[32] Though he never published his views on the monument, Vanderpool expressed them orally to a generation of American School students. We last spoke with him about the monument in August 1987. In print, one finds Vanderpool's view expressed first in ROSSITER 1967, p. 435, now in its 3rd edition (ROSSITER 1981, p. 456).

[33] See, for example, VOLKMANN 1958, pp. 216–18.

been insufficient time for the completion of a site plan. It was impossible, therefore, to publish anything more than a general description of the season's incomplete results and a large number of photographic views.[34] Consequently, this important monument still remains largely unknown to most scholars, and a unique example of a Roman *rostra* (i.e., ram) display slowly deteriorates in the middle of a briar patch.

On the positive side, the accomplishments of the 1974 season were significant. For the first time, a dirt road was cut through to the site. Intended to aid in the process of earth removal and to facilitate the movement of fallen blocks, the road still enables cars and trucks to reach the monument. In addition to this, exploratory trenches were sunk into the podium's surface and the stylobate of the stoa was located running east-west for a total length of 40.1 m. (cf. Figs. 6–7). Only one edge of the stoa's stylobate was uncovered before the work was terminated, but it is clear that this structure must be identified somehow with the *hedos ti . . . hypaithrion* mentioned by Dio 51.1.3.

In addition to discoveries made atop the podium in 1974, Petsas also cleaned the areas surrounding the podium of all vegetation. As a result, he found a number of the inscription blocks and two column drums, but most important, revealed clearly the cuttings in the face of the podium's retaining wall. Although the *testimonia* indicated that bronze warship rams originally filled these nose-shaped sockets, just how this worked was difficult to determine. And to make matters more complicated, the sockets were of different shapes and sizes, clearly reflecting in some way the differing dimensions of the ships that once carried the lost rams. Hoping to examine the matter more fully at a later date, Petsas published photographs of these cuttings in his 1974 reports for *Praktika* and *Ergon*.[35] But the key to the cuttings' interpretation—and by extension, the solution to the true appearance of the Campsite Memorial— had six more years to lie on the sea floor off the coast of Athlit, Israel.

In the meantime, the monument was briefly discussed in one book and two articles. In 1975 M. Karamesine-Oikonomidou published a study of the mint at Nikopolis. She argued that a temple of the Corinthian order appearing as a coin type during the reign of Septimius Severus ought to be identified with the Campsite Memorial.[36] Two years later, J.M. Carter published some confusing remarks on the nature of the monument and the placement of its inscription when he erroneously reported the existence of a new fragment in 1977.[37] And more recently, H. Jucker has tried to show that the monument is depicted on the reverse of a series of denarii issued by C. Antistius Vetus in 16 B.C.[38] Jucker revives an old view that Apollo stands near an altar on top of a high

[34] For the reports of the work in 1974, see PETSAS 1974a and 1974b.
[35] PETSAS 1974a and 1974b.
[36] OIKONOMIDOU 1975, pp. 56–58.
[37] CARTER 1977, p. 228; see infra Section 3.h. Carter was relying on observations he had made at the site in 1967.
[38] JUCKER 1982; cf. infra Section 5.

Fig. 6.

Fig. 7.

20

podium decorated with two anchors and three rams viewed frontally.[39] He advances this interpretation one step further by arguing that the scene is an abbreviated view of the Campsite Memorial. Even though the frontal views of the rams on the podium look quite odd, his argument seems persuasive, but is it correct? Unknown to Jucker, and to everyone else who had worked on the monument, the key to solving the problems of the Campsite Memorial had already been pulled from the sea off Israel.

In November 1980, Y. Ramon, a graduate student at the University of Haifa, discovered a well-preserved Hellenistic warship ram (Fig. 25). He found it on the sea bottom about 100 meters from the shore in Athlit Bay, some 15 km. south of Haifa.[40] The ram was cast in 465 kg. of high grade bronze, has an overall length of 2.26 m., a maximum width of 0.76 m., and a maximum height of 0.95 m.[41] When sectional drawings were published by J.R. Steffy in 1983, W.M. Murray recognized a similarity in shape between the ram's cross-section where it attached to the bow of its ship and the nose-like shapes of the Nikopolis sockets. After examining both the ram in Haifa and the monument at Nikopolis, he realized that 1) the monument could be used to determine the ship class of the Athlit ram, and 2) in return, the ram could help to explain the exact function of the sockets. Furthermore, an understanding of these sockets might allow for the reconstruction of the warship bows whose rams once decorated the monument.

When approached by Murray with this new information, Ph. Petsas agreed to help with a reexamination of the monument's cuttings. A collaborative project was proposed to both the Athens Archaeological Society and the Greek Archaeological Service, permission was granted, and the necessary fieldwork carried out in May 1986. Funding for the project was generously provided by the American Philosophical Society, the University of South Florida, and the city of Preveza.[42] To all those whose help enabled the successful completion of this project, the authors extend their sincere appreciation and thanks.[43]

[39] Cf. PICARD 1957, pp. 261–62. The alternate interpretation of the scene (put forth by H.A. Cahn in 1946; cf. PICARD 1957, p. 261 n. 1) has Apollo standing atop a podium decorated with laurel sprigs and three containers (*foruli*) for the Sibylline books.

[40] For the initial discovery and first reports of the ram in English, see LINDER-RAMON 1981; RABAN 1981, p. 292; BASCH 1982; FROST 1982; and STEFFY 1983. For a map identifying the findspot, see RABAN 1985, p. 33, Fig. 14; and LINDER 1988, p. 62, Fig. 1. For the date and provenience of the ram, see MURRAY forthcoming.

[41] Personal communication from J.R. Steffy, Dec. 11, 1986.

[42] The authors wish to thank the mayor of Preveza, Mr. N. Iannoulis, for sponsoring our request for assistance before the city council (which agreed to bear the expense of our lodging), and also for assigning to us at public expense two city workers to help with cleaning the site.

[43] The fieldwork in May 1986 was carried out with the help of S.P. Murray, D. Sagias and R. Evensen. R. and L. Kallet-Marx visited the site for a few days to help with the compass survey of the monument and also with the tedious job of laying the camera positions for the photo mosaic. Specific problems and questions raised by the preparation of this manuscript were reexamined and resolved by a visit to the site in July 1987, when we were aided by J.A. Maseman.

3. The Survey of 1986

During the 73 years prior to 1986, a half-dozen investigators of Octavian's Campsite Memorial had compiled the following list of some-times conflicting observations: 1) the dimensions of "a temple preserved only in its foundations"; 2) a few architectural elements such as column drums, one Corinthian capital, rooftiles, etc.; 3) 26 fragments from a large inscription carved on frieze blocks; 4) the stylobate of a stoa with cuttings in its surface (Fig. 8); and 5) a podium with nose-shaped cuttings of different sizes in its downhill face. Even when a list of ancient references to the monument was added, a clear picture of what actually existed here failed to emerge.[44] Our primary goal, therefore, was to record accurately the surviving elements of the monument currently visible above ground. In particular, this involved making a proper record

b

Fig. 8.

---

[44] For this reason, it is unfair to criticize excessively those who have misinterpreted the remains at the site; cf. supra nn. 12 and 14. It should be stated, however, that the arguments of Rhomaios and Gagé (supra Section 2) were largely ignored except for their comments on the monument's inscription.

of the cuttings, or "sockets," in the south retaining wall. To accomplish this goal we divided our investigation into three main tasks. Since we first needed to make an accurate plan of the site, we cleared away the considerable covering of thorns and weeds and mapped the exposed remains.[45] Next, we recorded the dimensions and spacing of the sockets preserved in the downhill face of the podium's southern retaining wall. And finally, to obtain an exact record of the cuttings' different shapes, exterior dimensions, and the relative positions of the constituent blocks, we made a photographic mosaic of the podium's south face.

When we first arrived at the site in early May, it was so overgrown with weeds, grasses, ferns and thorns that two days of work were required to expose the blocks of the southern retaining wall. A careful examination of the remains revealed the outline of the podium—a rectangular terrace supported by a stout retaining wall on three of its sides (Figs. 9–13). On the terrace's south side, the wall runs east to west some 62 meters; the western and eastern returns are preserved for 21 and 23 meters respectively. These remains are clearly the "temple foundations" reported by Philadelpheus in 1913.[46] Overall, the walls are fairly well preserved and reveal a clear understanding of the pressures they were designed to contain. Notwithstanding their sturdiness, both the western and eastern sides of the podium have suffered considerable damage at the hands of stone robbers.[47] On the steeper western side of the terrace, the wall is preserved in only one place to the height of three to four courses; elsewhere only the foundation course remains (Figs. 12, 14). Even this lowest course has been displaced in many sections of the surviving eastern wall (Fig. 10). The fact that the podium has not collapsed is due in large part to the extensive use of concrete in the core and the continued integrity of the southern retaining wall (Fig. 13).

On the positive side, the poor condition of the eastern and western walls reveals how the sides of the podium were originally constructed. Both retaining walls consist of heavy limestone blocks backed by a solid mass of concrete. Along the western side, where the remains are more complete, it can be seen that a few headers were placed at irregular intervals in a attempt to anchor the wall to its concrete core. On the downhill portion of both sides, the limestone facing blocks are stepped back into the hillside, resulting in a double row of blocks as a facing for the concrete core. This was done, presumably, where the architects thought greater pressures had to be contained. For further strength, the

---

[45] The area of the stoa on the podium's surface was not included in this cleaning of the site; its position was added to the survey in the summer of 1987.

[46] Cf. supra n. 15.

[47] Cf. PHILADELPHEUS 1913, pp. 90–91, who believes the monument may have been quarried during the reign of Justinian (following an incursion of the Goths) to help with the construction of a new, more defensible city wall. It also seems clear that local villagers have removed many blocks from the site in recent years. A comparison of Figures 3 and 13 shows how many blocks have been removed since 1913.

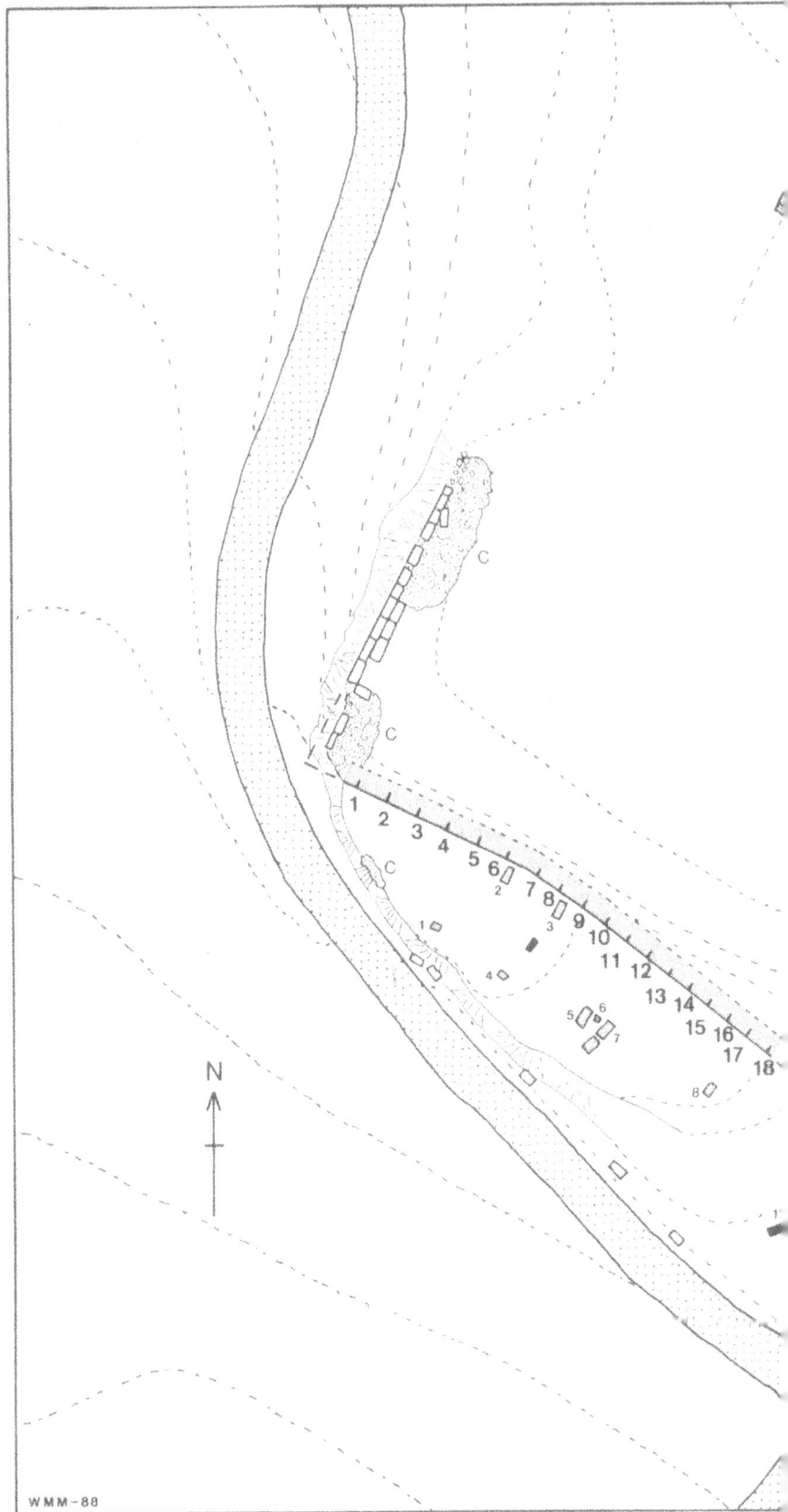

N

Fig. 9.

WMM-88

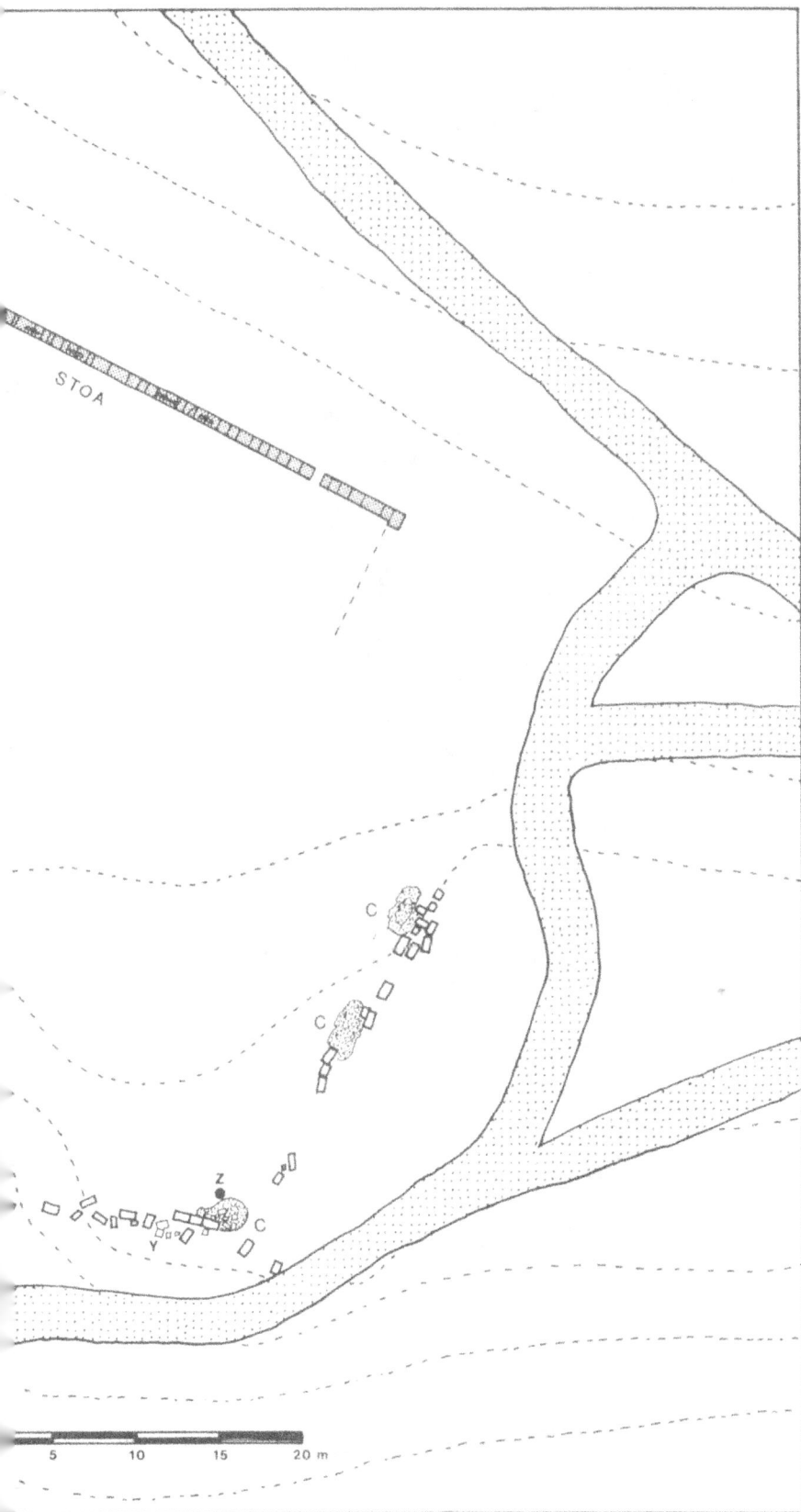

STOA

5   10   15   20 m

Fig. 9.

Fig. 10.

26

Fig. 11.

Fig. 12.

Fig. 13.

Fig. 14.

exterior line of blocks in this double row was clamped together by iron "double T" clamps (|-|) set in lead.

In addition to the double rows of blocks, the clamps, concrete core and headers, the blocks of the downhill portions were also bedded on a layer of concrete. Such a foundation can be seen at a number of places—beneath the robbed out blocks of the southwest and southeast corners, beneath the first block where the double row begins along the western wall (Fig. 14), and beneath several blocks still *in situ* near the east end of the southern wall (Fig. 15). From numerous gaps in the front (i.e., south) wall, it can also be seen that concrete was used here as well (Fig. 16). In fact, concrete was originally poured behind the entire length of the south wall as a means of binding the facing blocks together, thereby providing additional stability to the whole structure.

This exact type of construction is well attested in Rome as characteristic of the Augustan building program.[48] The usual concrete found in Rome during this period is "dusky red" in color and contains large rubble inclusions, called *caementa*.[49] These were usually taken from stone that was easily available, often from the same stone that served as the facing for the core. In the case of the Campsite Memorial, the concrete is basically gray (although it has a reddish cast to it in some places) with large *caementa* of limestone irregularly laid in the mortar. The *caementa* are clearly from the same stone that served as the facing for the core. Parallels for this type of construction (a concrete core boxed in by squared stone walls) can be found in numerous buildings of this period in Rome, most notably in the podium for the temple of Divus Iulius, the Mausoleum of Augustus and the *Rostra Augusti*.[50] But in many of the Roman examples, only fragments of the squared stone facing remain.

Fortunately for us, the main southern wall of the podium at Nikopolis is also the best preserved. It currently lies exposed for about 45 meters of its original 62 meter length and attains a height of four to five courses.[51] Two gaps currently exist in the wall: 2.65 meters are missing at its western end and a 4.68 meter stretch between sockets 18 and A has been ripped out. In addition, a 16.8 meter section of the wall's eastern end remains to be excavated (cf. Figs. 17–19). Slumped, broken and bent, the southern wall reveals the strain of containing the hillside for almost 21 centuries. Nevertheless, preserved along the entire length of its south face is the true measure of the skill exhibited by the monument's builders, for here remain the intricately carved sockets that once held the enemy's rams slightly recessed into the face of the retaining wall.[52]

---

[48] For a clear presentation of the evidence, see BLAKE 1947, pp. 333–52.

[49] BLAKE 1947, p. 343.

[50] BLAKE 1947, pp. 163–80, 334, 336.

[51] The wall reaches a height of four courses if one counts blocks that actually overlie one another. As can be seen from Figure 13, a fifth course is visible behind the top of the fourth course along much of the wall's length.

[52] Sufficient blocks remain from both the western and eastern walls to make it certain no rams were exhibited toward the west or the east.

Fig. 15.

Fig. 16.

Fig. 17.

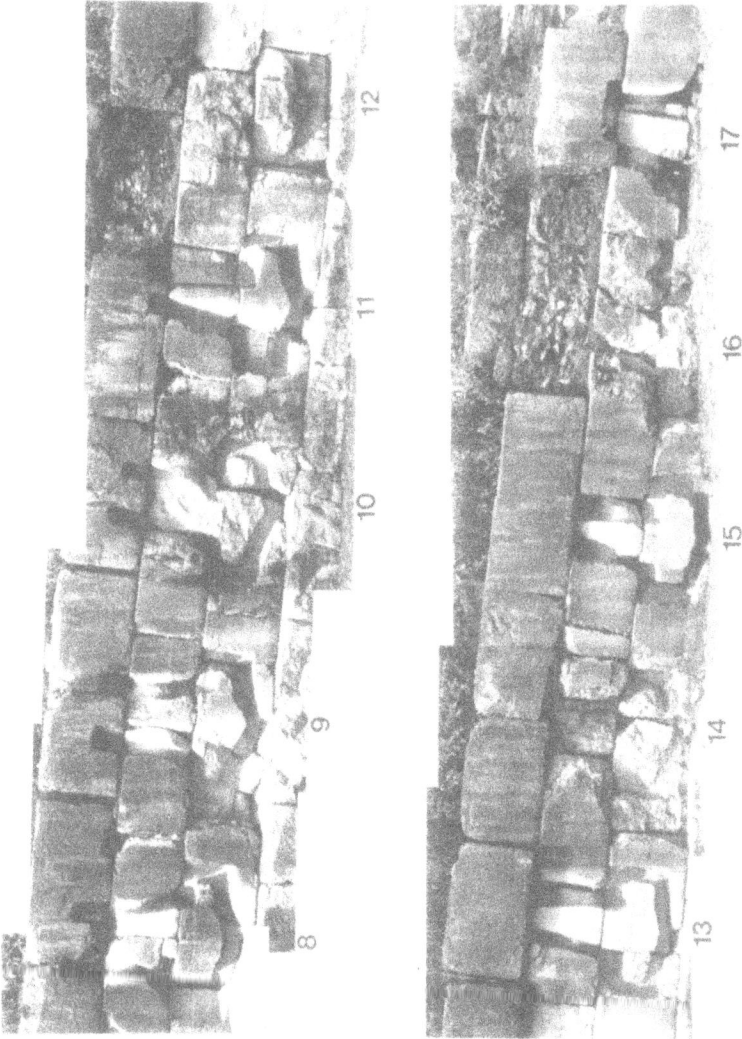

Fig. 18.

Fig. 19.

a. The Sockets and Their Importance

After all the weeds and thorns had been cleared from the front of the monument, the interiors of each socket were carefully cleaned to ground level. Thorn bushes have established thick roots behind and between many blocks in the wall, and it required dogged persistence to cut back the growth *below* the level of the cutting's surface. Throughout this process of cleaning the sockets, particular care was taken not to disturb the monument itself. In a number of places near the sockets' edges, the limestone blocks are badly weathered and cracked. In fact, we found four pieces that had previously broken off the face of the wall; each piece was set back into its original position, and it is hoped they will be reattached to the monument's face in the near future.[53]

Once the task of cleaning was done, 23 separate sockets were clearly visible, arranged from west to east in generally decreasing sizes (Figs. 17–22). Starting with the first cutting on the west, which was designated number 1 (hereafter socket numbers will be written [1], [2], [3], etc., to distinguish them from measurement numbers), we recorded a series of width and height measurements as well as a number of profiles. A full description of these measurements is given in Table 1.

So that the reader may understand what was recorded, we must now explain the reason for the sockets' peculiar shape, and this is best demonstrated by comparing Figure 23 with Figure 24. The first illustration represents a cross-sectional view of the Athlit ram 31.2 cm. forward of the port trough ear tip (along the A line in Fig. 25). If the Athlit ram were mounted on the wall at Octavian's campsite, this section would correspond to the plane of the wall's surface. Since the immense weight of the weapon was supported by the ground, the designers of this wall needed only to insure that the fit between the ram and the wall was tight. To accomplish this, they carefully cut back the timbers from each ram's interior to create a hollow. They then carved the socket for each ram leaving a central, uncut section or "core" which corresponded in shape to the ram's hollowed interior. Then, as they jockeyed the ram into its socket, the core of each cutting slid into the cavity created by the removal of the ram's timbers.

This "hand-in-glove" fit explains why no clamps held the rams in place on most of the cuttings, and why the core of each cutting corresponds so closely in shape to the wooden timbers found intact inside the Athlit ram: the chock, stem, ramming timber and wales. By measuring the dimensions of the sockets and their cores, priceless direct information from the bow timbers of Antony's fleet can be recovered.

There is more. Because the sockets were carved to receive the after-ends of each ram, they preserve the after-cowl curvature and rear contours of the trough ear and bottom plate (cf. Fig. 25). By carefully re-

---

[53] The affected areas occur in sockets [7], [8], [17] and [B]; for additional details, see infra.

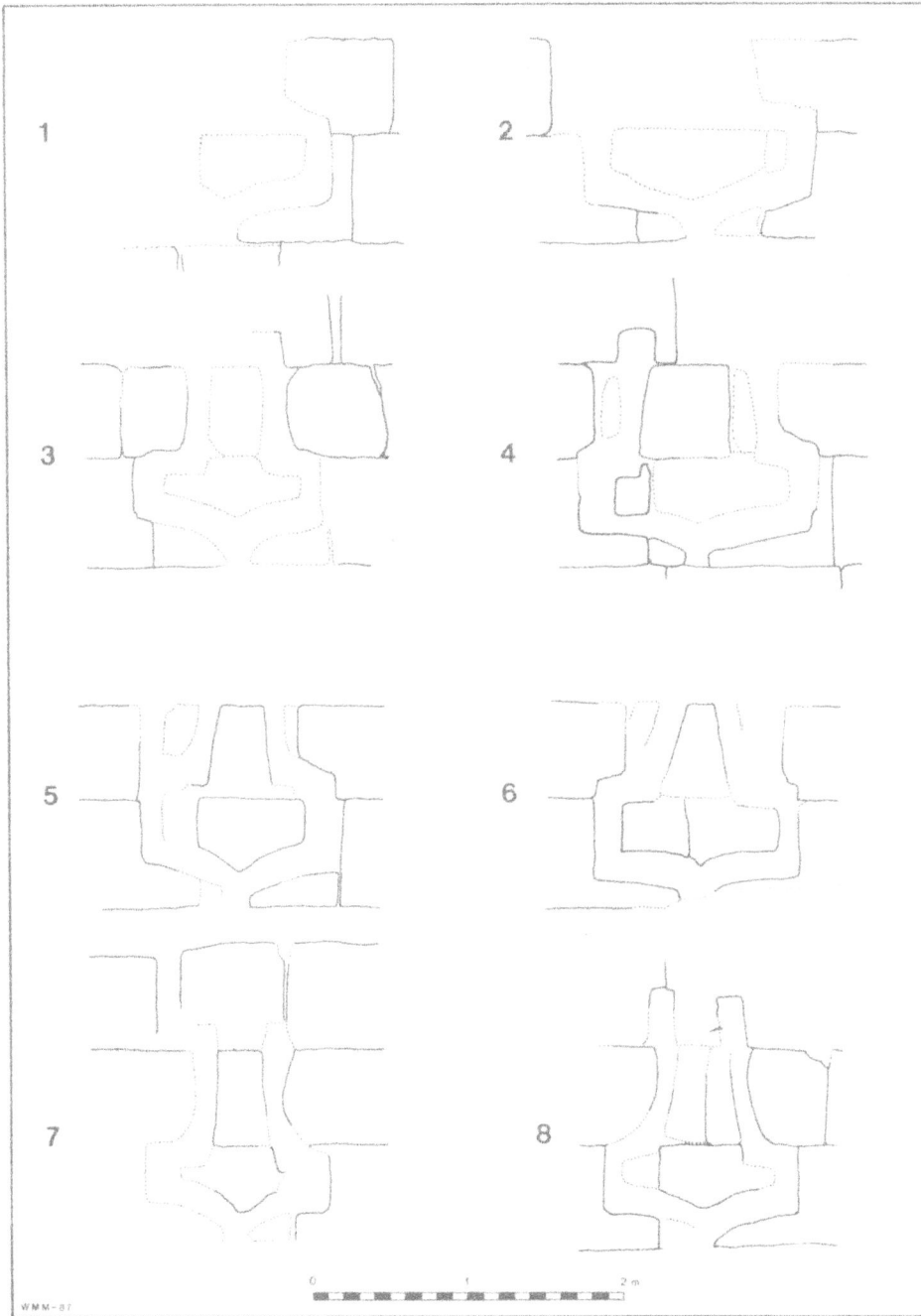

Fig. 20.

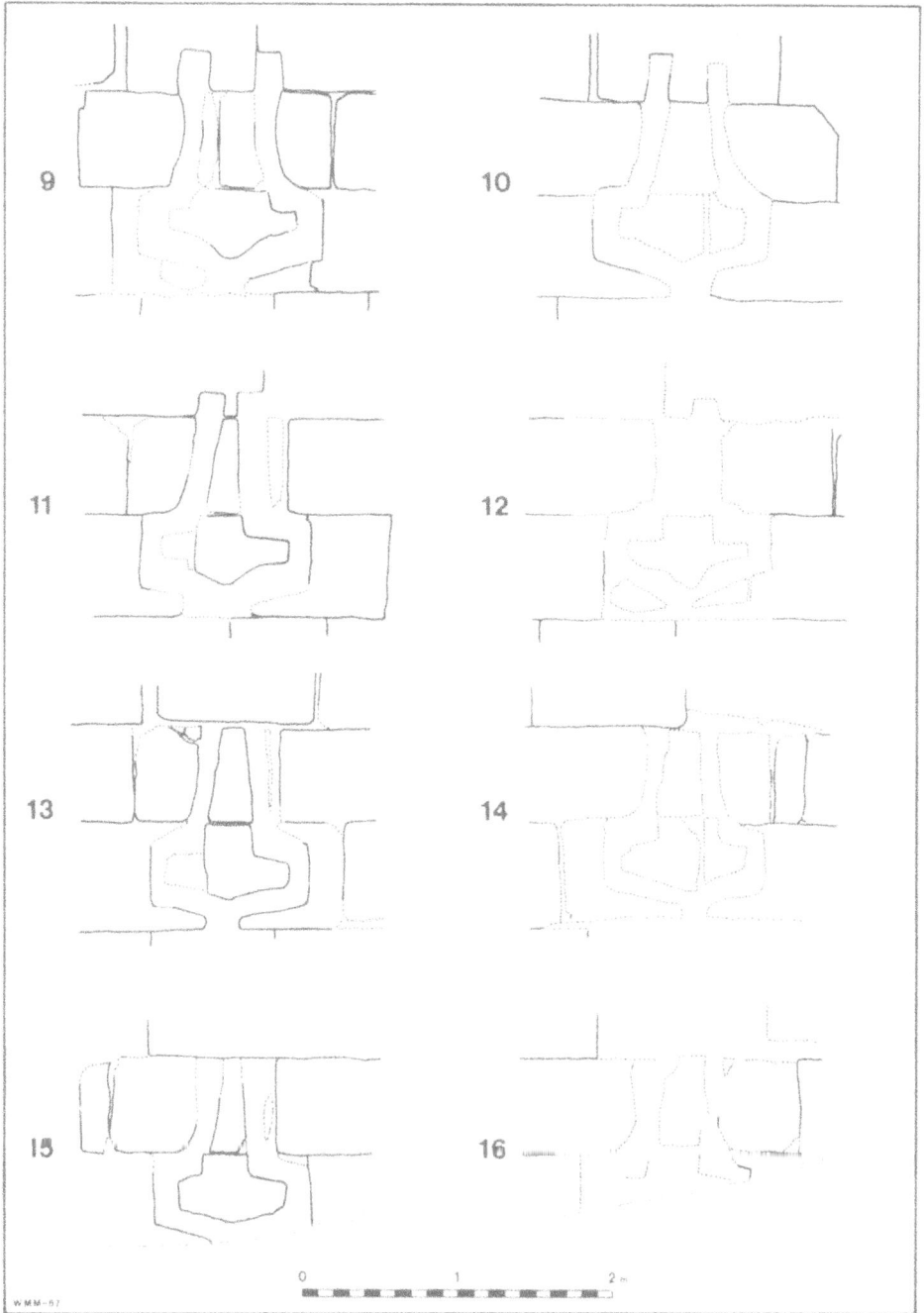

Fig. 21.

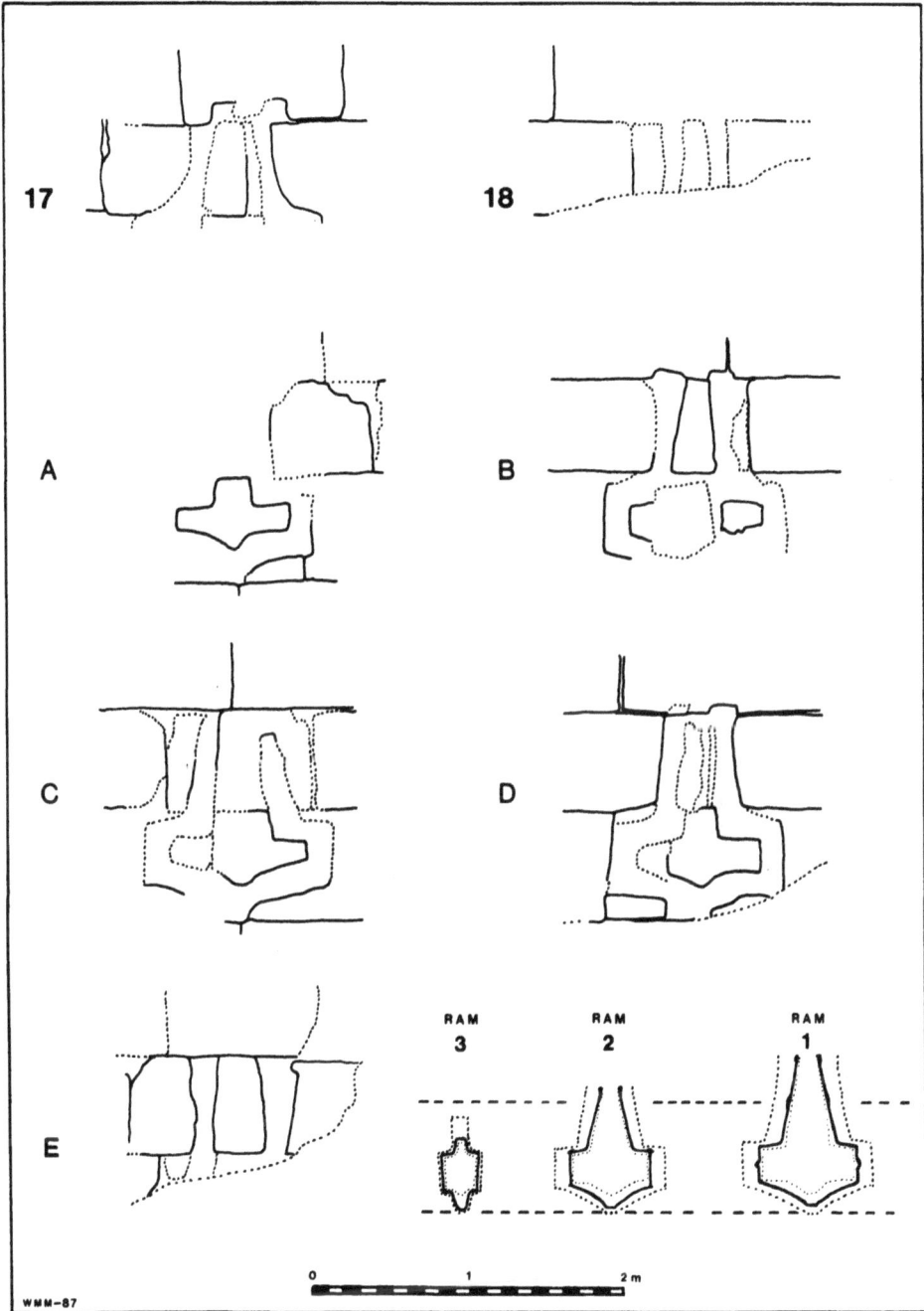

Fig. 22.

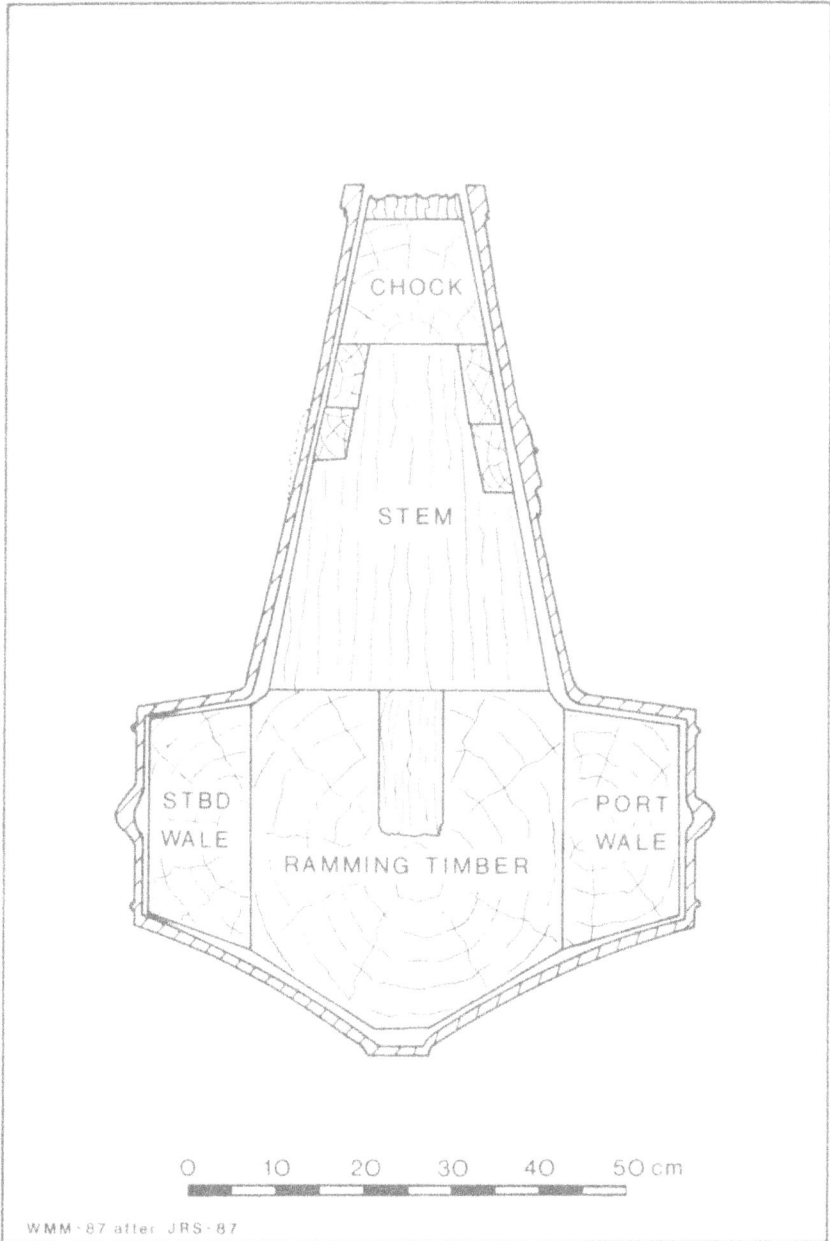

WMM·87 after JRS·87

Fig. 23.

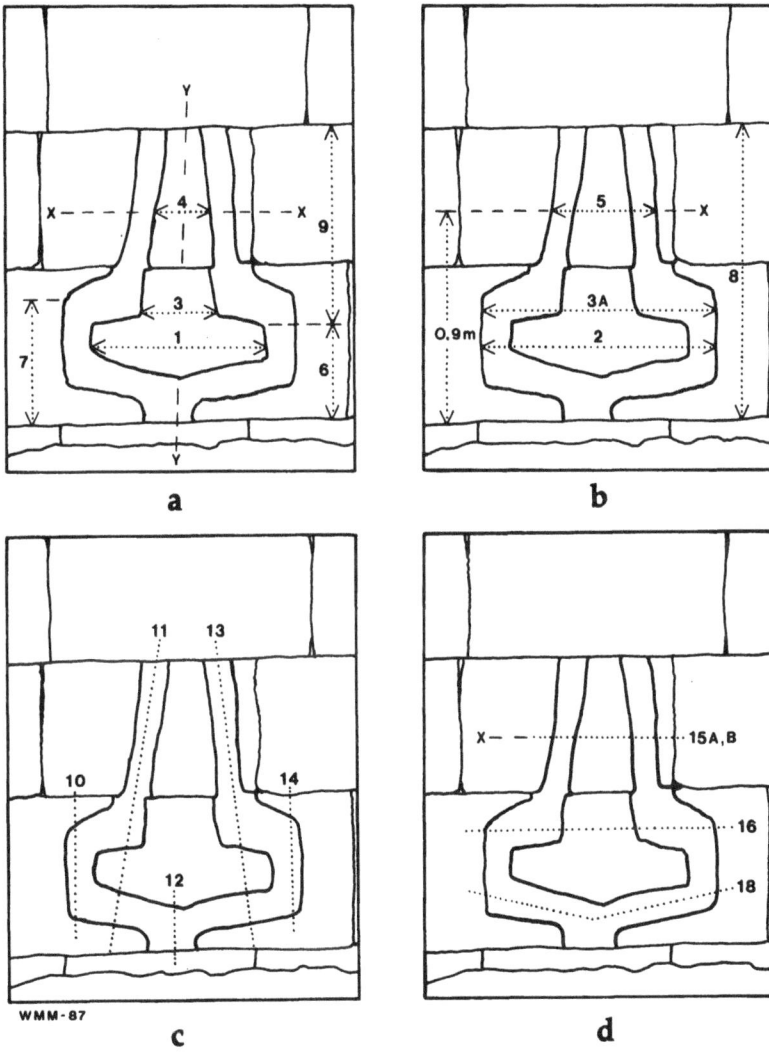

Fig. 24.

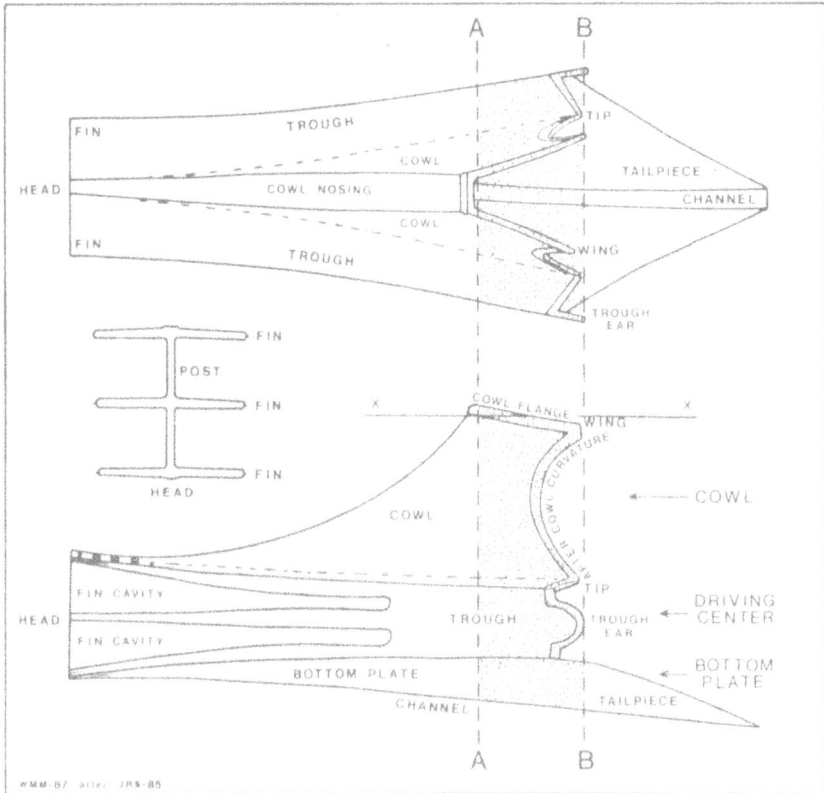

Fig. 25.

cording each socket's contours with a large profiler, the actual shapes of individual rams can also be recovered. Direct information, therefore, from the bows of 23 warships that fought in the Battle of Actium is provided by a careful analysis of these cuttings. More precious to nautical historians than a shipwreck full of coins, Octavian's Campsite Memorial graphically demonstrates the relative sizes of the large polyremes comprising the navies of the Hellenistic period. In effect, this memorial preserves information once thought lost forever.[54] In order to tap it, however, a system of measurements must be defined which accurately records the important features of each socket (see Table 1).

---

[54] For a discussion of the problems involved in identifying the various classes of ancient warships, see Chapter IV.

Table 1:
Measurement Definitions (cf. Figs. 23–25)

Note: the "core" designates the reserved, uncarved section of each socket which originally fit inside each ram mounted on the wall. The "x" line is 0.9 m. from the top of the first course and parallel to it; as it represents the approximate height of the Athlit ram, it is intended to provide a point of comparison between the different sockets and the Athlit ram. The "y" line is roughly perpendicular to the "x" line and is intended to represent the center-line of each socket; if the original placement of the socket was not exactly vertical, then the "y" line will not be perpendicular to the "x" line.

Measurement	Definition
#1:	the width of the core from wale to wale
#2:	the greatest exterior width of the cutting from wale to wale
#3:	the width of the core at the base of the stem
#3A:	the exterior width of the cutting at the base of the stem
#4:	the width of the core at the "x" line
#5:	the exterior width of the cutting at the "x" line
#6 L:	the height of the core at the top of the left wale[55]
#6 R:	the height of the core at the top of the right wale
#7 L:	the exterior height of the cutting at the top of the left wale
#7 R:	the exterior height of the cutting at the top of the right wale
#8 L:	the height of the cutting, left side
#8 R:	the height of the cutting, right side
#15A L:	the width of the cutting, left side at the "x" line
#15A R:	the width of the cutting, right side at the "x" line

Profile #	Definition
#10:	the after-end of the left trough
#11:	the after-end of the cowl and the depth of the bottom plate between the channel and the trough, left side
#12:	the depth of the bottom plate/tailpiece at the "y" line
#13:	the after-end of the cowl and the depth of the bottom plate between the channel and the trough, right side
#14:	the after-end of the right trough
#15B:	cross-section at the "x" line; cf. infra Table 2, #15B
#16:	the after-end of the top of the trough
#17:	see note 56
#18:	the after-end of the bottom plate

---

[55] It should be noted here that the left and right wales are terms which describe the *socket* and not the original ship. We should remember that from the perspective of the ship, what we call the socket's left wale represents the ship's starboard (i.e., right) side, and the socket's right wale the ship's port (i.e., left) side.

[56] A cross-sectional profile of the socket between #16 and #18 was originally designated as #17. Once we examined the cuttings, #17 was deemed superfluous because the depth of the profile was uniformly even and its shape could be roughly calculated from profiles #10 and #14, and measurements #1 and #2.

b. The Sockets: Methodology of Measurement

Measuring the cuttings involved many problems. Since our methodology determined the values we recorded, it seems appropriate to describe here the procedure we employed. First, we had to establish some fixed benchmark to which anomalies in the wall's structure could be referred. Because the wall slumped badly from west to east, and because we wanted to measure the degree of each socket's horizontal displacement, we decided to transect each cutting with a horizontal baseline. Three separate baselines were laid out along the face of the wall with a transit and marked in blue chalk with a carpenter's chalk line. BL1 (baseline) ran between sockets [1] and [13], BL 2 from [13] to [18], and BL3 from [A] to [E]. BL2 was placed 1.02 m. beneath BL1, and BL3 0.605 m. beneath BL2. Between the "y" axes of [1] and [D], the top of the first course has slumped downward, from west to east, 2.465 meters.[57]

Next, we developed a standard procedure for obtaining and recording the measurements we intended to extract from each socket. This was necessary in order to reduce the number and magnitude of errors made during the recording process. All measurements for each socket were recorded 1) on a separate standardized recording sheet, 2) in the same sequence, 3) according to the same system, and 4) by the same person, S.P. Murray.

Finally, we employed a measuring template specifically designed for the peculiarities of this monument. It consisted of two 2-inch by 0.5-inch pieces of stainless steel rectangular tubing, each a meter long and drilled with holes at 2 cm. intervals along the entire length of the steel (Fig. 26). For measuring the wide sockets at the western end of the wall, the two drilled sections could be joined end-to-end by means of a slip-joint. The holes in each section were just slightly larger than steel rods made from quarter-inch dowel stock which could be inserted through the template and thus pushed into the cutting at right angles to the surface of the wall. The depth of the socket at this particular point was then read from the rod which was marked in centimeter intervals. A second set of holes which accepted a support apparatus of moveable arms and pipes enabled us to position the template anywhere we desired along the face of the wall.[58]

By using this measuring device (hereafter abbreviated "MD"), we were

[57] An indication of the wall's horizontal undulation is provided by the distance from BL1 to the bottom of the socket (i.e., to the top of the first course) along the "y" axis for each socket. The following comparison of values reveals the progressive downward slumping of the wall between [1] and [D]: [1] = 0.38; [2] = 0.36; [3] = 0.34; [4] = 0.31; [5] = 0.315; [6] = 0.38; [7] = 0.46; [8] = 0.54; [9] = 0.665; [10] = 0.08; [11] = 1.0; [12] = 1.13; [13] = 1.315; [14] = 1.455; [15] = 1.605; [16] = NA; [17] = NA; [18] = NA; [A] = 2.18; [B] = 2.41; [C] = 2.635; [D] = 2.845; [E] = NA.

[58] The support device was made by Mr. Engolfios Sagias of Agioi Anargyroi (formerly of Amphyklia, Phokidos); the authors thank Mr. Sagias who created the support on short notice out of his Easter *souvles* (spits for roasting the Easter lamb). To honor the memory of an associate of Mr. Sagias who frequently created such "Rube Goldberg" contraptions, we named this device the "Braganza."

able to record the dimensions identified in Table 1 with a high degree of consistency. In addition, we adhered to the following procedures which were applied uniformly to each cutting. In the list below, each measurement-number is paired with a reference (in parentheses) to the appropriate segment of Figure 24, and is followed by a brief description of the procedure utilized to recover each dimension. The words "socket" and "cutting" are used interchangeably; "exterior" is used to define areas away from the center-line of the socket.

Table 2: Measurement Procedures	
Measurement #:	Procedure Utilized:
#1 (Fig. 24a):	Taken with a tape-measure from edge to edge where the core's surface was preserved and with the MD when the surface edge of the core was not preserved.[59]
#2 (Fig. 24b):	Taken with a tape from edge to edge at the narrowest surface dimension; if the original edges were not preserved, the MD was used to measure the distance between the preserved traces inside the socket of the cutting's exterior side.
#3 (Fig. 24a):	As with #1; taken with a tape or MD as appropriate. [This terminology will be used to indicate that the MD was used when the desired features existed only in traces on the back or side surfaces of the socket and were not preserved on the monument's original surface.]
#3A (Fig. 24b):	As with #2; taken with the tape or MD as appropriate (cf. #3).[60]
#4 (Fig. 24a):	Widest surface dimension taken with tape or MD as appropriate (cf. #3).
#5 (Fig. 24b):	Narrowest surface dimension taken with tape or MD as appropriate (cf. #3 and n. 60).
#6 (Fig. 24a):	Taken from the exterior upper corner of the core (at the wale) to the top of the first course with tape or MD as appropriate (cf. #3).
#7 (Fig. 24a):	Taken from the exterior upper corner of the socket (at the trough) to the top of the first course with tape or MD as appropriate (cf. #3).
#8 (Fig. 24b):	Taken with a tape or MD as appropriate (cf. #3).

[59] By positioning the MD flat against the face of the wall we were able to project all interior features to the wall's surface. Thus, when we wanted to measure the distance between broken features within the cutting, we projected the position of the desired features to points on the surface of the MD (and thus the plane of the wall's surface) and then obtained our measurement. On all such measurements, the points were projected from the first available traces that were closest to the original surface of the wall.

[60] The exterior edges of the cutting exhibited an inward expanding flare to accommodate the flaring shape of the cowl. At these places, we measured the most narrow preserved width toward the original surface of the wall.

#9 (Fig. 24a):	As this dimension could be calculated from #8 and #6, we omitted recording it on most sockets.
#10 (Fig. 24c):	Taken with the MD at the cutting's deepest point in the area of the desired profile.[61]
#11 (Fig. 24c):	As #10; also see "Offset" below.
#12 (Fig. 24c):	Since #18 provides the depth of the socket here, we generally did not record this profile.
#13 (Fig. 24c):	As #10; also see "Offset" below.
#14 (Fig. 24c):	As #10.
#15A (Fig. 24d):	Taken along the back wall of the socket.
#15B (Fig. 24d):	Taken with the MD when the interior of the socket exhibited an anomaly; if no anomaly existed, then #15A sufficed.
#16 (Fig. 24d):	Taken with the MD in such a way as to follow the deepest part of the socket.
#17:	Not necessary as a profile.
#18 (Fig. 24d):	Taken with the MD in such way as to follow the deepest part of the socket; as a result, the profile was not taken in a straight line.
Offset:	The face of the third course was set back from that of the second by about 4 cm. Variances in this dimension revealed that the positions of the second and third courses had shifted. The offset was measured on both the immediate left and right sides of each socket as well as on the core at the "y" axis. When taking profiles #11 and #13, we referenced the MD to the face of the second course block.

The catalog below presents in a systematic manner the surface measurements from each socket. If Figure 23 is compared with Figure 24, it can be seen that measurements #1, #3 and #4 represent width dimensions of the actual bow timbers inside each ram. If we compare Figures 24 and 25, we see that measurements #2, #3A and #5 represent the width dimensions of the ram's after-end somewhere between the cross-sections at the A and B lines in Figure 25.[62] The actual height of the wale from the ram's bottom is between the values for #6 and #7, and the total height of the ram is represented by #8. The "L" and "R" in measurements #6–#9 and #15A represent measurements from the left and right sides of the socket, respectively. An asterisk (*) next to the meas-

---

[61] We began measuring the profile one hole above the upper edge of the cutting and finished one hole below the bottom edge of the cutting. When the profile crossed a joint between blocks, the baseline, the "x" or the "y" lines, these points were noted on the recording sheet. Since the profile was not always taken on a truly vertical line, these fixed points allowed us to make the appropriate corrections when we combined them into a single side view (cf. Figs. 27–29).

[62] If the Athlit ram were inserted backwards into a socket on this wall, section B (Fig. 25), which is wider than section A, would necessarily correspond to the exterior dimensions of the socket. For another possibility, see infra Section 3.f.

Fig. 26.

urement indicates that additional observations appear in the "Remarks" section following the catalog; for the values in parentheses, see the "Remarks" for Socket [3]. All measurements are given in meters.

c. The Sockets: Catalog of Dimensions

Socket [1]

#1	1.07*	#5	0.77*	
#2	1.38*	#6	L=NA;	R=0.54
#3	NA	#7	L=NA;	R=0.64
#3A	NA	#8	L=NA;	R=NA
#4	NA	#9	—	
Offset	NA	#15A	L=NA;	R=NA

BL1 to bottom of socket=0.38

Socket [2]

#1	1.15	#5	1.22*	
#2	1.50	#6	L=0.67;	R=0.67
#3	NA	#7	L=NA;	R=0.81
#3A	0.84*	#8	L=NA	R=NA
#4	NA	#9	—	
Offset	NA	#15A	L=NA	R=0.18 (preserved)

BL1 to bottom of socket=0.36

#1	0.95
#2	1.32* (−0.03)
#3	0.37
#3A	0.715
#4	0.345
Offset	L=0.035

BL1 to bottom of socket=0.34

Socket [3]

#5	0.655* (−0.02)	
#6	L=0.60	R=0.565
#7	L=0.69	R=0.68
#8	L=NA	R=1.435* (+0.01?)
#9	L=NA	R=0.87
#15A	L=0.185	R=0.185

#1	1.105
#2	1.525
#3	0.725
#3A	1.035* (−0.02)
#4	0.73* (−0.02)
Offset	L=0.02 R=0.03

BL1 to bottom of socket=0.32

Socket [4]

#5	1.03* (−0.02)	
#6	L=0.57	R=0.58
#7	L=0.74	R=0.76
#8	L=1.465	R=NA
#9	L=0.90	R=NA
#15A	L=0.135	R=0.145

#1	0.85*
#2	1.23
#3	0.425
#3A	NA
#4	0.37
Offset	L=0.035 R=0.03
	core=0.045

BL1 to bottom of socket=0.315

Socket [5]

#5	1.05	
#6	L=0.67*	R=0.665*
#7	L=NA	R=0.82
#8	L=1.24	R=1.23
#9	—	
#15A	L=NA	R=0.34 (cf. #15B)

#1	1.02
#2	1.315
#3	0.52* (−0.02)
#3A	1.01?
#4	0.365
Offset	L=0.04 R=0.03

BL1 to bottom of socket=0.38

Socket [6]

#5	NA	
#6	L=0.665	R=0.635
#7	L=0.775	R=NA (under soil)
#8	L=NA	R=NA
#9	—	
#15A	L=0.09	R=0.12

#1	0.077*
#2	1.195
#3	0.51
#3A	0.60?
#4	0.305
Offset	L=0.03 R=0.035
	core=0.04

BL1 to bottom of socket=0.46

Socket [7]

#5	0.595* (−0.025)	
#6	L=0.50*	R=0.485*
#7	L=0.64*	R=0.575
#8	L=1.415	R=1.38
#9	—	
#15A	L=0.16	R=0.14 (Cf. #15B)

#1	0.925* (−0.045)
#2	1.235* (−0.045)
#3	0.545
#3A	0.78*
#4	0.415

Socket [8]

#5	0.625	
#6	L=0.53*	R=0.51
#7	L=0.65	R=0.65
#8	L=1.59	R=1.55
#9	—	

Offset L=0.03 R=0.04   #15A L=0.105   R=0.095
        core=0.06
BL1 to bottom of socket=0.54

Socket [9]

#1	0.86	#5	0.065* (−0.01)
#2	1.25	#6	L=0.485 R=0.505
#3	0.54	#7	L=0.59 R=0.0575
#3A	0.72	#8	L=1.49 R=1.47
#4	0.35* (−0.01)	#9	—

Offset L=0.03 R=0.055   #15A L=0.10   R=0.125
        core=0.055
BL1 to bottom of socket=0.665

Socket [10]

#1	0.845	#5	0.625
#2	1.15	#6	L=0.555 R=0.60
#3	0.525*	#7	L=0.67 R=0.685
#3A	0.815	#8	L=1.48 R=1.485
#4	0.40*	#9	—

Offset L=0.04 R=0.05
BL1 to bottom of socket=0.80

Socket [11]

#1	0.885	#5	0.555*
#2	1.12	#6	L=0.495 R=0.495
#3	0.335	#7	L=0.64 R−0.65
#3A	0.60*	#8	L=1.38 R=1.41
#4	0.16	#9	—
		#15	L=0.095 R=0.090

Offset L=0.045 R=0.04
        core=0.04
BL1 to bottom of socket=1.00

Socket [12]*

#1	0.86	#5	NA
#2	1.10	#6	L=0.46 R=0.46
#3	0.32	#7	L=0.66 R=0.655
#3A	NA	#8	L=NA R=1.39
#4	NA	#9	—
		#15A	NA

Offset L=0.035 R=NA
        core=NA
BL1 to bottom of socket=1.13

Socket [13]

#1	0.79	#5	0.48*
#2	1.03	#6	L=0.44 R=0.43
#3	0.33	#7	L=0.54 R=0.515
#3A	0.575* (−0.04)	#8	L=1.25 R=1.255
#4	0.25	#9	—
		#15A	L=0.11 R=0.12

Offset L=0.055 R=0.025
        core=0.00
BL2 to bottom of socket=0.295

Socket [14]*

#1	0.80*	#5	0.465	
#2	1.035	#6	L=0.49	R=0.50
#3	0.34*	#7	L=0.55	R=0.59
#3A	NA	#8	L=.124*	R=1.24*
#4	NA*; similar to [13]	#9	—	
Offset	L=0.03 R=0.05	#15A	NA	

BL2 to bottom of socket=0.435

Socket [15]

#1	0.69	#5	0.50*	
#2	1.005	#6	L=0.50	R=0.505
#3	0.30	#7	L=0.58	R=0.56
#3A	0.565* (−0.04)	#8	L=1.23	R=1.24
#4	0.175	#9	—	
Offset	L=0.04 R=0.045	#15A	L=0.12	R=0.12
	core=0.03			

BL2 to bottom of socket=0.585

Socket [16]

#1	0.72*	#5	NA	
#2	0.85*	#6	L=NA	R=NA
#3	0.35*	#7	L=NA	R=NA
#3A	0.53-0.56*	#8	L=NA	R=NA
#4	NA	#9	NA	
Offset	NA	#15A	NA	

BL2 to bottom of socket=NA

Socket [17]

#1	NA	#5	0.55*	
#2	1.12*	#6	L=NA	R=NA
#3	0.40*	#7	L=NA	R=NA
#3A	0.71*	#8	L=NA	R=NA
#4	0.345*	#9	L=NA	R=0.82
Offset	NA	#9A*	L=NA	R=0.73
		#15A	L=0.125*	R=0.085

BL2 to top of 3rd course=0.30

Socket [18]

#1	NA	#5	0.42*	
#2	NA	#6	L=NA	R=NA
#3	NA	#7	L=NA	R=NA
#3A	NA	#8	L=NA	R=NA
#4	0.205*	#9	L=NA	R=NA
Offset	NA	#15A	L=0.10	R=0.105

BL2 to top of 3rd course=0.19

Socket [A]

#1	0.715	#5	NA	
#2	0.98	#6	L=0.455	R=0.465
#3	0.24-0.26*	#7	L=NA	R=0.53
#3A	NA	#8	L=NA	R=NA

#4	NA	#9	L=NA R=NA
Offset	R=0.03	#15A	L=NA R=NA

BL3 to bottom of socket=0.555

Socket [B]

#1	0.83	#5	0.50*	
#2	1.105	#6	L=0.45	R=0.48
#3	0.335	#7	L=0.565	R=0.585
#3A	0.545	#8	L=1.29	R=1.285
#4	0.23	#9	—	
Offset	L=0.06 R=NA	#15A	L=0.14	R=0.12
	core=NA			

BL3 to bottom of socket=0.785

Socket [C]

#1	0.845	#5	0.555	
#2	1.175	#6	L=0.455*	R=0.45
#3	0.40*	#7	L=0.585	R=0.565
#3A	0.745*	#8	L=1.245	R=1.06
#4	0.285	#9	—	
Offset	core=0.06	#15A	L=0.14	R=0.14

BL3 to bottom of socket=1.01

Socket [D]

#1	0.755	#5	0.45*	
#2	1.025	#6	L=0.435	R=0.475
#3	0.235	#7	L=0.635	R=0.645
#3A	0.52	#8	L=1.18*	L=1.305
#4	0.195*	#9	—	
Offset	R=0.025	#15A	L=0.12	R=0.14

BL3 to bottom of socket=1.22

Socket [E]

#1	NA	#5	0.57* (−0.06)	
#2	1.03-1.12*	#6	L=NA	R=NA
#3	NA	#7	L=NA	R=NA
#3A	0.62* (−0.055?)	#8	L=NA	R=NA
#4	0.31	#9	—	
Offset	L=0.06 R=NA	#15A	L=0.12	R=0.16* (−0.06)
	core=0.03			

BL3 to bottom of socket=NA

1.) Remarks on the Catalog of Dimensions

Socket [1]: Measurements #1, #2 and #5 were calculated by doubling the appropriate distance from the preserved features to the "y" line. Since all cuttings are slightly asymmetrical, these "restored" measurements must represent approximate values only. Hereafter, such measurements will be denoted as being "calculated from the 'y' line."

Socket [2]: Measurements #3A and #5 are calculated from the "y" line; cf. [1] above.

Socket [3]: The upper right fourth course block of this cutting has shifted since its original placement and the original height of the socket (#8R) would have been about 1 cm. higher. Since other blocks have shifted from their original positions as well, this has resulted in the opening of gaps between the blocks of this cutting. As a result, the values indicated in parentheses must be subtracted from measurements #2 and #5 to arrive at the original dimensions.

Socket [4]: Block shifting has created a 2 cm. gap which must be subtracted from measurements #3A, #4 and #5; cf. [3] supra.

Socket [5]: Measurement #1 is calculated from the "y" line because the left side of the cutting is broken; the preserved width is 0.695 m. Measurements #6L and #6R are estimated from traces on the back wall of the socket.

Socket [6]: Measurement #3 was taken from the core where it is broken back from the wall's surface. Since the side of the core tapers inward (proceeding from the back of the socket to the surface), the width of #3 would have been originally about 2 cm. narrower at the wall's surface.

Socket [7]: The preserved width of measurement #1 is presented in the table, but the core is badly broken. If the measurement is calculated from the "y" line, the width would be 0.86 m. Since the end of the wales are preserved, measurements #6L and #6R are taken from the top of the preserved surface closest to the original end of the wales. Measurement #7L is taken from traces of what appear to be the original surface which has since largely broken away. Block shifting has created a 2.5 cm. gap which must be subtracted from measurement #5.

Socket [8]: Block shifting has created a 4.5 cm. gap which must be subtracted from measurements #1 and #2. Measurement #3A is calculated from the "y" line, and measurement #6L is taken from traces on the back wall of the socket.

Socket [9]: Block shifting has created a 1 cm. gap which must be subtracted from measurement #4 and #5.

Socket [10]: A 3.5 cm. gap exists between the two blocks that comprise the second course of the core which might affect measurement #3. But since no evidence of shifting is visible anywhere, this gap must have originally existed when the wall was constructed; it would have been invisible with the ram mounted in the cutting. Measurement #4 is calculated from traces on the right side of the socket and the "y" line.

Socket [11]: Measurement #3A is taken from traces on the right side of the socket; measurement #5 is also taken from traces on the right side.

Socket [12]: Since this cutting is poorly preserved, most measurements were taken from traces preserved on the interior of the socket.

Socket [13]: Block shifting has created a 4 cm. gap which must be subtracted from measurement #3A. The right side of measurement #5 was taken from traces of the original edge.

Socket [14]: Since this cutting is poorly preserved, most measurements were taken from traces. The traces for measurements #1, #3, #8L and #8R are very faint, and the values recorded must be accepted as approximate only. Measurement #4 is not preserved, but the width of the stem can be made out some 12 cm. higher as 0.25 m.

Socket [15]: Block shifting has created a 4 cm. gap which must be subtracted from measurement #3A. The right side of measurement #5 was taken from traces of the original edge.

Socket [16]: Because of the half-buried and poorly preserved nature of this cutting, measurements #1, #2, #3 and #3A are recorded from faint traces and are thus only approximate values.

Socket [17]: Because of the half-buried nature of this cutting and its broken left side, measurements #2 and #3A are calculated from an approximate "y" line; #3, #4, #5 and #15A are taken from traces. Measurement #9A represents the distance from the upper exterior edge of the wale to the top of the third course.

Socket [18]: Measurements #4 and #5 are taken from traces.

Socket [A]: Measurement #3 would be 0.24 m. but for the fact that a natural irregularity on the surface of the block makes it 0.26 m.; just above this bump, however, the width is clearly 0.24 m.

Socket [B]: Measurement #5 is taken from traces on the right side.

Socket [C]: Measurement #3 and #3A are calculated from the "y" line; measurement #6L is taken from traces.

Socket [D]: Although a gap of 5 cm. exists between the two blocks that make up the stem, it is possible that this gap is original and that no shifting has occurred. It is also possible that 5 cm. should be subtracted from measurements #4 and #5. Measurement #8L is taken from the true cutting at the top of the third course, not from the shallow impression in the bottom of the fourth course.

Socket [E]: Because of the half-buried nature of this cutting, measurement #2 is calculated from the "y" line. Possible traces on the left side of the socket might indicate that the left side is broken; if this is so, the original measurement should be restored as 1.03 m. A gap of 5.5–6 cm. exists between the two blocks of the third course. What appears to be a carved stone spacer still sits in the cutting which might indicate that the gap is an original feature of the wall. If so, the width of the gap should not be subtracted from measurements #3A, #5 and #15AR. Measurement #5 is taken from a broken right edge; as a result, its value is approximate. The value for measurement #15AR is also approximate.

d. The Profiles of the Sockets (Figs. 27–29)

We have already mentioned that the interior contours of the sockets preserve the outline of each ram's after-end. By overlapping profiles #13, #14 and #18, a composite view of the socket's right side can be drawn, and a similar view of its left side can be drawn from profiles

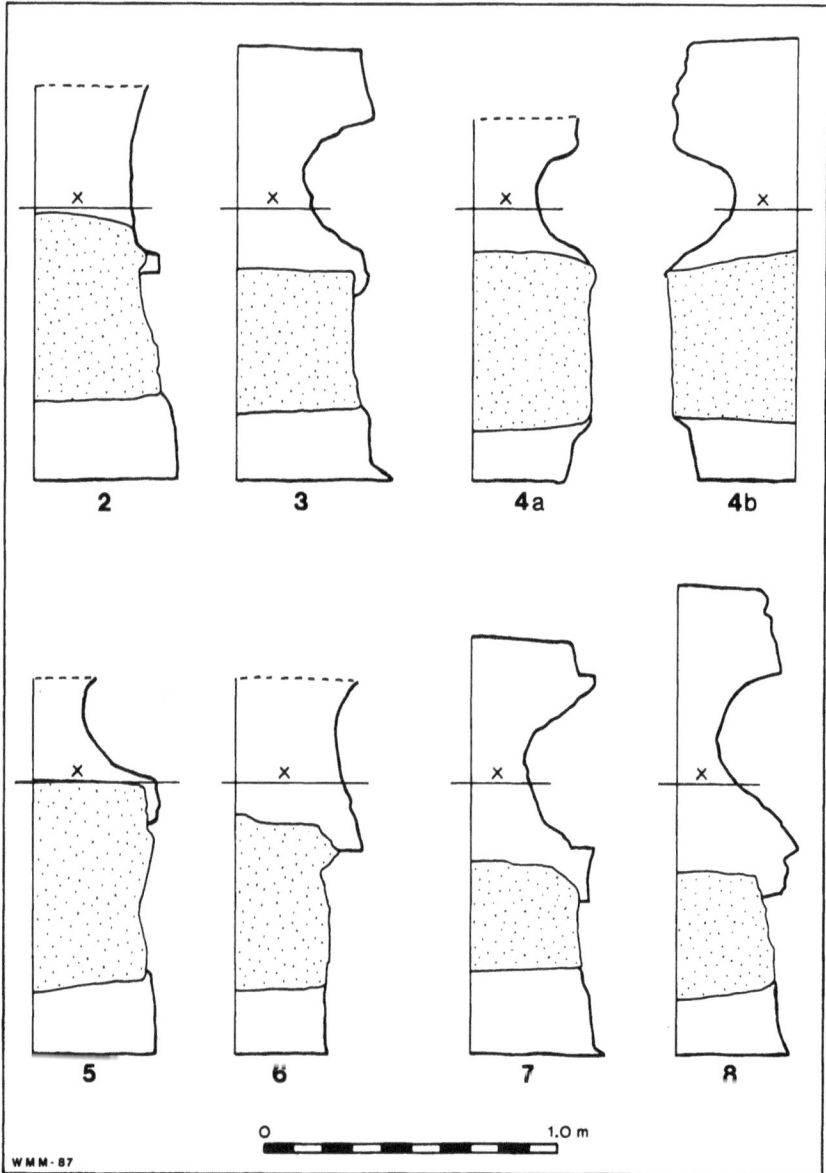

Fig. 27.

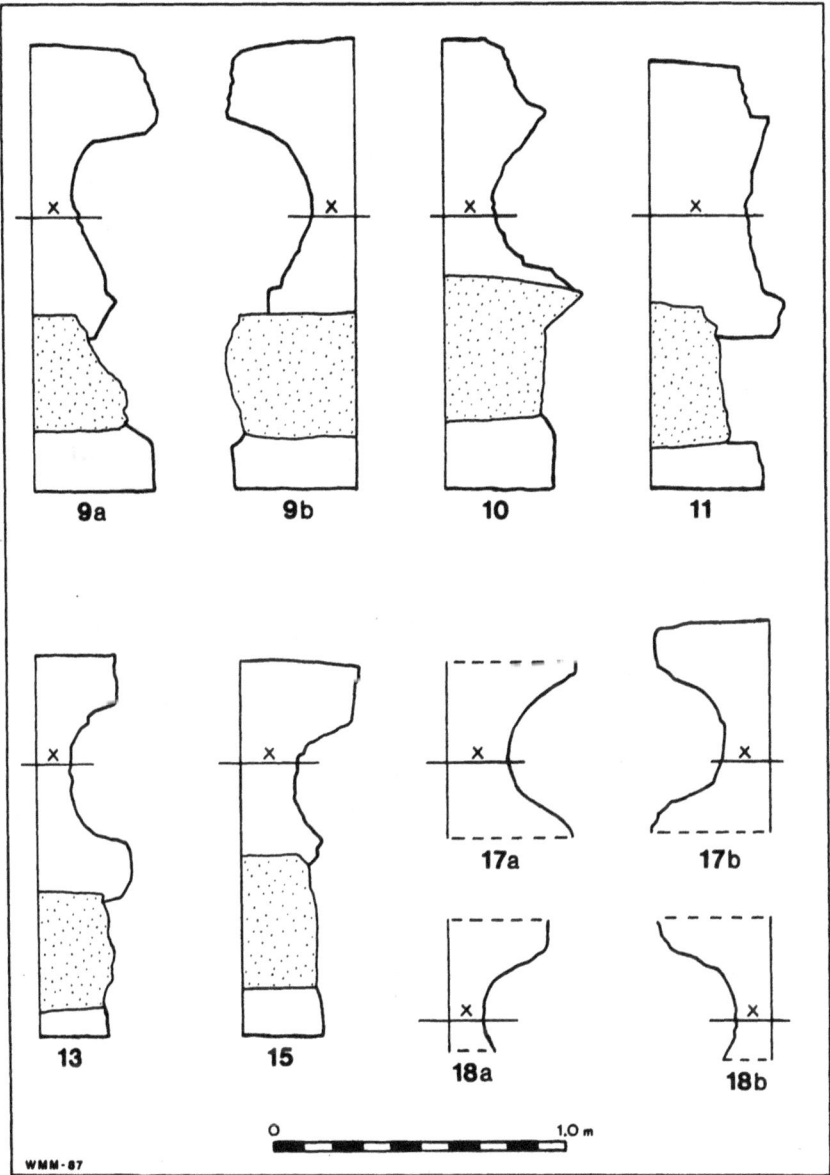

9a   9b   10   11

13   15   17a   17b

18a   18b

0   1.0 m

WMM-87

Fig. 28.

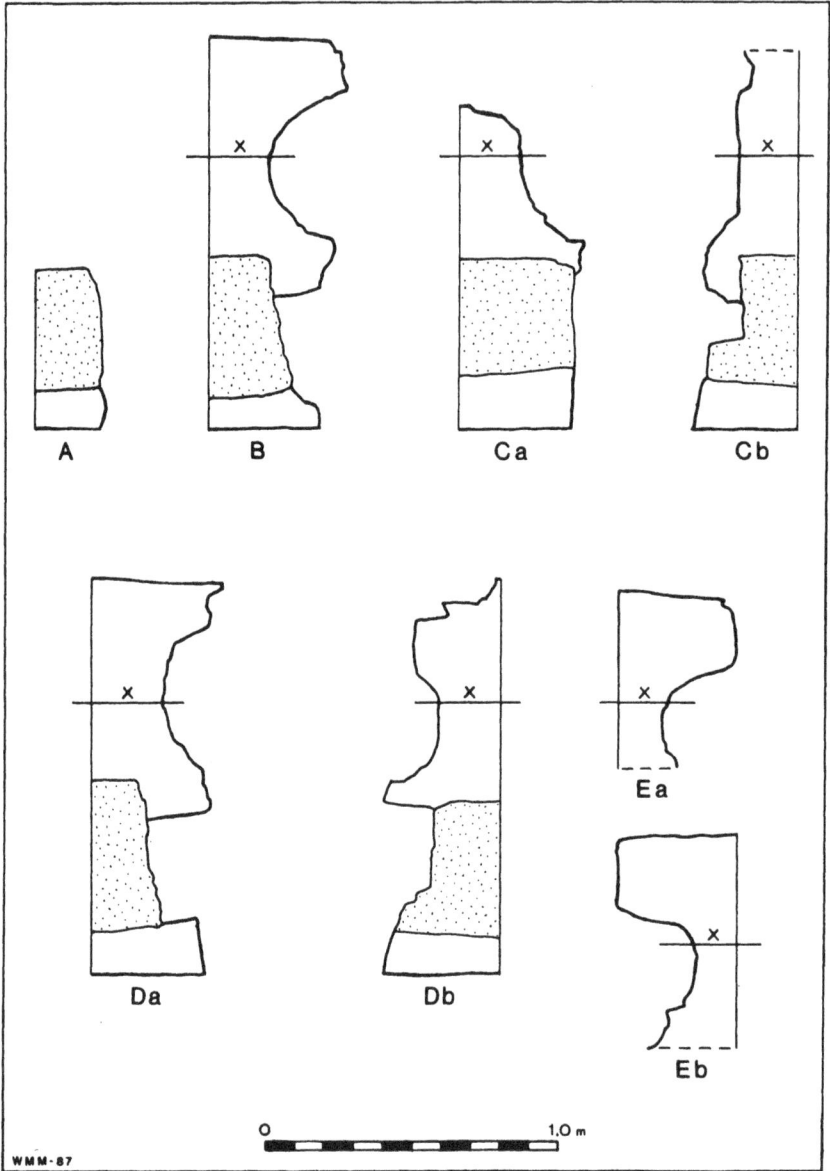

Fig. 29.

#10, #11 and #18. Unless the two sides differed significantly, we have chosen to represent only the sockets' right sides, in effect reproducing a view of each ram's port after-end.

Reference to Figure 25 will help the reader visualize what these profiles represent. If the Athlit ram were mounted on the Campsite Memorial, the stippled section between lines A and B represents the portion of the ram contained within the socket. The A line represents the surface plane of the wall, and the B line the deepest extent of the socket with the ram's tailpiece removed. Strictly speaking, were the Athlit ram to be mounted on this wall, an extra deep recess would have to be carved at the socket's bottom to accommodate its long tailpiece. We have represented the socket area in Figure 25 without the tailpiece, however, because this corresponds more closely to the actual profiles preserved by the sockets of the monument.

Figure 27 presents the after-ends of the rams that once occupied sockets [2]–[8], Figure 28 presents [9]–[18] and Figure 29 shows [A]–[E]. Sockets [4], [9], [17], [18], [C], [D] and [E] have been represented from both sides; "a" represents the left side of the socket (the ram's starboard side), and "b" its right side (the ram's port side). In each case the straight vertical line is intended to represent the surface plane of the wall, and the thick undulating line the depth of the cutting as plotted from the values recorded with the profiler (i.e., the MD). The trough section of each view (provided by profiles #10 and #14, depending on the side) is indicated by stippling. Note the "x" line indicated in each of the reconstructed views represents a height of 0.90 m. from the bottom of the socket and allows for an easy comparison with the highlighted section in Figure 25.[63]

e. The Original Number of Rams on the Campsite Memorial

In addition to the dimensions and profiles of each socket, we also measured the intervals between the cuttings. These intervals, expressed as the distance between the center lines of adjacent sockets, are presented in Table 3. A comparison of these values allows us to calculate the total number of rams originally displayed on the wall. Although it is impossible to be certain, socket [1] seems to have been for the first ram displayed on the western end of the terrace. Space exists for another ram to the west of [1], although it seems unlikely that such a large object would have been placed this close to the corner of the monument.[64] Two

---

[63] For further analysis of these cuttings and the type of rams revealed by these profiles, see Chapter III.

[64] If a ram equal in size to [4] were placed to the left of [1], its left side would have been cut about 0.7 m. from the western corner. Though possible, this placement seems a bit close to the edge of the terrace. If [1] were the westernmost cutting, its left side would originally have been 2.785 meters from the western edge of the terrace. This placement seems a bit more appropriate for such a large object and would correspond more closely to the beginning of the inscribed text (see infra Section 3.h.).

rams spaced 1.78 meters apart would have filled the gap between [18] and [A], and eight to ten rams spaced at intervals of 1.5–1.8 m. might have occupied the unexcavated section east of [E].[65] These 10 to 12 additional rams plus the 23 currently visible would make the appropriate total of rams originally displayed on the monument somewhere between 33 and 35.

It is also possible (though we think it unlikely) that the rams displayed on the eastern end of the wall were so small that a "y to y" interval less than 1.5 m. would have existed. For example, the small ram recently acquired by the Deutsches Schiffahrtsmuseum in Bremerhaven has a maximum width of 0.26 m. as compared to the 0.755 m. of cutting [D] (for this ram, see Chapter III, n. 33). Since three to four rams of this small size would fit into the linear space occupied by sockets [D] and [E], 33 should be seen as the minimum number of rams originally displayed on the monument. If very small weapons occupied the extreme eastern end of the wall, 40 or more rams may have been originally displayed on the Campsite Memorial.

There are good reasons, however, to prefer the lower total over the higher one. First, one wonders if the original number (whatever it was) does not represent a tithe from the total number of captured ships. A tithe is certainly what one would expect in a dedication to the gods of captured war equipment. If the dedication represents a tithe, as we think it must, then the total 33 to 35 corresponds well with the number of ships Augustus himself recorded as having been captured from the enemy. According to Plutarch (*Ant.* 68.1), Augustus wrote in his *Memoirs* that 300 ships were captured in the battle (or, more likely, in the war; see Chapter VI, Section 2.a). Since Augustus fails to count vessels smaller than triremes for the total of captured warships presented in his *Res Gestae* (cf. Chapter III, n. 25), 330 to 350 seems to represent a more accurate value for the complete total of ships captured from Antony and Cleopatra during the Actian War. And for this reason, we prefer not to restore a large unknown number of small rams on the eastern end of the wall.

---

[65] If 3 rams were restored in the gap between [8] and [A], the y-y intervals would have averaged 1.338 m. Although this is theoretically possible, no other y-y interval is so small. We have therefore chosen the larger interval resulting from the restoration of two rams in this section.

Table 3:
"y to y" Measurements

Note: The value for the 0–[1] measurement represents the distance from the calculated western edge of the terrace to the center line of socket [1]. The distance from 0–[E] measures 45.08 m. along the face of the wall.

Socket #	y-y	Socket #	y-y
0-[1]	3.475	[12]-[13]	1.615
[1]-[2]	2.02	[13]-[14]	1.54
[2]-[3]	1.97	[14]-[15]	1.565
[3]-[4]	1.96	[15]-[16]	1.50
[4]-[5]	2.015	[16]-[17]	1.67
[5]-[6]	1.88	[17]-[18]	1.61
[6]-[7]	1.78	[18]-[A]	5.35
[7]-[8]	1.76	[A]-[B]	1.59
[8]-[9]	1.775	[B]-[C]	1.68
[9]-[10]	1.73	[C]-[D]	1.635
[10]-[11]	1.66	[D]-[E]	1.68
[11]-[12]	1.62		

f. The Sequence of Construction

During the process of mapping the podium and recording the dimensions of the cuttings, we observed certain construction details. These led, in turn, to the following speculation on the sequence of the monument's construction. Although the hillside terrace had probably been leveled somewhat to receive Octavian's tent, it was no doubt "regularized" further after the decision was made to build a memorial on the site. This would have involved the smoothing of its surface and the trimming back of its sides to receive retaining walls. At this stage, the length of the upper finished terrace was measured according to the number of rams to be displayed and the desired spacing between them. Next, a terraced "step" was cut in the southern flank of the hillside beneath the level of the original campsite to serve as a platform for the ram display. Shallow trenches were then dug along the trimmed-back margins of the hillside terrace and filled with *caementa* and mortar to serve as a foundation for the retaining walls to be built along the west, south and east sides of the upper podium. Heavy rectangular blocks of limestone were then laid on this concrete foundation and were clamped together with iron "double T" clamps (|–|) set in lead.

Concrete masses in front of cuttings [2], [11]–[13] and [A]–[E] reveal that a retaining wall backed by a core of concrete was built to contain the pressures of the lower terraced "step" as well. The original limestone facing of this lower terrace which supported the ram display has not survived except for six large blocks along the side of the modern road. Nevertheless, a retaining wall must have existed, and would have been laid in a manner similar to the surviving retaining wall of the upper terrace or podium. According to evidence from the south wall of the podium, the core for this lower terrace was probably poured behind the wall in stages, as the masonry rose course by course.

Along the western retaining wall, there is clear evidence of concrete on top of an *in situ* facing block of the inner row. It seems likely that after the two rows of blocks were laid on their concrete footer, additional concrete was poured behind them. Next, the second course was laid on the exterior block only, and then concrete was poured over the inner block up to the level of the exterior second course. The inner block was intended to serve, therefore, as a large regular *caementum*. The irregular use of headers in the retaining walls indicates, as well, that the architect who built this podium conceived of the wall and its concrete core as an integral structure. This perception on the part of the architect is remarkable for the time.[66]

After the lower terrace for the ram display was finished, and after at least two courses of the main southern retaining wall were clamped firmly in place, it seems that the rams were placed on the lower terrace near enough to the wall for their sockets to be carved. Superfluous clamp cuttings in the sides of the cores in sockets [8], [11], [B] (Fig. 30) and [D] show that these sockets were carved into one side of the "double T" clamps holding the second course together. Obviously the clamps were removed (or were never installed), but the unaffected half of the clamp cutting still bears witness to the original sequence of construction.[67]

At this point, the rams were placed in their sockets and the outward flares of their cowls carefully measured. This enabled the masons to carve carefully the third blocks of each socket to match the expanding flare of each ram's port and starboard cowl. When these blocks were carefully lowered into place, they served to lock each ram into its individual socket by the flare they exhibited. This sequence of construction seems amazingly difficult, yet any other fails to take into account the socket's outward flare at the level of the third course (i.e., the back of

---

[66] According to BLAKE 1947, p. 352, clear examples of bonding between the facing wall and its concrete core are rare before the end of the Augustan period. The fact that headers were used in the Campsite Memorial is probably due to the architect's concern over the pressures the terrace walls would have to contain since they were built on the side of a hill.

[67] In other words, the blocks of the second course were set side by side and cuttings were carved in their surface to receive "double T" clamps. In sockets [8], [11], and [D], the clamp occurred on the left side of the core block; in [B], it occurred in the right side of the block. Perhaps these clamps were thought necessary to keep the blocks from shifting when the concrete was poured behind them. In any event, the clamps must have been removed when their sockets were carved. A similar looking clamp cutting in the second course core of socket [1] clearly anchored the left block of the core (now broken away), and would have remained in place when its socket was carved.

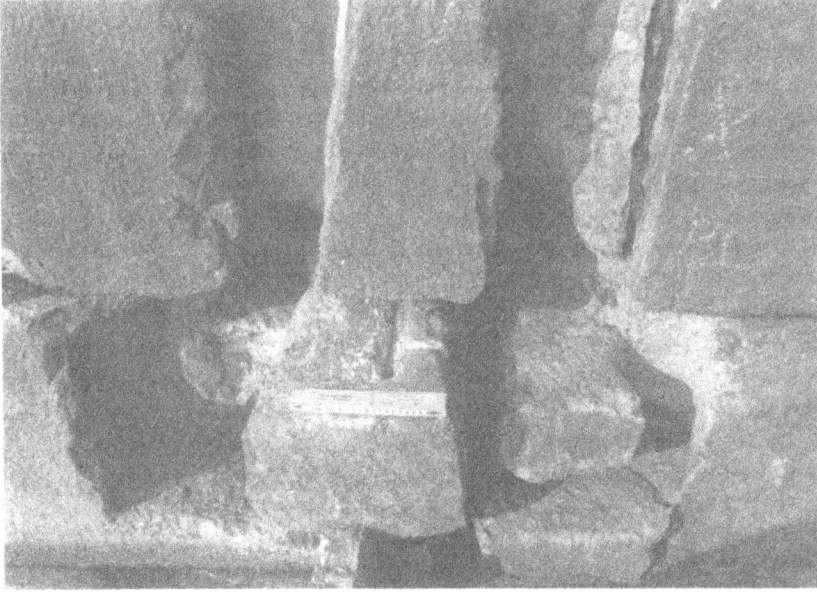

Fig. 30.

the cutting was wider than its front). There can be no other explanation: the curious expanding flare in the cuttings of this course was clearly intended to follow the exterior dimensions of each ram (cf. the difference in sections along the A and B lines in Fig. 25).

After the third course had been set and clamped in place, concrete was again poured behind the wall to create a bond with the headers placed at irregular intervals in this course.[68] Once this concrete backing had set, double rows of blocks (i.e., one laid in front of the other) were laid as the fourth and fifth courses although the inner row of blocks seems not to have been continuous.[69] Although no exterior blocks from the fifth course remain, the mass of tumbled blocks appearing in the 1913 photograph (Fig. 3) must originate from this course. The inscription may then have occupied the sixth course which was crowned in turn by at least another course as indicated by dowel cuttings in the tops of the inscribed blocks. We do not know if these upper courses were laid in double or single rows, nor do we know the wall's original height or exact placement of its upper portion, which may, for example, have been stepped back into the hillside.

---

[68] The left, third course block of socket [2] has not survived. A clear impression of its back side remains, however, in the concrete still *in situ* that was originally poured behind the block.

[69] Evidence for this feature can be seen clearly above sockets [2]–[7] and [16]–[18]. Gaps in the inner row of blocks were filled with concrete (and thus are original to the monument) in the fourth course at cuttings [5], [12], [16] and [18].

g. The Photo Mosaic

Because of the increasing damage caused by the roots which grow
behind and between the blocks, we wanted to record as accurately as
possible the relative positions of the blocks currently *in situ*. We decided
to do this by making a photographic record of the podium's south facade.
The problem involved minimizing the optical distortion from the camera
lens. The procedure we employed is described in detail to substantiate
the accuracy of our final image (Figs. 17–19).

First, we utilized a 50 mm. macro lens to keep the image as sharp as
possible at the borders of the frame. Next, we established 5.0 m. as the
maximum distance from the wall that the terrain would allow us to align
our tripod with the middle of each socket. When the front of the lens
was set at this distance, approximately 2.15 m. of the wall's facade was
included in the camera's field of view. Allowing for a 30 percent overlap
between each frame to minimize distortion at the edges of each image,
we repositioned the camera at 1.50 m. intervals along the face of the
wall before shooting adjacent images.

To help lay out these points, we used a straight piece of wood, 1.5
m. long. A long line which had been knotted half-way along its length
was attached and the string pulled tight (see Fig. 31), its length was
adjusted to form an isosceles triangle with a height of exactly 5.0 m.
from the leg formed by the stick. Beginning at the east, one person
positioned the stick on the south wall's face and marked its end positions
on the stones with blue chalk. A second person held the string's knotted

Fig. 31.

center and pulled it tight. Once a proper isosceles triangle had been formed, this same person dropped a plumb bob from the apex of the triangle and a third person marked the spot on the ground with a long nail thrust through a bright yellow piece of surveyor's tape. This procedure produced focal points for the camera lens at 1.5 m. intervals regardless of the wall's slumping undulations, except at the wall's western end. Here the terrace which once supported the rams stops abruptly. As a result, the frames shot to the left of socket [3] had to be taken from the top of our car at a distance greater than 5.0 m. and enlarged in the darkroom to the same scale when we printed the final segments of the mosaic.[70]

For each position marked in front of the wall, the tripod was positioned so that the front of the camera lens sat directly over the nail head; a plumb bob was dropped from the lens to the ground to verify its position. The camera was set in a horizontal position by means of a bull's-eye level attached to its flash shoe, and its elevation was adjusted to correspond to the center of the cutting. After the camera's position was judged to be correct, a 40 cm. square was placed along the wall's face near the edge of the frame (in an area destined to be cropped from the final print), and the picture was taken. A second frame was exposed with the camera turned in a vertical position (i.e., with the longer axis of the camera's field of view placed at right angles to wall's line) after the lens was again positioned over the nail head. Before the pictures were taken, a thin yellow line was run across the surface of the wall at the level of the various baselines. Since this line was horizontal, its position in each photograph acted as a guideline which helped immensely in the final process of joining the individual prints.

Although the image we obtained is satisfactory, we would make the following changes were the task to be repeated. First, the camera lens should be kept at the same precise elevation relative to the wall's courses for each photograph. Second, a camera with a larger format (like one which produces a 4 by 5 inch negative) would yield a much sharper image. Third, a line marked in meters should be placed in the gap between [18] and [A], and to the left of [1] to insure the correct joining of the printed photos. And finally, a taller tripod or ladder should be used to record the images between [A] and [E] since the wall leans backward at an angle from the camera. The camera could then be tilted forward at an angle equal to the wall's backward tilt so that the image taken is exactly perpendicular to the wall's surface. Even with all these shortcomings, however, the final result of the mosaic is much more accurate than any single camera view could record. Our final image contains 31 photos.

---

[70] The focal points of the lens were still placed 1.5 m. apart, but a longer string was used to center the lens.

h. The Dedicatory Inscription (Figs. 32–46)[71]

Since the first discovery of blocks in 1913, the inscription found here was recognized as a very important text. Notwithstanding its importance or the attention focused on it by numerous scholars, the inscription has yet to be fully illustrated or understood as an element of the monument. Twenty-six fragments of the text have been published to date, although the twenty-sixth fragment is really a misreading of a previously recorded block. Nine blocks were found by Philadelpheus during the excavations of 1913 and four more were located by Rhomaios during the summer of 1922 (Fig. 32). In 1926, I. Miliadis excavated the section of the retaining wall east of socket [18] and located twelve more blocks. Ten years later, the whole collection of 25 blocks was presented in an "epigraphic note" at the end of Gagé's article on the Actian War memorials. These fragments are listed below according to Gagé's numbering system for the convenience of reference. To minimize confusion with the system of Rhomaios and our sequential numbering of the fragments still preserved at the site, Gagé's block numbers will be indicated by the prefix "G."

Table 4: The Fragments as Numbered by Gagé[72]			
Fragment #		Fragment #	
G1	R·DIV	G14	PRO
G2	F·VICT	G15	BLIÇ
G3	MPERAT	G16	IS
G4	VL	G17	A·
G5	PTIM	G18	GES
G6	VM·PA (A joins with G7)	G19	T·IN·HAC (C joins with G13)
G7	AC	G20	TVNO
G8	E[·]PARTA	G21	ASTRA
	(A joins with G9; cf. n. 72)	G22	QVIBV
G9	A·TERRA	G23	SEÇ (or perhaps SEQ?)
G10	ON	G24	RṬ
G11	O·Q	G25	ESSV
G12	VOD		
G13	C·REGI		

---

[71] A complete bibliography on the inscription, arranged in chronological order, includes the following studies: PHILADELPHEUS 1913; RHOMAIOS 1922 and 1925; PHILADELPHEUS 1927, p. 225 [= PHILADELPHEUS 1938, p. 16]; GAGÉ 1936, pp. 98–100; GAGÉ 1937, p 114; OLIVER 1969; EHRENBERG-JONES 1976, p. 57, #12; CARTER 1977 (the same text appers in CARTER 1982, pp. 111–112); and KOS 1979, pp. 69–70, #158. Blocks G1–G13 were originally illustrated by RHOMAIOS 1925, p. 1; his drawing appears as our Figure 32. Blocks G2, G6, G11, G13, and G19–G24 were originally illustrated by PETSAS 1974a, Pls. 67–70; and Pl. 61b shows the new block we call G28 (see text); these fragments appear as Figures 33–46 here.

[72] Although Gagé never saw the blocks he lists, he seemingly failed to consult RHOMAIOS 1925. His reading of G8 as "PART" ignores the horizontal stroke which Rhomaios showed was an E; and he never would have recorded G10 as "IO" had he seen Rhomaios' illus-

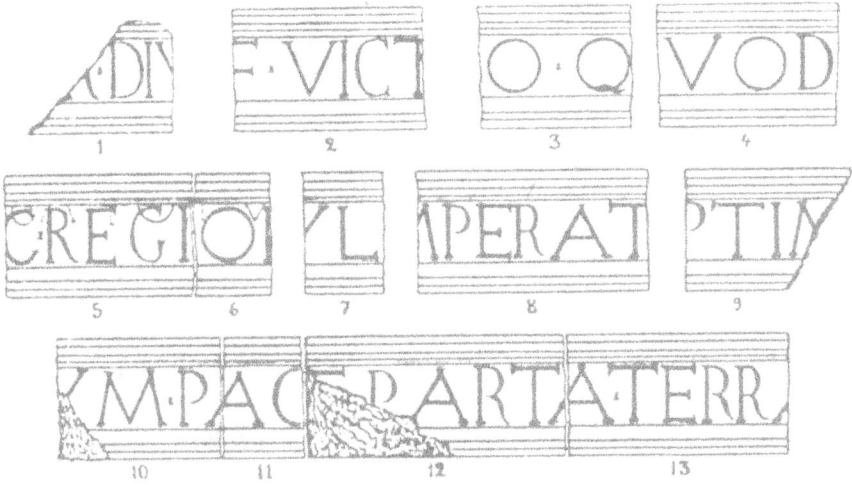

Fig. 32.

Fig. 33.

In 1969, J.H. Oliver constructed a proper text from these 25 fragments. His article unfortunately was overlooked by Ehrenberg and Jones when they revised their collection of texts in 1975, and as a result many students of this period know only an inferior version of this important inscription. In 1977, Oliver's own text was altered slightly by J.M. Carter when he claimed to have found a twenty-sixth block during a visit to the site in the 1967.[73] Although Carter published no drawing or photograph of the new block, it is clear that he misread G15 (currently lying upside down 5.8 m. to the south of socket [8]) as ṚIT. Since Carter listed all the blocks he saw and G15 is not among them, since this block currently lies in full view, and since it is unlikely that Carter (or anyone else looking for inscription blocks) would have failed to notice it, we are certain that Carter's twenty-sixth block is really G15 (BLIÇ), read upside down in deceptive light. For this reason, Carter's restoration "vict[oriam ma]rit[imam" has been abandoned in our restored text.

To make the list of fragments complete, three additions must be appended to Gagé's list. In 1922, Rhomaios noted the existence of two uninscribed blocks at the western end of the lower terrace which clearly came from the same inscribed frieze course; we add them to Gagé's list as G26 and G27.[74] Today, one of these blocks (which we arbitrarily designate G27) still remains on the terrace, 5.2 meters south of socket [5] (Fig. 33). An additional fragment (which we call G28) was partially uncovered in 1974 by Petsas who published a picture of it in his 1974 *Praktika* report (Fig. 43).[75] From the position of the column drum in the photo, fragment G28 should be located roughly 7 meters south of socket [B]. We say "should" because we are unable to detect the block on the surface in 1987, although it probably still lies buried in the soil. From the photo, however, we can clearly make out a P and the lower horizontal stroke of an L or an E. If we read the letter as an E, and restore an interpunct between the two letters, this new fragment would fit with G15 as R]Ẹ[·]P[U]BLIÇ[A.

During a visit to the site in July 1987, Murray noticed traces of a C, G, O or Q on the right side of G17 and of the right horizontal stroke of a T on the block's left side (Fig. 38). The reading of a T before the A agrees with Rowell's restoration "ornata" but the C demands a reevaluation of the inscription's concluding verb. It seems that Oliver's "de-

---

tration of the block (Fig. 32). For the remainder of the blocks, he reported the readings of I. Miliadis, who missed the horizontal stroke of the T and the interpunct on G19 (which he recorded simply as "IN · HAC"), and misread G24 as RI instead of RT. We have placed dots under certain letters to indicate that there are traces on the stone compatible with the letter which we print, which would not, apart from the context of the inscription, necessarily dictate the reading of that letter. Because the steeply slanted side strokes of the "A" are reproduced in no other letter of the alphabet, partial A's (such as in G6) have not been dotted. Letters which are inscribed across joins are listed on both fragments and are not dotted when the combined letters are unambiguous.

[73] CARTER 1977.

[74] RHOMAIOS 1925, p. 2.

[75] PETSAS 1974a, Pl. 61b.

Fig. 34.

Fig. 35.

Fig. 37.

Fig. 36.

Fig. 38.

Fig. 39.

Fig. 40.

Fig. 41.

Fig. 42.

Fig. 43.

Fig. 44.

Fig. 45.

Fig. 46.

dicavit" must now be abandoned in favor of something like "consa-cravit."[76]

At this juncture it may help to review what Suetonius says about the dedication in his biography of Augustus (18.2): . . . locum castrorum, quibus fuerat usus, exornatum navalibus spoliis Neptuno ac Marti con-secravit ("the site of the camp which he had used, adorned with naval spoils, he consecrated to Neptune and Mars"). The similarity between the words of the text and the "spoli]is [ornata]a c[onsacravit," of the monument's inscription is striking. We believe that this is more than simple coincidence and think it likely that Suetonius had a copy of the dedication text from so famous a monument, or more likely, that he knew the text from the *Memoirs* of Augustus, which he tells us he con-sulted on numerous occasions.[77] For this reason, we have decided to follow the vocabulary of Suetonius' sentence and restore the inscription's concluding words as "navalibus spoli]is [exornat]a c[onsacravit."

If we accept that Suetonius was accurately informed concerning this

---

[76] For the spelling "consacravit," cf. *Res Gestae* 2.30 (c. 11).

[77] Suetonius, in his biography of Augustus, refers specifically to this work as a source on five separate occasions: sections 2, 27, 42, 62, 74. He refers to the work twice in his life of Caesar (section 55), and once in his treatise on grammar (*de Grammaticis* 16). For unacknowledged references to the *Memoirs* in the works of Suetonius (made certain by fragments gathered from other author's works), see PETER 1906, pp. 54–64 (fragments #2, #4, #5, #20). It should also be remembered that of all the ancient authors who mentioned this monument, Suetonius alone correctly attributed the camp's dedication to Neptune and Mars.

monument (he is the only author to identify correctly the deities honored here), it seems that only naval spoils were displayed at Octavian's campsite. Other than the rams, the only items displayed there for which we have any record are the statues of Eutychos and Nikon. Although it might first appear otherwise, these conform to our hypothesis because the bronze for their manufacture would have come, most likely, from one or two of the captured rams.[78] Furthermore, Strabo's observation that the entire precinct (both on the hill and in the grove below) was adorned with spoils might lead us to speculate further. If naval spoils alone were displayed at the Campsite Memorial, then spoils taken primarily from the army would have been displayed near the athletic fields in the sacred grove at the base of the hill.

We have checked Carter's statement that G23 cannot read SEÇ because the last letter must be an O or a Q.[79] The total outside width of the letter from the upper right edge of the preserved stroke to the exterior of the curved left side measures 19 cm. while the width of the C in G2 from a point just before the flare of the serifs to the exterior of the curved left side measures 20 cm. Although the G in G13 also measures 20 cm. from a point just before the serif atop the vertical stroke to the exterior of the curved left side, its top appears flat in comparison with the letter on G23. This block, therefore, could have read SEÇ, SEQ or SEO. We accept Carter's proposal that it reads SEQ because of its probable position in the text (see below).

As concerns the placement of the inscription on the monument, most scholars have either accepted the view of Philadelpheus that the text came from the building above the wall, or they have remained silent on the matter.[80] Our research, however, has shown that this is simply not possible. To demonstrate why this is so, and to explore the implications of this fact for the word order of the text, we must carefully examine the inscribed fragments still remaining at the site.

Table 5 presents the dimensions and locations of the 13 blocks we identified at the site in 1986, plus the new fragment G28 attested only

---

[78] We know from Servius (ad. Georg. 3.29) that after the conquest of Egypt, Octavian melted down many of the captured rams and constructed four columns, which were later removed by Domitian from unknown positions and placed on the Capitoline hill. According to Pliny (HN 34.13), Agrippa made the capitals for the columns of the Pantheon from Syracusan bronze. The source for this metal was no doubt the rams from Sextus Pompey's ships captured at Naulochus in 36 B.C. It seems that rams were frequently melted down for use in commemorative and public monuments. The statues at the Campsite Memorial would have been cast from the metal that was at hand, and the obvious source was the rams of the captured fleet. According to Zonaras 10.30 (p. I 526 D), the two statues were carted off to Byzantion at a later date and set up in the hippodrome.

[79] CARTER 1977, p. 230; "Gagé-Meliades reported SEÇ as the reading of block 23, but the dot has disappeared in Oliver's publication. My own observation was that the right hand third of the Q had been broken off, but the letter was definitely not a Ç. SEQ remains a possibility, but unlikely one for reasons of vocabulary."

[80] Only RHOMAIOS 1925, p. 2, and GAGÉ 1936, p. 57, attempted to demonstrate that this was not the case.

in the 1974 photograph. The position of each block is noted on Figure 9 and is described in relation to the sockets along the face of the wall in Table 5. Our numbers correspond to each fragment's relationship to the beginning of the inscription, i.e., they are numbered sequentially beginning at the west. For example, block #1 (G27) lies 5.2 meters out from socket [5], #3 (G11) lies adjacent to the wall at socket [8], and block #12 (G21) lies between #11 and #13 in front of socket [B].

Fragment numbers preceded by an asterisk (*) are headers with the length of the inscribed surface presented in the "block length" column and the length of the header given in the "block depth" column. "Space units" are equivalent to letter widths regardless of the letter's shape or size; interpuncts have not been counted because in all but one case they seem not to occupy a full letter space. Only the letters, therefore, are counted as space units, and two partial letters are counted as one space unit. Included among our 14 fragments is one uninscribed block (our #1). Gagé's numbers are indicated with a "G" prefix, and we have noted the numbers of the new fragments (not numbered originally by Gagé) by placing them in parentheses.

Table 5:
Sizes and Locations of Fragments (cf. Fig. 9)

Fragment #	Space units	Text	Block length	Block depth	Position of block
1 (G27)	0	Uninscribed	0.85	0.56	[5] (5.2 m. out)
2 G2	4	F·VICT	0.98	0.54-0.68	[6] (0.5 m. out)
*3 G11	2	O·Q	0.70	1.36	[8]
4 G15	3	BLIÇ	0.48	0.60	[8] (5.85 m. out)
5 G19	5	T·IN·HAC	1.14	0.59	[11] (4.8 m. out)
6 G17	1	ṬA·Ç	0.53	0.41	Adj. to #5
7 G13	5	C·REGI	0.96	0.48-0.50	[13] (5.4 m. out)
8 G6	3	VM·PA	0.85	0.65-0.70	[17] (3.4 m. out)
9 G22	5	QVIBV	1.29	0.44	betw. [18] & [A]
10 G20	4	TVNO	1.15	0.56	Adj. to #9
11 (G28)	–	Ẹ[·]P	?	?	?[A] (7.5 m. out)
12 G21	4	ASTRA	1.24	0.43	[B]
*13 G24	2	RṬ	0.36	0.80	Adj. to #11
14 G23	3	SEQ	0.72	0.64	Adj. to #12

Total letter spaces: 41
Total inscribed length: 10.4 m.

The fact that two of these blocks (G11 and G24) are inscribed headers demands that the inscription be placed on the wall over the rams. It would be impossible to fit a deep block like G11 into an architrave corresponding to the column elements found at the site.[81] This evidence is conclusive, and it is supported by the varying widths and irregular back sides of the inscribed blocks themselves (cf. Fig. 35). Most of these blocks were clearly intended to be set directly into the hillside and therefore little attention was paid to finishing their back faces. As a result, their thicknesses vary widely (cf. "Block depth" values, Table 5). Of the blocks currently visible, only G21 is cut down to a uniform thickness and this is simply because it was clamped to a backer serving as a *caementum* in the concrete core of the podium.

The original length of the text can be *roughly* calculated from the lengths of blocks #2–#13. Since 41 letters of different widths randomly preserved from the entire length of the original dedication (see infra) occupy a space of 10.4 m., the total restored text of 220 letters (see infra) should occupy a space of approximately 56 m. This is clearly too long to fit easily on a stoa whose preserved stylobate measures 40.1 m., but quite appropriate for placement along the southern face of the podium whose length is 62 m. If the dedication was centered over the rams, we should restore a *vacat* of approximately 3.0 m. before and after the inscribed text. Such a blank space explains the two uninscribed frieze blocks noted by Rhomaios in 1922, one of which we record as block #1 (G27) on the western end of the terrace. It might be more than coincidence that a *vacat*, about 3.0 m. long, locates the inscription's first word over the center of socket [1].

The fact that the inscription was originally placed above the rams on the retaining wall has important implications for the word order of the proposed restoration. Although we cannot prove this conclusively, it seems unlikely that the larger blocks have strayed far from their original positions on the monument.[82] For example, the positions of blocks #9 and #10 next to the base of the wall imply that they have simply dropped from their original locations on the wall above. If this is true, then other individual blocks (and particularly the large, heavy ones) may be close to their original positions in the inscribed text on the wall. The physical locations of the blocks currently at the site, therefore, might be significant in determining their original positions in the restored text (cf. Table 5 and Fig. 9).

<del>___</del>

[81] If the text is placed over the rams, we also need not be concerned, as is CARTER 1977, pp. 227–28 and n. 3, with matching the proportions of the inscribed frieze to the column elements found at the site (for these, see infra Section 4). Presumably because of the dense weeds at the site, he wrongly identified the column base near the southeast corner of the podium as a Doric capital, and believed another structure lay in the weeds nearby. Since Octavian's memorial is the only visible structure in the vicinity, he must have confused the ruins of the eastern retaining wall with a separate structure and assigned the nearby column base to it as a "Doric capital."

[82] To our knowledge, none of the 13 blocks currently visible at the site was moved significantly by the excavators from the positions in which they were originally found.

Table 6:
Blocks Reported by Rhomaios in 1922

(Rhomaios' numbers are preceded by an "R," Gagé's by a "G")

R1 = G1	R·DIV	R8 = G3	MPERAT
R2 = G2	F·VICT	R9 = G5	PTIM
R3 = G11	O·Q	R10 = G6	VM·PA (A joins with R11)
R4 = G12	VOD	R11 = G7	AC
R5 = G13	C·REGI	R12 = G8	E[·]PARTA (A joins with R13)
R6 = G10	ON	R13 = G9	A·TERRA
R7 = G4	VL		

To his credit, Rhomaios realized the importance of this fact in the early 1920s and in his publication of the fragments gave the general locations of the blocks then known to him.[83] According to his report, the blocks were arranged as follows: R1 and R2 (see Table 6) lay about 10 meters from the western end of the wall, blocks R10–R13 lay about 25–28 meters from the western end, and the rest lay in between. We cannot be sure of the precise sequence of individual blocks, since he may have rearranged them slightly to make sense of the inscription. Nevertheless, some general observations can be made on the basis of this evidence.

A comparison of Tables 6 and 5 shows that, of Rhomaios' 13 blocks, only R2 (G2), R3 (G11), R5 (G13) and R10 (G6) remain visible at the site today. From our measurements, however, we are certain that R2 and R10 have not been moved appreciably since 1922, nor apparently have the other two. Of the additional blocks discovered since 1922, G22 and G20 are the most important, since they were unknown to Rhomaios and were presumably still buried when he wrote that "it would be logical to expect from a consideration of symmetry, that almost one half of the full inscription should be sought in the future to the right [i.e., to the east] of block #13."[84] Undisturbed until the section east of socket [18] was excavated by Miliadis in 1926, they remained buried next to the wall, close to where they fell when dislodged from their original positions in the text. For this reason, we have followed Carter's reading of G23 as SEQ, and place it in the text roughly where it can be seen today, close to socket [C]. With this in mind, we present the following restoration as the most likely version of the monument's dedication. Our block numbers appear above the appropriate places in the text; Rhomaios' numbers are preceded by an "R".

---

[83] RHOMAIOS 1925, p. 2.
[84] RHOMAIOS 1925, p. 2

1.) The Dedication Text from Octavian's Campsite Memorial
(for a translation, see infra Section 5)

#1   R1   #2 = R2
vacat Imp · Caesa]r · Div[i · Iuli ·]f · vict[oriam · consecutus

#3 = R3   R4   #11   #4   #5   #7 = R5
· bell]o · quod · pro [·r]e[·]p[u]blic[a] · ges[si]t · in · hac ·

R6   R7   R8   R9   #8 = R10 R11   R12
region[e · cons]ul [· quintum · i]mperat[or · se]ptimum · pace [·] parta ·

R13   #10   #13   #12   #9
terra [· marique · Nep]tuno [· et · Ma]rt[i · c]astra [· ex ·] quibu[s ·

          #14
ad · hostem · in]seq[uendum egr]essu[s · est · navalibus · spoli]is

    #6
[· exorna]ta · c[onsacravit *vacat*

Restorations[85]: [Imp], Gagé; Caesa]r Div[i, Rhomaios; [Iuli], Oliver; vict[toriam con]sec[utus est, Gagé; victoriam ma]rit[imam, Carter; bell]o, Rowell; pro [re pu]blic[a, Oliver; pro r]e p[u]blic[a, Murray; cons]ul, Gagé; [quintum], Oliver; [quinctum], Carter; i]mperat[or se]ptimum, Gagé; terra [marique, Rhomaios; c]astra [e] quibu[s egr]essu[s, Gagé; ad hostem in]seq[uendum, Carter; egr]essu[s est, Oliver; ornat]a, Rowell; [navalibus spoli]is [exornat]a c[onsacravit, Murray.

Note that the relative positions of the blocks currently at the site have been followed as closely as possible in constituting the word order. The fragments that depart significantly from this rule, #11 and #6, are small enough to have strayed far from their original positions. We obviously do not maintain that all the blocks at the site are in their original positions after falling from the wall; certainly they are not. Some have obviously been dragged away at unknown times for reuse elsewhere. We found a few large blocks from the retaining wall up to 50 meters downhill from the site, clearly abandoned because it was too difficult to drag them further. Fragment #6 is a relatively small one which could have been easily moved from its original position when other blocks were removed from the site; the exact size of fragment #11 is as yet unclear.[86] Our blocks #9, #10, #12 and #13 might seem to have been moved, but their close proximity in the original text makes their current jumbled state insignificant. If our argument is accepted that the current positions of these blocks correspond roughly to their placement in the original text,

[85] H.T. Rowell suggested some of the restorations published by OLIVER 1969.
[86] It would be helpful to know how many of the 26 inscribed blocks still exist. Sixteen were found by Oliver in 1968, 13 by Carter in 1967, and 12 by us (excluding the uninscribed block) in 1986. Another block from the inscribed course currently lies face down (and thus unreadable) beside our #7 (G13). CARTER 1977, p. 228, notes that no one person has ever seen all the reported blocks. And since Rhomaios gives the positions of blocks no longer visible at the site, we can only assume that some were removed by the local villagers after 1922.

then the order of the major grammatical units that make up the dedication can certainly be recovered.

The placement of Caesar's name as donor in the nominative case at the beginning of the dedication would thus be warranted by the locations of R1 and our block #2 (= R2) at the west end of the wall. The names of the deities to whom the monument was dedicated, in the dative, then occur in the middle of the inscription near the place where the blocks can be found today, wrenched from their original positions in the gap between sockets [18] and [A]. And finally, the verb "consacravit" will conclude the text near the eastern end of the wall.[87]

The form of the dedication, essentially nothing more than a long sentence, corresponds closely in structural arrangement to the inscription placed by Augustus in Rome on the bases of two obelisks dedicated to the god Sol in 10/9 B.C. (*ILS*[3] 91 = *CIL* VI 701 and 702):

> Imp. Caesar divi f.
> Augustus
> pontifex maximus,
> imp. XII, cos. XI, trib. pot. XIV,
> 5   Aegupto in potestatem
> populi Romani redacta
> Soli donum dedit.

Both texts begin with Caesar's name, followed by the date of the dedication expressed in the titles of the ruler. An extra subordinate clause precedes Octavian's titles in the Nikopolis text to stress the fact that time has passed since the date of the Actian War: "victoriam consecutus bello quod pro re publica gessit in hac regione."[88] Following the titles, an ablative absolute occurs in both texts to describe the circumstances which have brought about the dedication, and finally there follows the name of the deity (or deities) to whom each monument is dedicated. Future excavation of the section beyond socket [E] may produce additional fragments which will slightly modify the text; otherwise, we are fairly certain that the general tone, word order and position of the dedication on the monument have finally been settled.

4. The Stoa

Although the existence of a stoa or portico atop the podium was documented in 1974 by four separate photographs, a full account pre-

---

[87] Given the placement of our blocks #9 and #10, it still seems possible that additional fragments of this inscription will turn up when the area east of cutting [E] is finally excavated.

[88] CARTER 1977, p. 230, argues that these titles were delayed to the end of the inscription to stress the fact that the monument postdates the victory by almost two years. We believe that the subordinate clause "victoriam consecutus . . ." ("following after the victory . . .") adequately alerts the reader to this fact. Although CARTER 1977, p. 230, prefers the spelling "quinctum" on the evidence of the contemporary *ILS*[3] 81 (= EHRENBERG-JONES 1976, p. 57, #17) erected by the Senate, Augustus uses the normal spelling "quintum" in his *Res Gestae* (cf. 8.1; 15.1, 3; and 21.3). Since Octavian presumably composed the text on the Campsite Memorial, we feel that "quintum" is to be preferred over "quinctum."

senting all the details of the discovery never appeared in print. One hopes that someday the excavation of the stoa will be resumed and that a proper account of its original design and subsequent history will be prepared. What follows does not presume to fill this need; it is simply an attempt to describe the fragments of the building that have come to light over the years and to make some simple observations concerning the building's original form. In general, the pieces discussed below are currently visible at the site or reside in the courtyard and storerooms of the museum at Nikopolis.

Among the elements still at the site are two limestone column drums, one of which (Fig. 47) still bears traces of its original stuccoed surface. This drum lies 7.2 m. out from [A] and exhibits clear traces of fluting. The other (Fig. 48), 4.5 m. out from [10], has no flutes and a diameter of 0.56 m.; the columns may have been fluted only part-way down their shafts, like those in the Stoa of Attalos in Athens.[89] Also at the site, currently lying near the southeast corner of the podium, is a column base (Fig. 9 at "z"; Fig. 49) which corresponds in diameter to the two drums. The setting surface that would have roughly corresponded to the column's lower diameter measures 0.575 m. and the dimensions of its square plinth are approximately 0.79 m. on a side.

The single Corinthian capital found at the site in 1913 (Fig. 4) was moved to the Nikopolis museum with a second column base in 1967 and now sits atop this base outside the museum's northwest corner. The capital's lower diameter was impossible to measure directly in its present position, but a rough measurement of its circumference (ca. 1.60 m.) corresponds well with the diameters of the base and the column drums at the site.[90] The capital's preserved height (including the abacus) is 0.35 m. It is interesting that neither the capital's proportions nor its decoration are Augustan and seem to be much later in date than the monument's original construction.[91] Although this matter remains for further analysis, we propose that this capital (and the column elements?) belongs to a later phase of the stoa.[92]

[89] In 1986, this drum was located out from socket [8], but in 1987 the same drum had been rolled down a small incline and now lies as described in the text. Figure 9 represents the position of the column as it appeared in 1986.

[90] Because the capital is not complete, it was difficult to get a precise measurement of its circumference. One measuring 1.60 m. would equal a diameter of 0.509 m., and this corresponds well with Vitruvian proportions for the capital's diameter when the lower diameter of the column equals 0.589 m. This value is calculated from the Augustan foot revealed by the interaxial spacings of the columns; see text below. Philadelpheus recorded the diameter of the capital as ca. 0.75 m., but he must be referring to the width of the abacus.

[91] For examples of Augustan capitals from Greece, see HEILMEYER 1970, pp. 55–56 with the appropriate plates; for examples of Augustan capitals at Nikopolis, see HOEPFNER 1987, p. 133 with Pls. 12 and 13 on pp. 455–56.

[92] This capital's late appearance must lie behind Rhomaios' belief (RHOMAIOS 1925, p. 3) that the architectural elements found at the site come from some later structure built at the site. We must stress, however, that the placement of the stoa atop the podium reveals it as an integral part of the monument and presumably part of the monument's original plan. We must also point out that the suggestion of OIKONOMIDOU 1975, pp. 56–58, that a

Fig. 47.

Fig. 48.

Fig. 49.

In addition to these elements from the columns, we found a few
fragments from the building's roof in 1986, namely, large Corinthian tile
fragments (from both pan and cover tiles) as well as fragments of smaller
Laconian tiles. In 1987, on the road southeast of [E], we also found a
fragment of a terracotta water spout, molded in the shape of a lion's
head (Fig. 50). This fragment, measuring 0.087 m. in height and 0.06
m. from the back of the lion's head to the tip of its nose, preserves the
eye and left side of the beast's head down to its open mouth. No traces
of teeth are visible.[93]

We also found a few fragments from the building's marble decoration:
two white moldings (Fig. 51), and a small fragment of a thin (0.011 m.)
white revetment slab flecked with gray spots. A bit of sculpture has
even turned up at the site. H. Jucker reported finding at the eastern end
of the podium in 1979 a "carefully chiseled fragment of marble sculpture"
0.077 m. in height. According to Jucker, the piece came from the dress

---

temple was built here during the reign of Septimius Severus is unsupported by the foundations preserved at the site; see infra, Section 5.

[93] The fabric of the fragment is a fine, light buff clay with a few large gray and many
fine sparkling inclusions. There are a few fine voids throughout the clay, and one large
void on the back broken edge of the fragment. The thickness of the spout's wall is 0.02
m. This fragment was removed from the site (along with the two marble moldings mentioned below) and deposited in the Nikopolis museum.

Fig. 50.

Fig. 51.

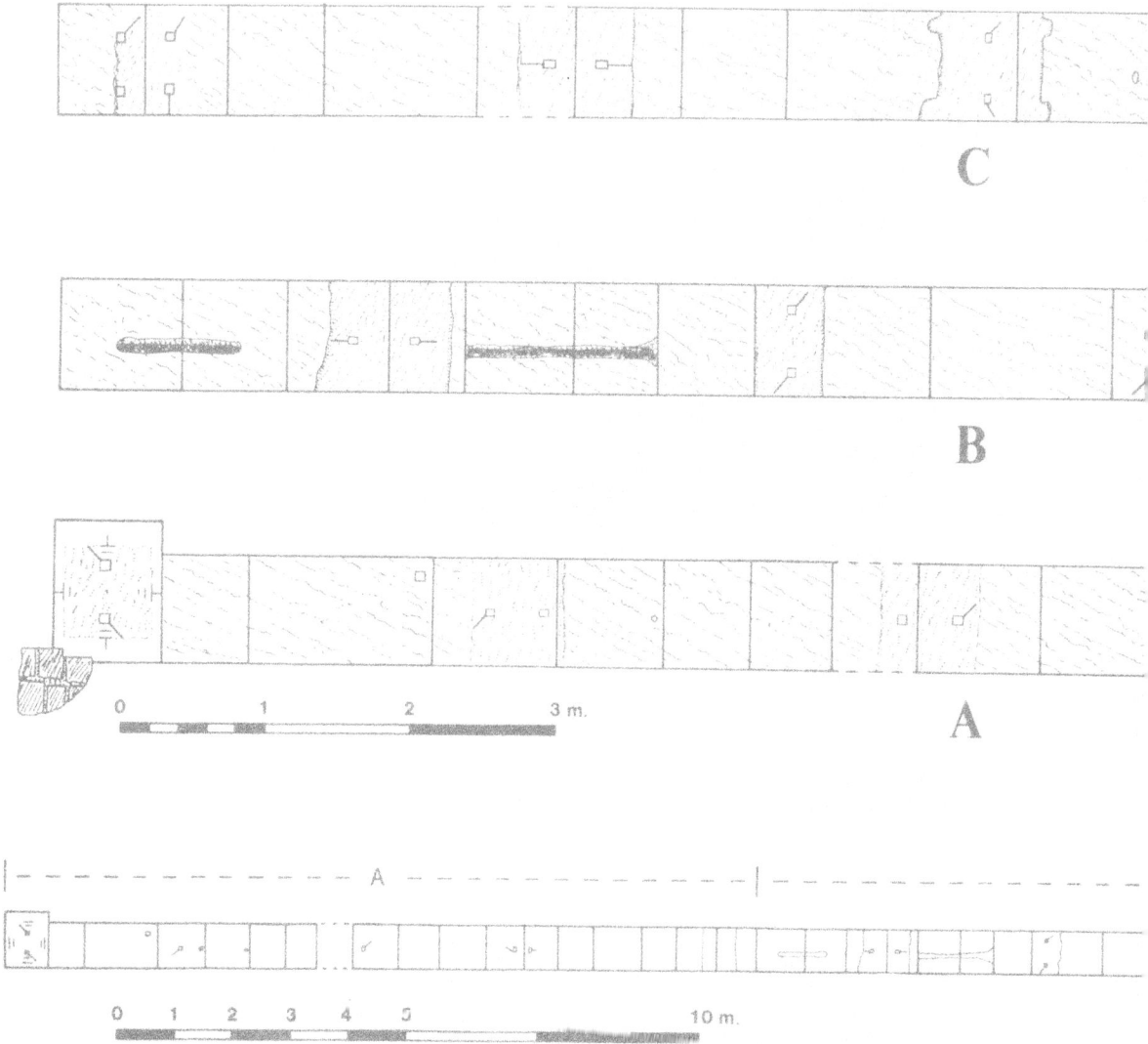

Fig. 52.

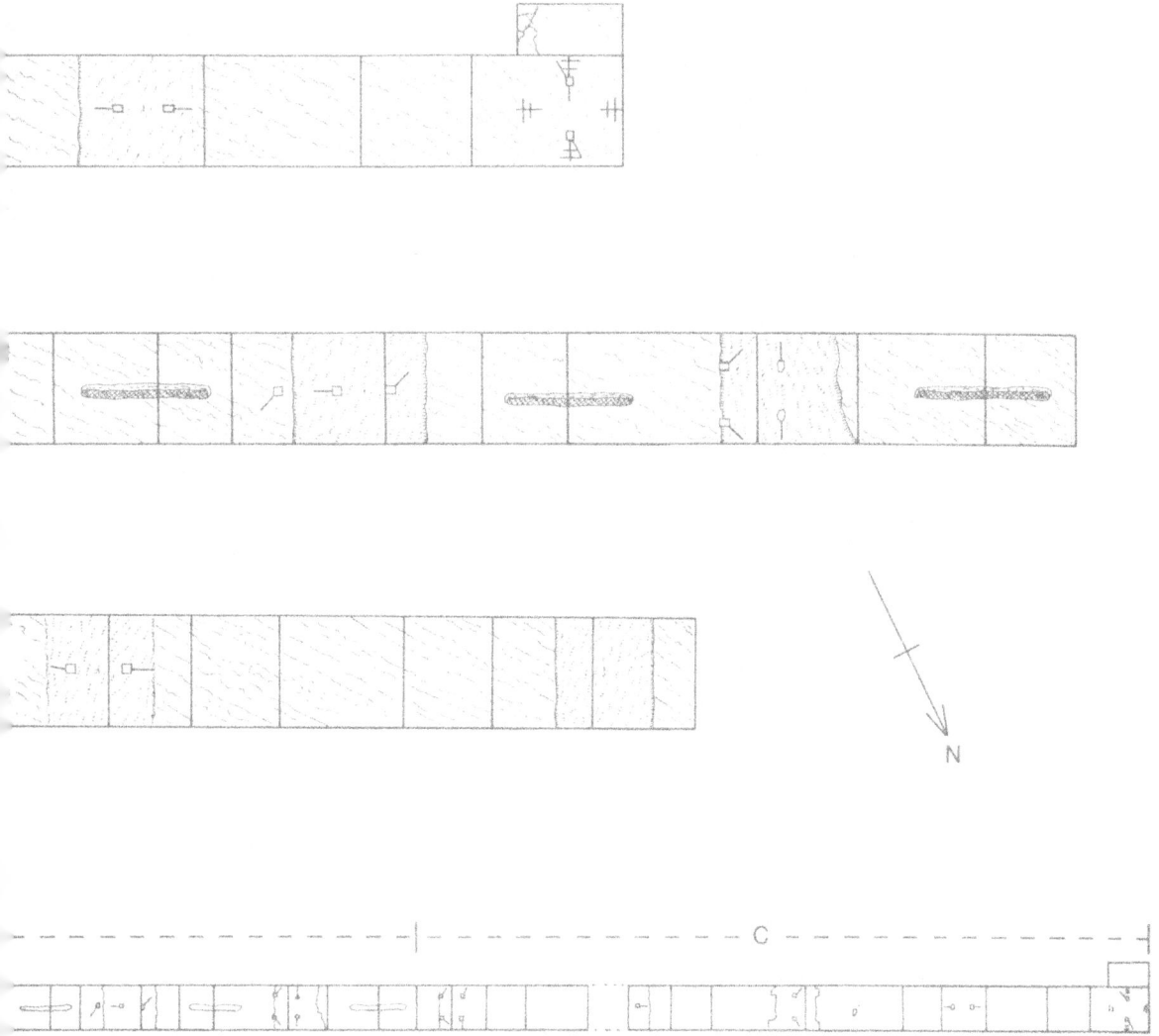

Fig. 52.

of a life-sized female statue. The fragment's present location is not stated.[94]

As for the foundations uncovered in 1974, a plan of the exposed blocks was hurriedly prepared, but for various reasons was not included in the preliminary report. We now include this plan as Figure 52, and comment simply that it represents a "restored view" of what must be the inner (south) side of the stoa's northern section. A comparison with the photographs of the north foundation reveals that the plan does not represent the actual present-day condition of the excavated blocks. As preserved, the foundation measures 40.1 m. from east to west. The beginnings of the southward running foundations at both its eastern and western ends (Figs. 6–7) are clearly preserved.[95] These returns indicate that the original groundplan must have resembled the Greek letter Π with its open end facing southwestward toward the site of the naval battle. The stoa would have essentially wrapped around the sacred site of Octavian's tent.

Without further excavation and careful measurement of the exposed remains, it would be unwise to conclude much about the details of this structure. Nevertheless, the 1974 plan plus the fragments preserved at the site allow for some general observations. The large rooftiles, column elements (two bases, one capital and two drums) and waterspout justify the restoration of a simple roofed portico atop the terrace behind the ram display. Dowel cuttings and setting marks on the foundation's upper surface reveal the placement of 15 square plinths set roughly 2.81 m. apart (center to center). This spacing corresponds to an interaxial distance of 9.5 Augustan feet, allowing us to compute the Augustan foot utilized in this building as 29.578 cm.[96] It also allows for the following proportional suppositions about the building's columns and their spacings in Augustan feet:

a) lower diameter (l.d.) of column = 2 Augustan feet (estimated from the diameter of the setting surface on the column base: 0.575 m.)
b) interaxial spacing = 9.5 Augustan feet
c) inter-columnar spacing = 7.5 Augustan feet
d) column height (base, shaft and capital) = 10 × l.d. = 20 Augustan feet (or roughly 5.9 m.)

From these values, it would seem that the building's architrave and roof

[94] JUCKER 1982, p. 98 and Pl. 16.
[95] Clear evidence for a return exists at the western end of the foundation but we do not know how far to the south this line of blocks originally ran. A hint of the eastern return is indicated by the greater width of the easternmost foundation block of the exposed stylobate.
[96] The inter-axial distance between columns 4 and 5 measures roughly 3.39 m. on the plan, but it is uncertain whether this increased spacing was original to the plan or simply the result of earth movements subsequent to the stoa's construction. From the displaced conditions of the blocks, one can see that the latter is a distinct possibility. It must be stressed that we did not clear or remeasure the exposed blocks of the stylobate. A full study of the campsite area remains for the future.

were constructed in wood and explain why fragments of stone architrave blocks have never been found at the site along with the column elements.

Additional cuttings in the stylobate's upper surface attest to the erection (whether originally or later, we cannot say) of dedications and *stelai*. (cf. Figs. 8b and 52) The absence of a step, the fact that the columns are set at ground level, and the clear wooden clamp cutting that mars the surface of at least one block (a sign that the block was reused) indicate that the stylobate was probably not intended to be seen.[97] It may have been covered originally with a thin layer of earth or clay, appropriate for the simple site of a Roman general's tent. For this reason, we envision the center of the open-air enclosure as a simple paved area which would have indicated the site of Octavian's tent. Here too may have stood altars and/or statues of Neptune and Mars.[98]

Additional fragments of marble at the site reveal that the stoa (or its contents) was decorated with marble moldings (such as the dado molding illustrated in Fig. 51) and with some surfaces clad in a thin (0.011 m.) veneer of white marble flecked with gray spots. Laconian rooftiles found at the site may indicate that the stoa was repaired at a later date when the original heavy Corinthian tiles were replaced, and perhaps, when at least one capital was replaced as well.[99] On the other hand, the Laconian tiles may indicate the presence of one or more additional roofed structures on the terrace. For example, remains of what appear to be a basin plastered with hydraulic cement (Fig. 9 at "x") may correspond to a cistern. Regardless of all the precise details, there can be little doubt that the Π-shaped stoa with its central open-air courtyard represents the *hedos ti . . .hypaithrion* mentioned by Dio 51.1.3.[100]

5. A Reconsideration of the Campsite Memorial

The finished monument must have been impressive. As one approached from the grove at the base of the hill, a massive podium fronted by a lower terrace some five to six meters wide first came into view. Resting on this lower terrace, with their back ends fixed to the podium's long retaining wall, was a continuous line of green warship rams. Arrayed in generally increasing sizes from right to left, these weapons led one's attention smoothly to the west end of the wall where the inscription

---

[97] The swallow-tailed cutting appears in the third block from the eastern end of the stylobate (the right block of the upper photo in Figure 8). This exact type of cutting has been noted in many of the fortifications of Epirus, Aetolia and Akarnania where they definitely served to hold wooden clamps. For the evidence in Akarnania, see MURRAY 1982, p. 456.

[98] We thank E.-L. Schwandner for this suggestion, as well as for observations on the stoa's proportions.

[99] A mass of tiles and cement at the eastern end of the preserved stylobate indicate that some repairs were undertaken at the site at a later date. Since both types of rooftiles were found at the site, we presume that the more substantial tiles would have been utilized in the initial construction phase, if the Laconian tiles come from the stoa.

[100] Cf. supra n. 7.

began above the first ram—a monster weighing over two tons.[101] Like those who see a modern aircraft carrier for the first time at close range, most visitors would have been unprepared for the massiveness of these weapons. And if the amazing sight had left the visitor forgetful of the important facts, the inscription clearly paraded them in foot-high letters across the entire length of the wall: IMPERATOR CAESAR, SON OF THE DIVINE JULIUS, FOLLOWING THE VICTORY IN THE WAR WHICH HE WAGED ON BEHALF OF THE REPUBLIC IN THIS RE- GION, WHEN HE WAS CONSUL FOR THE FIFTH TIME AND COM- MANDER-IN-CHIEF FOR THE SEVENTH TIME, AFTER PEACE HAD BEEN SECURED ON LAND AND SEA, CONSECRATED TO NEPTUNE AND MARS THE CAMP FROM WHICH HE SET FORTH TO ATTACK THE ENEMY NOW ORNAMENTED WITH NAVAL SPOILS.

Atop the terrace sat a Π-shaped stoa more than 40 meters wide. Its placement on a lofty terrace reminded one of the upper terrace at the Asklepieion on Kos, or of two Italian sanctuaries thought to be influ- enced by the Koan complex: the sanctuary of Fortuna Primagenia at Praeneste (particularly the Cortina Terrace), and the sanctuary of Her- cules Victor at Tivoli.[102] Though less elaborate in execution than these plans, the intended effect of Octavian's Campsite Memorial was no less grand. Here "under the open sky" on a wide terrace supported by a Roman rostra of grandiose proportions was a portico which focused the visitor's attention on two images. The first was near at hand: the simple consecrated place where Octavian's tent had stood. The second was in the distance, where one could see on the horizon the site of the glorious Battle of Actium; and in the middle ground hummed the living city which celebrated the great victory (Fig. 53).[103]

In order to help the reader visualize the original appearance of the monument and its south facade, we give two restored views—one from the southeast (Fig. 54), the other from a point near the present-day gap between sockets [18] and [A] (Fig. 55). Our reconstruction is not intended to be accurate in every detail because, quite frankly, too much remains unknown. We do not know the original height of the wall, nor the exact course at which the inscribed frieze was set, nor the precise disposition of the wall's upper courses. We also know little about the overall di- mensions of the portico's east and west wings atop the upper terrace.

---

[101] This estimate of the ram's likely weight was provided by John Coates of the Trireme Trust in a personal communication from J.S. Morrison dated December 16, 1985. For a discussion of the sizes of the rams mounted on this wall, see Chapter III.

[102] For reconstructed views of the Asklepieion on Kos, the Sanctuary of Fortuna Pri- magenia at Praeneste (Palestrina), and the temple of Hercules Victor at Tivoli, see re- spectively BIERS 1987, p. 287 (Ill. 10.14), p. 25 (Ill. 12), and BOETHIUS-PERKINS 1970, p. 142 (Fig. 78) and p. 141 (Fig. 77).

[103] GAGÉ 1955, pp. 509–10, makes the suggestion that Octavian took the auspices before the battle from this spot, i.e., that here was his *auguraculum*. He is no doubt correct. This spot was not only the site of Octavian's *praetorium* or command post from which he could survey his entire army; its height made it the best place in the area for observing the flight of birds and other heavenly signs.

Fig. 53.

In addition, we know nothing about the entrance to the complex, nor do we know the precise shapes of the rams, although we thought it reasonable to model them after the example from Athlit. Even so, we have attempted to follow the facts of which we are certain, and a conjectural view is better than no view at all.

With Octavian's Campsite Memorial thus defined, let us turn once again to the problems posed by the ancient *testimonia* (supra Section 1). A simple comparison of these statements with the physical remains leads us to conclude tentatively that the monument was dedicated to Neptune and Mars as recorded by Suetonius (*Aug.* 18.2). If Apollo was included in the dedication, no evidence has yet been found to substantiate this fact. We recognize that there are obvious strong connections between Octavian, Apollo, Neptune, Mars and Actium that would make it appropriate for Apollo to be included among the deities honored here.[104] Indeed, the site is still known locally as "The Temple of Apollo." Nevertheless, we believe that Suetonius' description of the monument displays a knowledge of the dedication text. And therefore, we consider his testimony preferable to that of Dio (51.1.3), who not only says that the site was sacred to Apollo, but omits mention of Neptune and Mars altogether. Since Apollo is extensively represented elsewhere in the neighborhood, it is possible that Dio simply made a mistake. Strabo's account (7.7.6), which implies that the whole complex in this suburb was sacred to Apollo, can also be interpreted in a manner that is perfectly compatible with Suetonius' text. As Strabo tells us, the hill on which

---

[104] GAGÉ 1955, pp. 499–522, presents the most forceful case for doing just this. It is a well-established fact that Apollo was adopted by Augustus as his own patron deity and that he identified quite closely with the god well before he entered public life; cf. for example LAMBRECHTS 1953 and KLEINER 1988, pp. 353–57.

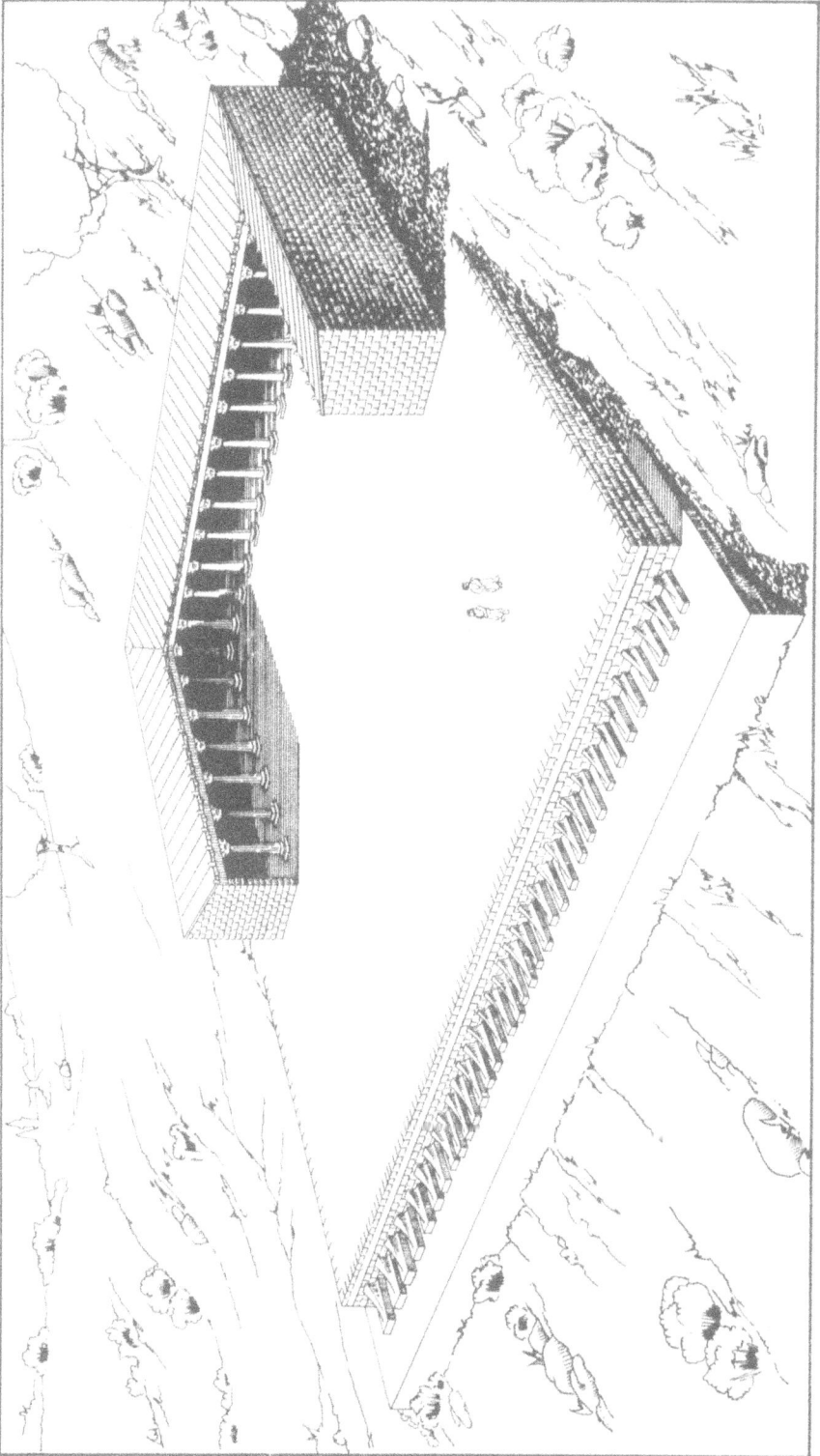

Fig. 54.

Fig. 55.

the monument was built, and which lay behind the *temenos* of the *Aktia*, was itself sacred to Apollo. On this hill, a *temenos* was specifically set aside by Octavian at the former site of his camp, decorated with naval trophies, and dedicated to Neptune and Mars.

What little we know about these three deities of the Actian War makes it quite appropriate for a *temenos* of Neptune and Mars to be built in an area otherwise sacred to Apollo. Gagé has examined the relationship between these deities and Octavian, and has pointed out an interesting connection which emerged after the Battle of Actium—a connection that he feels was personally forged by Octavian. The evidence is provided by the *Fasti Arvalium* which report that on the birthday of Augustus (September 23), cults of Mars and Neptune were received in the Campus Martius, and of Apollo "ad theatrum Marcelli" (i.e., at Apollo's ancient extrapomerial temple, near the triumphal gate). Although the *fasti* fail to list the connection between these anniversaries, Gagé shows that their falling on the same day as the *natalis Caesaris* is more than mere coincidence. He concludes that these festival days were instituted on Octavian's birthday in commemoration of the victory at Actium. "The gods of 23 September are the gods of Actium."[105]

In trying to show that the Campsite Memorial was sacred to all three deities, Gagé articulates a convincing argument that applies equally well to our modified view. We believe that a *temenos* of Neptune and Mars was particularly appropriate on a hill sacred to Apollo, and that the whole sacred area—hill and *temenos*—overlooked a suburb of the city which hosted the games of Actian Apollo. As the center of the Actian Games, this suburb of the city must have evoked strong images of Apollo, and for this reason Dio has mistakenly assumed that the Campsite Memorial was sacred to Apollo as well. Since Neptune is clearly mentioned in the inscription (Mars is as well, but the reading is less certain) it seems unnecessary to defend Dio's contradictory account. He simply made a mistake. Otherwise, Dio's description of the site as an "open-air shrine" (*hedos ti . . .hypaithrion*) makes sense if we view the centrally placed site of Octavian's tent as the consecrated focal point of the *temenos*. In all other respects, when one restores the monument as we have described it, the ancient accounts really supplement one another.

What then of the alternate views recently expressed concerning the monument's form? We have already referred to Oikonomidou's argument, based on coin types, that a temple was constructed at Octavian's campsite during the reign of Septimius Severus.[106] We have shown that the foundation uncovered in 1974 corresponds to a Π-shaped stoa with 15 columns along the inner side of the northern wing. What is more, the column drums, bases and capital (even though it is late) found at

[105] GAGÉ 1936, pp. 58–66 (the quote is on p. 62); cf. also GAGÉ 1955, p. 512.
[106] OIKONOMIDOU 1975, pp. 56–58; her views have been recently reiterated by SOULE 1987, pp. 171–73.

the site correspond perfectly with this stoa and not with some temple. The coins of Severan date which depict a large temple of the Corinthian order must, therefore, refer to some other building at Nikopolis.

Equally impossible is Picard's view that the Campsite Memorial is similar to the monument depicted on the coin minted by Antistius Vetus but with statues arrayed in a composition akin to that of the St. Bertrand trophy.[107] A similar verdict must be made concerning Jucker's recent identification of the Campsite Memorial with the image on Vetus' coin.[108] Considering what we now know about the Campsite Memorial, the coin's reverse must depict some other monument.[109] First, were a monumental statue of Apollo (or a statue group) originally placed above the wall, it is inconceivable that its existence would have been left unmentioned by Plutarch, Strabo or particularly Suetonius. The general correlation between Suetonius' description of the site and the surviving remains implies, at the very least, that he was working from accurate information.[110] It would be doubly hard to explain how he could have overlooked a statue of Apollo or a statue group had it been the central feature of the monument. Furthermore, all the physical evidence gathered from the site itself points to the existence of a portico atop the podium, and not a large statue of Apollo (or of others) set in the open air.

Second, a comparison of the sockets' shapes with the frontally viewed projections beneath the statue of Antistius' coins reveals that we are not dealing with rams of the type mounted on the Campsite Memorial (if we are dealing with rams at all). The projections on the coins have a clear outward flare at their tops, while the sockets on the monument clearly flare outward at their bottoms. And finally, no sockets for anchors are preserved anywhere along the face of the podium's retaining wall. The main point of Jucker's thesis, that the statue of Apollo Aktios on the coin is separate and distinct from the statue of Apollo Palatinus, remains unaffected by our conclusions. The statue and base depicted on these coins, however, cannot be located at the Campsite Memorial. This image also seems inappropriate to us as a representation, even on an abbreviated scale, of the type of monument preserved at Octavian's campsite.

As concerns the stoa's function, it is quite possible that naval spoils from the battle were displayed here. The naval spoils that Suetonius says adorned the sacred enclosure (*Aug.* 18.2) might simply be the rams which studded the podium's south face, but they might also include other items separately placed inside the stoa atop the terrace. The act of dedicating military equipment in stoas was a common practice among

---

[107] PICARD 1957, pp. 260–62.

[108] JUCKER 1982.

[109] This is essentially the observation of TRILLMICH 1988, p. 523, #364, and ZANKER 1988, p. 85.

[110] It must be remembered that he, alone of our sources, correctly identified Neptune and Mars as deities honored here.

the Greeks, who filled their porticos with all types of military armor and naval gear.[111] As concerns naval dedications in stoas, the most famous example is the one constructed by the Athenians at Delphi during the fifth century. The inscription preserved along its stylobate reads: "The Athenians dedicate the stoa and the *hopla* and *akroteria* having taken them from the enemy."[112] Although one is unsure whether *hopla* means the cables from the great bridges of Xerxes, or simply "arms," *akroteria* must refer to ships' figureheads or perhaps their stern ornaments.[113] Another example is known at the sanctuary of the Great Gods at Samothrace, where inscriptions reveal that anchors were dedicated in the stoa.[114]

In general throughout the Greek world, stoas (as well as temples) were a customary repository for armor of all kinds. At Athens, shields taken from the Lakedaimonians at Sphakteria in 425 B.C. and from the Sikyonians at some unknown date were displayed in the Stoa Poikile.[115] At Thebes, the armor taken from the Athenians near Delion in 424 B.C. was nailed to the stoas in the marketplace.[116] At Thermon, Philip V found some 15,000 suits of armor displayed in the stoas when he sacked the sanctuary in 219 B.C.[117] And at Samothrace, K. Lehmann discovered pieces of armor and a fragment of a spear in the stoa he called the "Hall of Votive Gifts."[118]

Although the evidence for Roman dedications of armor in stoas is not as extensive as that for the Greeks, they too seem to have made such dedications on occasion in their porticos. Customarily, Roman soldiers displayed the spoils they won in single combat in the vestibules of their homes.[119] Victorious generals, however, were allowed to make a special dedication of the arms taken from the enemy leader in single combat. Three grades of dedication are known. Those of the first rank, the *spolia opima*, were dedicated to Jupiter Feretrius, while those of the second and third rank were dedicated to Mars and Quirinus respectively.[120] Dedications of military spoils were also made in public places such as the *Forum Romanum*. Livy relates (10.46.7–8) that so many spoils were captured from the Samnites by L. Papirius in 293 B.C. that he was able to decorate the temple of Quirinus and the *Forum Romanum*, and still

---

[111] For Greek dedications of military equipment, see PRITCHETT 1979, pp. 240–95; cf. also COULTON 1976, pp. 12–13.

[112] See MEIGGS-LEWIS 1969, pp. 53–54.

[113] Cf. PRITCHETT 1979, p. 281.

[114] PRITCHETT 1979, p. 267.

[115] Paus. 1.15.4. A shield from the Pylos dedication appeared in the excavations of the Athenian Agora; see SHEAR 1937. Because a column drum from this stoa has a hole in it, THOMPSON-WYCHERLY 1972, pp. 92–93, have suggested that the shields were hung from the columns.

[116] Diod. 12.70.5.

[117] Polyb. 5.8.9.

[118] LEHMANN 1962, p. 93, and #118–#119 on p. 160.

[119] Cf. Livy 10.7.9, 23.23.6, 38.43.11; Suet. *Nero* 38; Pliny *HN* 35.2.7; in general on the origins of the Roman trophy, see PICARD 1957, pp. 103–48.

[120] For *spolia opima*, see CAGNAT 1911, p. 1441 and LAMMERT 1929.

distribute the remainder to the allies and neighboring colonies for the decoration of their own temples and public squares. He also writes (22.57.10) that after Cannae in 216 B.C. the spoils from former wars were removed from temples and porticos in order to equip the makeshift army being raised to resist Hannibal.[121]

Octavian himself is known to have made such a dedication in Rome. In 33 B.C., he commemorated his Dalmatian victory of the same year by restoring the Porticus Octavia near the Theater of Pompey. According to Appian (*Illyr.* 28), Octavian placed inside the portico the standards (originally captured from A. Gabinius in 48/7 B.C.) just recovered from the Illyrians. Is it not logical, therefore, to expect that the stoa at Octavian's campsite was built to house the naval dedications referred to in Suetonius' account?

We know of at least two offerings which might have been placed inside the stoa: the bronze statues of Eutychos and Nikon, cast most likely from one or two of the captured warship rams. If we are correct in assuming that other naval spoils were placed inside the building, the arch at Arausio (Orange) shows us what they would have looked like (Fig. 56). There would have been figureheads, coils of line, sets of blocks and tackle, anchors, stern ornaments, gangplanks, tridents, steering oars, masts, standards and naval ensigns.[122] Renewed excavation of the podium's surface might reveal the fragmentary remains of such equipment. But until such evidence is found, questions concerning the stoa's exact contents (or, for the matter, its true function) must remain unresolved.

Whatever its precise function, this stoa must not have been as extraordinary a sight as the ram display, because the ancient authors who specifically mention the Campsite Memorial either fail to describe the building in detail (Dio and Suetonius), or ignore it completely (Plutarch and Philippus). We must conclude, therefore, that the most memorable feature of the monument was its ram display—the monstrous ships' *rostra* that studded the southern wall of the upper terrace. These were intended to command the visitor's attention, and to shed glory on the man who managed to capture them.

In order to appreciate the massiveness of these rams, and to recapture a sense of the awe this display was intended to inspire, we need to place these rams in perspective. To this end, we must now turn our attention to the different sizes or classes of ancient warships that were used in the navies of the Hellenistic Age.

---

[121] Appian (*Hann.* 7.11) records a similar story after the Roman defeat at Lake Trasimenus in 217. Clearly, a tradition existed at Rome that recorded the use of trophy armor during the Hannibalic War, whether it happened in 217 or one year later.

[122] It is quite possible that the spoils on the arch were directly modeled from the wide array of equipment captured at Actium. For the profound influence of Actium on the representational art of the early Principate, see HÖLSCHER 1984 and 1985, and ZANKER 1988, p. 84.

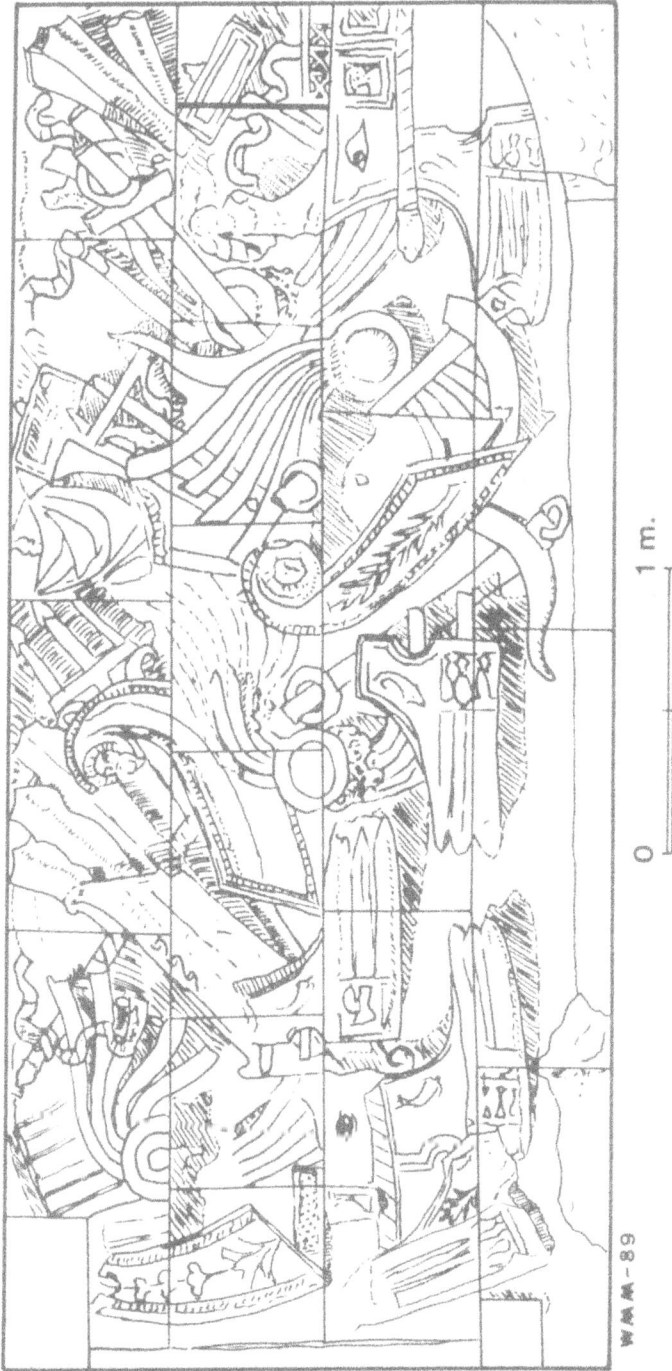

Fig. 56.

III: The Relative Sizes of Ancient Warship Bows

1. The Problem of Ancient Ship Classes

Ancient navies, like their modern counterparts, were composed of different sizes or classes of ships introduced at various times for various purposes. Although the names and partial descriptions of some of these classes exist in ancient written sources, no complete warship of known class has yet been located on the sea floor.[1] In the near total absence of physical evidence for the designs of these different ship classes, it has been difficult to appreciate fully the complexity of these war machines and the differences that accounted for the various classes. The class about which we know the most, the "three," or *trieres* (usually translated as "trireme," from the Latin *triremis*), is one of the most popular and long-lived classes utilized in the ancient navies of the Mediterranean powers.

According to Thucydides, the trireme was developed at Corinth in the late eighth century B.C., and Zosimus makes it clear that the class was still in use a thousand years later.[2] From literary, epigraphical, archaeological and iconographic evidence, a reasonably clear picture of the vessel has emerged over the years, which is now expressed in a full-

---

[1] Partial remains of two narrow vessels, interpreted as Punic warships, were excavated by H. Frost between 1970 and 1973 near Marsala, Sicily. One ship retains a prow structure of two up-curving (ramming?) timbers, while the other retains its stern and a section of its port side up to the beginning of the parallel midships section; cf. FROST 1972, 1974, 1975a, 1975b, 1981a, and 1981b. Although Frost interprets this latter ship as a Liburnian— a fast, light galley of the Hellenistic Age—this identification is by no means secure. Its presumed length of 35 meters is equal to that of the *Olympias*, the "three" (a ship supposedly larger than a Liburnian) designed by John Coates and built by the Greek navy. Furthermore the Punic ship's supposed weight of 120 tons is almost triple that of the *Olympias*, which according to Coates weighs about 48 tons with spars, oars and a full crew (personal communication, August 8, 1987); on the *Olympias* reconstruction, see infra n. 3. A partial section of an undisputable warship was found attached to its bronze ram near Athlit, Israel in 1980; cf. STEFFY 1983. Here, the bow timbers were preserved along with 3.08 m. of the vessel's port wale. J.R. Steffy has completed a full analysis of these 16 timbers which will soon appear in a monograph he is editing with L. Casson titled *The Athlit Ram* (forthcoming, Texas A&M Press); cf. LINDER 1988.

[2] Thuc. 1.13.2–3 and Zosimus 2.22.1–2, 24.1. BASCH 1969 argues that Thucydides says only that the first *Greek* trireme was built at Corinth; according to Basch, the class first appeared in Phoenicia. Against this view, cf. LLOYD 1972 and 1975; and MORRISON 1979. Morrison follows the belief that Thucydides' date is inaccurate due to a "faulty generation count," and that the first trireme, therefore, was built around 650 B.C.; cf. MORRISON-COATES 1986, pp. 39–40. According to CASSON 1971, p. 148 with n. 31, the latest secure reference to the active use of triremes occurs in the Zosimus passage.

scale replica of an Athenian trireme of the Classical period.[3] Although different types of triremes were built throughout its long history of use, the standard "covered" example seems to have carried a full crew of 200 men. This included 170 oarsmen arranged in three superimposed files per side, with each man pulling his own oar.[4] The dimensions of the class have been deduced from the covered slipways in which triremes were stored. On this evidence, a trireme's length and width must be just under the dimensions of the Zea shipsheds preserved at Piraeus, Athens' port city. These had a maximum dry length of about 37 m. and widths of about 6 m. each.[5]

Before the introduction of the trireme, smaller ships with 20, 30 and 50 rowers (the *eikosoros, triakontoros* and *pentekontoros*) seem to have been the preferred warship classes.[6] Representations on Greek pottery of the Geometric and Archaic periods make it clear that the oarsmen on these vessels might be arrayed in either one file per side, or in two, one superimposed above the other.[7] The development of a two-banked vessel (a *dikrotos* or bireme) is thought by L. Casson to be an outgrowth of ramming warfare, since the new design shortened the length of the vessel, strengthened the integrity of the hull without any loss of oar power, and greatly narrowed the turning circle, thereby decreasing the time needed to turn the vessel in combat.[8]

During the fourth century, classes larger than the trireme were introduced into the navies of the Mediterranean. Pliny says (on the evidence of Aristotle) that the Carthaginians were the first to invent a "four" and their lead was soon followed by Dionysius of Syracuse who added both "fours" and "fives" to his navy.[9] By the time of Alexander the Great, these new classes had apparently been adopted into all the major fleets.[10] By this time as well, the "six" had just been introduced at Syracuse by Dionysius II (367–344 B.C.).[11] Following upon Alexander's death, a naval arms race between his generals and their successors produced ships of still greater sizes, some of which were enormous. We hear of "sevens," "eights," "nines," "tens," "elevens," "thirteens," "fifteens," and "six-

---

[3] See MORRISON-COATES 1986. In the following notes, we refer frequently to this book chiefly for the sake of convenience, but we do not mean to imply that a consensus has been reached on all matters relating to this warship class. Interested readers may examine the controversies for themselves by referring to notes cited by Morrison and Coates throughout their book.

[4] MORRISON-COATES 1986, pp. 107–108 (crew size), 130 (one man, one oar); 137 (170 oarsmen); 137–51 (arrangement of rowers in the hull).

[5] See D. Blackman in MORRISON-WILLIAMS 1968, pp. 181–82 with notes; and MORRISON-COATES 1986, p. 134.

[6] On these classes, see CASSON 1971, pp. 43–65.

[7] Cf. CASSON 1971, pp. 53–60.

[8] Cf. CASSON 1971, p. 56, who believes this may have resulted in bireme pentaconters that were about 65 feet long, and triaconters that were about 45 feet in length.

[9] Pliny HN 7.207; cf. CASSON 1971, p. 97.

[10] They fought on both sides at the siege of Tyre in 332 (Arr. *Anab.* 2.22.3–5); "fives" appear in the navy of Sidon by 351 (Diod. 16.44.6); and both classes are mentioned in the naval inventories at Athens dated to the year 325/24 B.C. (*IG* II² 1629, lines 808–11).

[11] Ael. *VH.* 6.12; Pliny HN 7.207.

teens," in the fleet built by Demetrius Poliorcetes. And at the height of his power, the fleet of Ptolemy II contained one "twenty" and two "thirties."[12]

The largest ship produced at this time was a "forty," launched during the late third century by Ptolemy IV Philopator (221–203 B.C.). Primarily because of its incredible size, the ship's dimensions were written down and preserved.[13] Its length measured 128 m., its beam 17.4 m., its stern and bow towered more than 20 m. above the water (24.2 m. and 21.9 m. respectively), and when empty its draft measured a surprisingly shallow 1.8 m. The four steering oars were each 13.7 m. long, while the longest oars measured 17.4 m. On its maiden voyage, the vessel had 4,000 oarsmen, 2,850 marines and 400 men who served as officers, ratings and deckhands.[14] According to Plutarch (*Demetr.* 43.5), it could be moved only with great difficulty and danger, and was intended solely as a showpiece.

Even if we dismiss the "forty" as an extraordinary freak, we are still left with the task of explaining the differences that marked one ship class from another. Since no physical remains of these monsters have survived from antiquity, most scholars have focused their attention on describing their oarage system as an outgrowth of their class names. Originally it was thought that these polyremes (i.e., vessels larger than triremes) were, on the model of the trireme, named for increasing numbers of superimposed oar banks.[15] Now most would agree that the ship's classification refers to the number of oarsmen in each "rowing unit."[16] If each oar was seen as belonging loosely to a vertical unit, then the number of oarsmen who worked in that unit, regardless of the total number of oars, would provide the name for the ship's class. A "three" has three oarsmen per unit and the unit consists of three superimposed oars.[17] A "four" would then consist of four men per unit, and the unit would consist of two superimposed oars each handled by two men, or one oar handled by four men. A "five" would consist of five men per unit, and they could be arrayed in one, two or three superimposed banks with the appropriate number of men per oar.[18] Such a system can be extended to explain adequately the oarage systems of the various sizes,

---

[12] For the evidence, cf. CASSON 1971, pp. 98–99, 103–16, and 137–40.

[13] The details are preserved by Athenaeus (5.203e–204c). Casson's discussion of this vessel provides the basis for our remarks in the text; cf. CASSON 1971, pp. 108–12.

[14] CASSON 1971, pp. 108–109.

[15] Cf., for example, the literature cited in COOK 1905 (= TORR 1964, pp. 196–204). TARN 1905 showed convincingly that the ancient evidence simply cannot be reconciled with the view that the larger classes are defined by superimposed banks greater than three in height.

[16] For this unit, see MORRISON-COATES 1986, p. 134.

[17] Note that the placement of the oars in each unit may not be exactly in a vertical line, but in the standard "complete unit" of the "three" there are three oars and three oarsmen; cf. MORRISON-COATES 1986, Fig. 36 on p. 140 and Figs. 40 and 41 on pp. 147 and 149.

[18] Cf. for example, CASSON 1971, pp. 100–103.

although one still wonders how this worked on the larger polyremes such as a "twenty," "thirty" or "forty."[19]

Attention has focused on the oarage systems because we simply did not have much more to go on. Nevertheless, the differences between these ship classes must have extended beyond simple variations in how oarsmen were arranged in each rowing unit. Presumably this juggling of men per unit had something to do with differences in the dimension and weight of each class. This observation might seem obvious, but it needs to be stressed. In spite of the known fact that some types of "fours" and "fives" seem to have been similar to triremes except for their reduced number of oars, *in general* it seems that "fives" were larger and heavier than "fours" and that "fours" were larger than "threes."[20] This distinction is important; if we cannot presume that a "ten" was physically larger than a "nine" and that both were larger than an "eight," how can we reasonably explain the different sized sockets on the front facade of Octavian's Campsite Memorial?

In general, the hypothesis that "tens" had more freeboard, and were heavier than "fives," is defensible. For example, Florus could maintain that Antony's fleet of "sixes" to "nines" was on average heavier, higher out of the water and more difficult to maneuver than Octavian's "twos" to "sixes."[21] Plutarch says much the same thing, as does Dio.[22] As stated above, there is clear evidence that on average a "five" was heavier and higher out of the water than both a "four" and a "three." Livy, for example, makes it clear that a "five" was slower than a "three," and was probably heavier.[23] In a passage describing events of 200 B.C., Livy tells of three Carthaginian "fours" that were unable to ram a Roman "five" as it rounded a promontory because, he says, the Roman vessel was too fast. In the end, however, the "fours" seem to have been faster, since the crew of the "five" eventually drove their vessel on shore to escape. That the "five" was higher out of the water, and thus heavier than the "fours" chasing it, appears certain from this same episode. While the chase was on, the Carthaginian marines were unable to board the "five" from their "fours" because of the "five's" higher freeboard.[24] If we knew more about these classes, we would no doubt find that the dimension and weight of each class were critical variables in the design

---

[19] CASSON 1971, p. 100 n. 20 and p. 105 n. 37, placed eight men per oar as the upward limit to this type of system because it is the greatest number to be found in better documented periods of history (in this case on "galeasses" of the seventeenth and eighteenth centuries). Although this system accommodates a "twenty" (i.e , two banks of eight men per oar, and one bank of four per oar), it does not account for a ship larger than a "twenty-four," an unattested ship class. CASSON 1971, pp. 107–16, argues therefore that classes above the "sixteen" were essentially large catamarans with expansive decks bridging two parallel hulls. This would also help to explain the amazingly shallow draft of the "forty."

[20] CASSON 1971, p. 101.

[21] The validity of Florus' statement is not at issue here. That he and his readers would accept that larger classes meant heavier, higher and less maneuverable ships is the issue.

[22] Plut. *Ant.* 65.4–66.2; Dio 50.32.

[23] Livy 28.30.5.

[24] Livy 30.25.5–7.

formula which determined the number of men placed in each rowing unit.

2. The Ship Classes of the Sockets

From this evidence, we feel justified in assigning the largest sockets with the largest cores to the largest ship class captured by Octavian. The sockets next in size should correspond to the second largest class, and so on. This, at any rate, is a reasonable theory with which to start, particularly since we lack sufficient evidence for a more accurate approach in determining the various ship classes of the sockets.

It is important now to ascertain as accurately as possible the "pool" of classes available to Octavian for selection after the battle's conclusion. Although the surviving accounts of the battle differ concerning the classes in Antony's fleet, Strabo provides us unwittingly with the answer we seek when he mentions the war memorial built by Octavian at the sanctuary of Apollo Aktios.[25] Its grandiose scale made the dedication so noteworthy that Strabo described it for his readers even though a fire had consumed it by the time he composed his account. Thanks to Strabo, therefore, we know that one each of the ship classes fighting in the battle was dedicated "from a *monokrotos* to a *dekeres*." If we remember that Octavian himself claims to have captured 300 ships from the enemy, we can reasonably conclude that he had a full range of classes to dedicate at his campsite from "ones" to "tens."[26]

Adhering to the methodology outlined above, the largest sockets, such as [4], should correspond to a "ten." When we attempt, however, to

---

[25] Strabo 7.7.6. Plutarch (*Ant.* 64.1) says Antony used "threes" to "tens"; Dio (51.1.2) reports that Octavian dedicated "threes" to "tens" at Actium (i.e., they were captured from Antony's fleet); while Florus (2.21.5) asserts that his fleet consisted of "sixes" to "nines." Strabo's account is preferable to all the others because it is based on an actual dedication whose impressive size made it so famous that it was given a name— ἡ δεκαναΐα, "the ten shipper." From the *Res Gestae* (3.4), we see that Augustus did not include vessels smaller than "threes" in his lifetime total of captured warships; cf. infra n. 30. Since we know that Plutarch consulted Augustus' *Memoirs* for the total number of ships captured in the battle (or perhaps in the war—see Chapter VI), he (and perhaps Dio as well) may have wrongly inferred that no ships smaller than "threes" were taken from the enemy. The Florus passage is more difficult to explain and may simply represent an elaboration on the part of an author known to be unreliable in maritime details; cf. BASCH 1980, p. 368.

[26] The number 300 is preserved in Plut. *Ant.* 68.1. According to TARN 1931, pp. 181 and 186, there was only one "ten" in Antony's fleet, his flagship. If we judge from the "tens" in other recorded fleets we might conclude, on the contrary, that more than one probably existed in Antony's fleet. In the fleet of Ptolemy II, we see that although the largest ships are limited in number he still possessed 17 "fives," 5 "sixes," 37 "sevens," 30 "nines," 14 "elevens," 2 "twelves," 4 "thirteens," 1 "twenty" and 2 "thirties" (Athenaeus 5.203d). The ship classes "ten" and "nine" are among those that were not so exceptional as to be severely limited in number. Furthermore, we have the direct statement of Plutarch (*Ant.* 61.1) that Antony began the war with "no fewer than 500 fighting ships, among which were many vessels of eight and ten banks of oars, arrayed in pompous and festal fashion" (trans. PERRIN 1920). As a result, we believe it quite probable that Octavian captured more than one "ten" from Antony's fleet, *pace* Tarn.

determine the class differences among sockets smaller than [4], we are seriously handicapped by not having a full range of sizes visible for examination. Even though we know that ten classes are possibly exhibited here, the possibility for error in determining class differences is very great because we do not know how many classes are represented between [1] and [E], nor do we know the size of a "one." Fortunately, additional evidence, independent of the Campsite Memorial, is available for filling this gap at the lower end of our series. But before we turn our attention to it, we should discuss the problems inherent in the evidence we are forced to use.

a. The Significance of the Profiles

If we possessed a wealth of detail concerning warships of known classes from many periods of history, it would be soundest, methodologically, to utilize only that information from the mid-first century B.C. The different types of symbols cast onto the surface of the Athlit ram may indicate that it was made on Cyprus during the reign of Ptolemy V Epiphanes or, at the latest, during the early years of Ptolemy VI Philometor (i.e., between 204 and 164 B.C.).[27] If this supposition is correct, the Athlit ram would come from a ship more than a century older than the vessels which fought in the Battle of Actium.[28]

Certainly, changes in ship design will have occurred during this interval of time. For example, the depth profiles of the cuttings reveal that the Actium rams either had no tailpiece (cf. Fig. 27, all examples), that the tailpiece was quite short (cf. Fig. 28: 9, 11; Fig. 29: B?, D?), or that they were cut off before the rams were mounted. We will leave the full significance of this fact for others to determine, but the evidence independent of this monument implies that the rams had no tailpieces. If this is true, one wonders if some structural change lies behind this alteration of the ram's design.[29] One also wonders if this change affected the sizes of the rams assigned to each ship class. The evidence presented below for the size of a trireme ram seems to imply that this class remained largely unaffected by the tailpiece change (if there even was such a change for this class). Again, we must leave considerations of hull design to others more competent to judge, but the possibility that profound differences existed among ships of the same class over time must be admitted.

---

[27] MURRAY (forthcoming); cf. LINDER 1988, p. 65.

[28] The normal life of a well-built warship seems to have been between 20 and 30 years; cf. CASSON 1971, p. 90 with n. 68 and pp. 119–20. The older ships among those at Actium might have been built, therefore, around the middle of the century.

[29] J.R. Steffy (personal communication) has told us that the dropping of the tailpiece may correspond to some strengthening of the ship's keel such as the later addition of a keelson. He cautions, however, that the earliest surviving archaeological evidence for this particular element in Greco-Roman hull construction dates from the fourth century of our era. Even if such a change had already occurred in the vessels at Actium, the effect this might have had on the overall size and weight of each class is unknown.

The overall appearance of the rams on the Campsite Memorial can best be discerned from the types of rams illustrated on other monuments of this period.[30] The closest parallels we have found to the profiles preserved in the monument's sockets appear on a triumphal arch built during the first century of our era at Arausio (modern Orange, France).[31] The arch is triple in form with each of the three subsidiary arches framed by Corinthian columns that support a continuous entablature running above all three arches. Between the tops of each side arch and the entablature is a space in which war spoils are depicted. Directly above these two sculptured areas are two rectangular panels located in the entablature (two panels appear on either side of the monument) which depict naval spoils. And among the items illustrated are a large number of warship rams whose after-ends match perfectly the shapes recorded in the sockets of the Campsite Memorial (Figs. 56 and 57).

After Actium, no major sea battles were fought in the Mediterranean. A good possibility exists, therefore, that the design for the rams on the Arausio arch derives from the mass of naval spoils Octavian displayed in Rome upon his return in 29.[32] Furthermore, except for their lack of tailpieces, the rams of the arch are similar in appearance to the example from Athlit. Whatever the structural differences determined by this dropping of the tailpiece in the years between 204 and 31 B.C., it seems to have had little effect on the rest of the ram's appearance.

Other considerations lead us to suspect that the ram size for each ship class was determined by additional factors only partially related to its lack of a tailpiece. J.R. Steffy's analysis of the 16 bow timbers preserved in the Athlit ram makes it clear that this weapon was carefully designed to transfer the enormous shock of a ramming blow as equally as possible to the hull timbers of its ship. Such careful design was necessary if the attacking ship was to avoid damage from its own blows during combat. The ram, like a well-designed hardhat, would have to withstand the tremendous force of impact without bending or cracking. Such strength could be partly achieved by the careful design of the head and fins, but it would also depend partly upon the quality of the bronze used, the thickness of the driving center, cowl and bottom plate, and the integrity of the casting. A well-designed, well-cast, heavy ram would be necessary

---

[30] So many vessels were captured during the Principate of Augustus (some 600 according to *Res Gestae* 3.4) that many official monuments erected during his lifetime (and in the period immediately following his death) allude to the mass of naval spoils dedicated at temples during this period. For a discussion of this phenomenon, particularly as concerns spoils from the Battle of Actium, see HÖLSCHER 1984 and 1985, and ZANKER 1988, pp. 79–85. None of the naval spoils illustrated by Hölscher, however, corresponds as closely to the profiles on the monument as do these examples from the arch at Orange.

[31] On this arch, see PICARD 1957, pp. 319–25 and AMY 1962.

[32] Propertius 2.1 writes of seeing "Actian prows breasting the sacred way." For the view that Actium represents a starting point for the representational art of the Augustan age, see HÖLSCHER 1985. PICARD 1957, p. 322, argues that the naval spoils were depicted on the arch without any particular connection to a known historical event. He argues that they alluded to the universality of power wielded by the *princeps* on land and sea; cf. also the remarks of ZANKER 1988, p. 84.

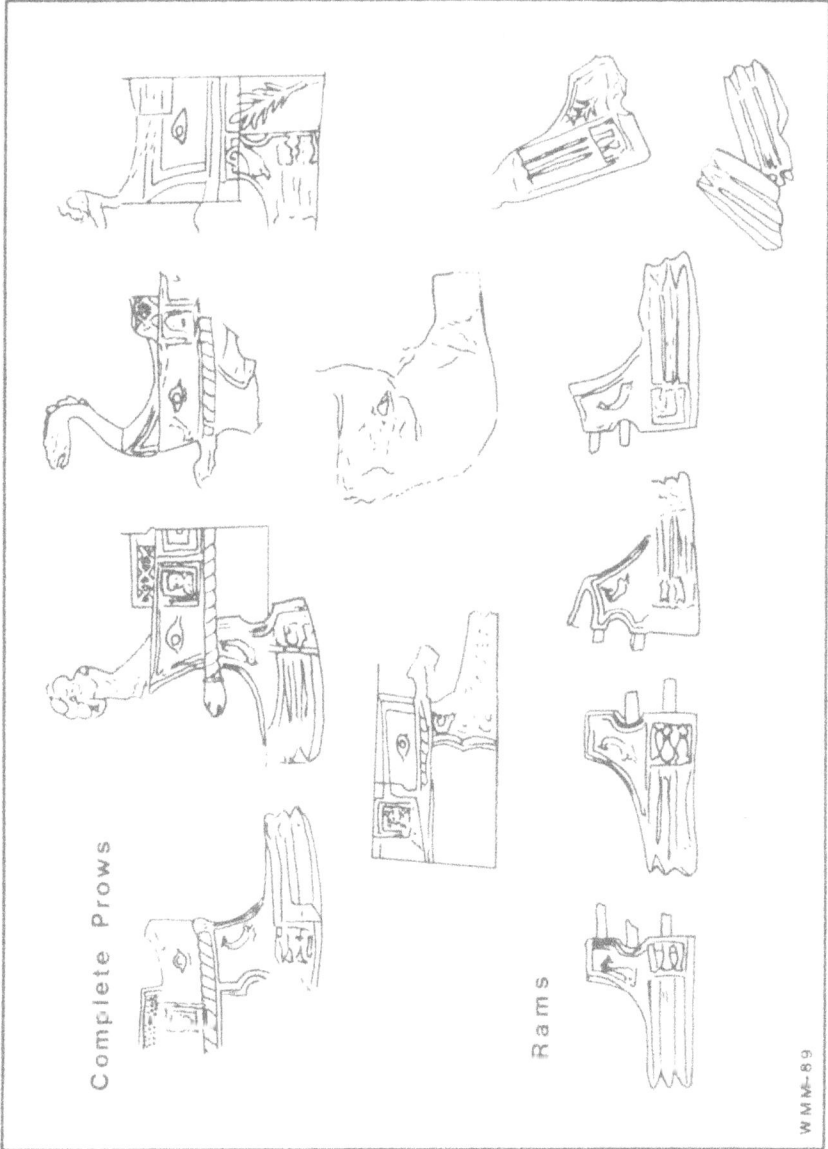

Complete Prows

Rams

WMM-89

Fig. 57.

for a ship of immense size and weight, or it would fail under the stress of impact. And, if the dropping of the tailpiece was the result of heavier structural timbers, this too should have had an effect on the mass of the rams used by these vessels.

To be honest, we must admit our ignorance in all these matters. Even so, the paucity of evidence concerning ship classes from any period demands that we use whatever information is available. If we admit, however, that all conclusions based on such evidence are open to question, and keep this cautionary statement firmly in mind, we can now turn to the available evidence.

b. The Weight of the Athlit Ram

The most important information is provided by the two *bona fide* warship rams surviving from antiquity because they represent the actual sizes and weights of two different ship classes. The larger example was found in 1980 off Athlit, Israel (Fig. 25), and the smaller one was purchased in 1987 by the Deutsches Schiffahrtsmuseum in Bremerhaven (Fig. 58).[33] Since both these rams are too small to fit into any of the sockets, they clearly must come from smaller ship classes. The problem is, of course, how small are they? Following the Athlit ram's discovery, some experts concluded that the weapon was quite large and must have come from a class considerably larger than a trireme. The evidence for this view rested primarily on the ram's immense weight of almost half a ton (465 kg.). According to C. Torr's calculations from the sale of five trireme rams in 325/4 B.C., one ram weighed roughly 77 kg. (170 lbs.). Although no one ventured a precise guess in print, some scholars be-

---

[33] Both rams have already been mentioned in the discussion of the socket's function and original number of rams on the monument. The first public notice of the Bremerhaven ram appeared in *Nefer 5* (1987), the catalog of the Nefer Galley in Zurich, p. 25. Dr. D. Ellmers, the director of the Deutsches Schiffahrtsmuseum, kindly provided us with the ram's dimensions, weight and appropriate cross-section (used in Fig. 22 as Ram 2) in a letter dated April 24, 1987. Recently, HAGY 1986, pp. 226–27 and Fig. 13, writes that three rams are known. Of the examples he cites, two can be dismissed for the purposes of this study. The "ram" in the Fitzwilliam Museum (Hagy's Fig. 13) is more likely a *proembolion*, or subsidiary ram which was mounted above the *embolion* or true ram (cf. CASSON 1971, p. 85). Another such example, called the "Turin ram" (cf. TORR 1964, Pl. 8, Fig. 43), preserves a bronze sheath in the shape of a ram's head that once served as the reinforced covering of a *proembolion*. A similar bronze sheath in the shape of a boar's head (not a sea monster as reported by BROUSKARI 1985, p. 46) is exhibited in the Kanellopoulos Museum in Athens. The "ram" found by H. Frost off Marsala is really a pair of upcurving timbers at the bow of a long narrow vessel thought by FROST 1975 to be the core for the ram. Since she followed Torr's light calculation for the weight of a trireme ram (cf. infra text) she believed (p. 224) that the ramming timbers were wrapped with a thin sheathing of bronze, a piece of which she found tacked to one of the timbers; cf. also FROST 1981a, pp. 70–75. In light of MURRAY 1985 (cf. infra text), this view of lightly sheathed Greek rams is no longer tenable. If ramming timbers are indeed present at Marsala, they must come from a completely different design than is expressed in the Athlit, Bremerhaven and Campsite Memorial examples; cf. BASCH 1975, pp. 215–17, for the evidence behind such a view.

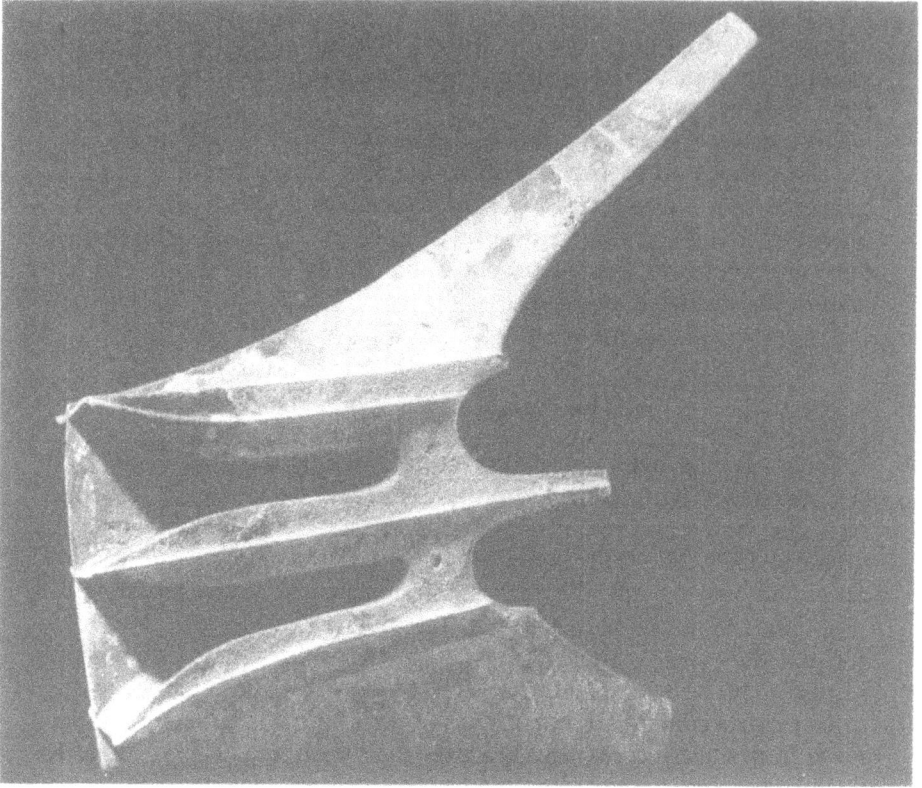

Fig. 58.

lieved that the Athlit ram came from a ship larger than a "four" or "five" and perhaps from one as big as a "nine" or "ten."[34]

Under close examination, however, Torr's calculations of 1894 do not stand up to inscriptional evidence found since his day. It now seems more likely that the rams in question were recovered from damaged ships, were themselves damaged, and were collected in fragments to be sold off as scrap. The average weight of the five rams sold was really about 44.5 kg. (98 lbs.), clearly too light to be serviceable trireme rams.[35] And since the rams were collected over a period of years before being

[34] Cf. for example BASCH 1982; POMEY 1983, p. 248; and MORRISON 1984, p. 217.

[35] For a full discussion of the evidence, see MURRAY 1985. The Bremerhaven ram, which we believe is from a "one," weighs only 53 kg. The vivid description of a trireme battle in the harbor at Syracuse (Thuc. 7.70), makes it certain that a 44.5 kg. ram would not have survived long on the bow of its ship before being smashed to bits. This is particularly evident when we remember that triremes were some 34 meters long and were powered by 170 oarsmen. J. Coates informs us that the trireme replica built by the Greek navy weighs about 40 tons with a full crew on board. The hull weighs roughly 22 tons; a full set of oars, about 2 tons; and the crew, about 15 tons. Spars, rigging, sails and personal gear (not carried on board during combat) may have raised the total weight to around 48 tons. A 44.5 kg. ram would have been much too light to withstand the enormous stresses generated by the impact of a 40-ton mass (the vessel's combat weight).

sold, it may be that the Curators in charge of the Athenian shipyards waited for sufficient bronze to accumulate before "selling" the metal to the foundry for the casting of a new ram. If this is so, the 216 kg. sold in 325/4 may be significant as a lower limit for the weight of a trireme ram.[36] We are not obliged, therefore, to interpret the Athlit ram solely in light of its weight. It may, in fact, correspond to a trireme, or to a "four" or "five" if we accept around 200 kg. as a minimum weight of a serviceable trireme ram.

c. The *Anaglypha Traiani* and the Sizes of Suspended Rams

Another piece of evidence that can be brought to bear on the size of a trireme ram is a pair of detailed reliefs called the *Anaglypha Traiani* showing the *Forum Romanum* at the time of Hadrian.[37] The right panel (Fig. 59, bottom) depicts the burning of record tablets from the Tabularium on the occasion of a remission of taxes in A.D. 118; the *Rostra Augusti* is partly depicted on the extreme preserved right edge of the panel. According to the generally accepted view, the left panel (Fig. 59, top) shows the emperor (either Trajan or Hadrian) standing on the *Rostra Aedis Divi Iulii* (the Rostra before the Temple of Divus Iulius) while a woman expresses thanks for the establishment of a program to help feed the children of needy families (the "institutio alimentaria").[38] The great value of these two reliefs is the fact that the rams depicted on both rostra are roughly similar in size (cf. Figs. 59–61). Since such care is lavished on the proportional details of the foreground (figures, platforms, trees, statues and tablets), it seems likely that the artist has attempted to illustrate the rams of the two rostra in correct proportion to the figures that surround them. In both cases, human figures appearing in close proximity to the rams allow for a comparison of their sizes with the Athlit and Bremerhaven rams, as well as with the sizes of the sockets on Octavian's Campsite Memorial.[39]

These rams are clearly smaller than the Athlit ram and yet significantly larger than the example from Bremerhaven. To what class do they correspond? In order to answer this question, we must determine the classes of the ships whose rams were chosen for display on these two rostra. As for the *Rostra Aedis Divi Iulii*, we know only that the rams came from ships captured at Actium in 31 B.C. The historical accounts tell us noth-

---

[36] MURRAY 1985, pp. 149–50. It is interesting to note that the ram of the replica weighs 200 kg., a weight considered by the modern founder as providing a minimum reasonable thickness for the weapon.

[37] For photos of these reliefs, and a bibliography of their interpretation up to 1968, see NASH 1968, Vol. II, pp. 176–77; more recently, see TORELLI 1982, pp. 89–118. Concerning the base for these reliefs, see GIULIANI-VERDUCHI 1987, pp. 79–80.

[38] For a different interpretation, see TORELLI 1982, pp. 87–118.

[39] We are not arguing that the proportions exactly correspond to real life. Nevertheless, it is striking that the sizes of the rams on both monuments depicted in the reliefs are roughly the same size. In addition, roughly similar proportions appear on coin depictions of these monuments which include figures: cf. Figs. 62, 63, 64 and 66.

Fig. 59.

Fig. 60.

Fig. 61.

ing about their sizes. We are fortunately in a better position to classify the sizes of the rams on the *Rostra Augusti* at the other end of the Forum.[40]

1.) The Rams of the Roman Rostra

Although the Republican speaker's platform was rebuilt numerous times and physically moved from its original position in 45 B.C., we know of at least two occasions (up to the reign of Hadrian) on which different groups of rams were affixed to its facade. The first was in 338 B.C. when six Antiate ships were stripped of their rams in order to decorate the platform for the first time. If we can trust the statement of Polybius that before 261 B.C. the "five" had not yet been introduced into any Italian navy, we can conclude that the Antiate ships were probably "threes."[41] Even though "fours" are not ruled out by Polybius' statement, the Antiate navy could not have been very large, and the standard ship of the line in the small navies of this period was the "three."[42] The first rams placed on the Republican Rostra, therefore, were most likely from triremes.

The second occasion occurred in the censorship of M. Antonius (97 B.C.) and is somewhat less certain than the first. According to Cicero (*de Orat.* 3.3.10), Antonius decorated the Rostra from the "manubiae" (i.e., money realized from the sale of booty) resulting from his naval triumph over the Cilician pirates (probably won in 100 B.C.).[43] The verb used by Cicero to describe Antonius' action ("ornarat") implies that he adorned the platform with some decoration. The clear implication of the passage is that Antonius adorned the platform with spoils from his naval victory, most logically the *rostra* from the ships he had captured. Considering what we know of Antonius' campaigns, the rams would have come from Cilician pirate vessels. According to Appian (*Mith.* 92), during the decade of the 80s the Cilician pirates began to add "twos" and "threes" to their fleets as a result of their association with Mithridates.[44] The ships captured by Antonius, therefore, would have been no larger than "threes," and in fact might have been from various classes of Hellenistic light vessels like the *myoparo* (a "one") and the *hemiolia* (literally a "one-and-a-half"), or from "twos."[45]

When the Rostra was moved farther to the west in 45–44 B.C., the selection of the censor's grandson to oversee the project implies that the

---

[40] Cf. as well, Chapter IV, Sections 1 and 2.

[41] Polyb. 1.20.10.

[42] In 330 B.C., even the fleet of Athens, a naval super-power by comparison to Antium, had only 18 "fours" as compared to 492 "threes"; cf. CASSON 1971, pp. 97 and 124.

[43] See also Chapter IV, Section 1.

[44] Cf. ORMEROD 1924, pp. 29–30, 208–209.

[45] For the *myoparo* and *hemiolia*, two classes of light vessels, see CASSON 1971, pp. 128–32. Since our sources preserve no detailed record of Antonius' campaign, and since the pirates seem so bold during the decades of the 80s and 70s, it has been presumed that Antonius' naval successes were overemphasized; cf. for example ORMEROD 1924, p. 209. The fact that Antonius was allowed to decorate the Rostra with his naval spoils, however, implies that his successes were not completely insignificant.

original rams were reapplied to the new structure.[46] Since Florus says that the original six from Antium were still visible in his day (the mid-second century of our era), we can presume that Antony also reutilized the rams dedicated by his grandfather.[47] We simply do not know if Antony selected additional rams from dedications elsewhere in the city, like those displayed by Pompey in his house (cf. Chapter IV, n. 12), to cover the face of the finished platform. We can be reasonably certain, however, that the ram-classes from the previous two Rostra (attested in the literary record) were from vessels no larger than the "three."

A recent study of the Forum's pavements suggests that between 14 and 12 B.C. Augustus enlarged the Rostra by raising the platform and adding a rectangular front (cf. Chapter IV, Section 2). If this was indeed the case, we must then assume that the rams were once again moved and remounted on the facade of this new rectangular structure. This much is implied by Florus' statement mentioned above. Once again, we do not know if Augustus added additional rams to those obtained from the previous monument, although the greater length of the facade would imply that he did. If new rams were added, however, their sizes are unknown. Nevertheless, from the right panel of the *Anaglypha Traiani*, from coins dated to 13 and 12 B.C. (Figs. 66 and 64), and from the positions of the holes in the facade of the Rostra itself, it is clear that the rams were suspended off the ground. This simple fact can be used to determine their maximum size.

2.) The Sizes of Suspended Rams

In order to determine the maximum sized ram the Romans normally suspended off the ground, we must first consider the *Rostra Aedis Divi Iulii*. Although we are not told the sizes of its rams, their maximum size can still be deduced. From the clear representations of this rostra that have survived, one on the left panel of the *Anaglypha Traiani* (Fig. 61), the other on a coin type minted during the reign of Hadrian (Fig. 62), we see how the rams were mounted. Both examples illustrate weapons

Fig. 62.

---

[46] Cf. Chapter IV, Section 1.
[47] Florus 1.11; cf. Chapter IV, n. 31.

smaller in size than the example from Athlit, and both show the rams mounted midway up the face of a wall. The fact that these rams were suspended off the ground is a fair indication of their size. The Athlit ram, for example, which weighs half a ton, is simply too heavy to be mounted in this manner on such a wall.

If we consider the sizes of rams mounted on rostral columns, we arrive at a similar conclusion. Both its size and weight make the Athlit ram ill-suited for placement on a column such as that depicted on a denarius of Octavian (Fig. 63).[48] The rams available for placement on the rostral column of Duillius came from those ships that he captured, and these are recorded on the surviving inscription as one "seven," and 30 "fives" and "threes."[49] To judge from the sequence of sockets on the Campsite Memorial (cf. infra) which certainly includes "sevens" and perhaps also "fives," the "threes" were probably the rams mounted on his column.[50] Let us now review the facts at our disposal:

1. The rams on the Rostra at the west end of the Forum (those for which we have any evidence at all) are likely to be from ships no larger than the "three."

2. Judging from the two panels of the *Anaglypha Traiani*, the rams on the *Rostra Aedis Divi Iulii* are similar in size to those depicted on the west side of the Forum. They are by comparison, therefore, no larger than "threes." If we remember that Augustus considered ships smaller than "threes" not worth counting in his lifetime total of captured warships (*Res Gestae* 3.4), our conclusion that the rams mounted on this platform were no smaller than "threes" receives additional support.[51]

3. The rams on the *Rostra Aedis Divi Iulii* are of a size (i.e., from a ship class) that is smaller than the smallest socket currently visible on the Campsite Memorial.

4. The Athlit ram is too long and heavy to be suspended easily off the ground on the face of a wall in the manner revealed by the Hadrianic reliefs, and by the various coin types.

5. The Bremerhaven ram (Fig. 58), weighing only 53 kg., could be

---

[48] For the *columna rostrata* on the coin of Octavian, see SUTHERLAND 1984, p. 60, #271; cf. also the remarks of ZANKER 1988, pp. 41–42 with Fig. 32.

[49] See Chapter IV, n. 10.

[50] If the smallest socket corresponds to a "six," then the largest class the Athlit ram could come from is a "five." If the smallest socket corresponds to a "five," then the Athlit ram corresponds to a "four." Since this ram is clearly too heavy to be mounted on such a column and since Duillius did not capture any "fours," we believe it likely that only the "threes" were used on the column. As for the "seven," its size is clearly represented somewhere in the sockets of the Campsite Memorial and thus is too large for mounting on a column.

[51] *Res Gestae* 3.4 (text of EHRENBERG-JONES 1976, p. 4): Naves cepi sescen[tas praeter] eas, si quae minore[s quam trir]emis fuerunt. "I captured 600 warships, not counting vessels smaller than 'threes.' " Although the precise designation of the ship size is not completely preserved, the number of spaces available on the stone plus the fact that under Augustus the standard unit in the major Italian fleets was the trireme make the restoration certain; cf. CASSON 1971, p. 141.

Fig. 65.

easily suspended off the ground on the face of a wall, column or statue base.

The pattern emerging from these facts implies that the Romans were capable of suspending rams up to "threes" off the ground on the facades of their monuments. If they were capable of mounting "fours" in this manner, we have no clear evidence for it. This likelihood has two implications. First, the Athlit ram cannot come from a trireme. And second, the smallest sockets in the face of the wall are for rams larger than the "four," since the Athlit ram must represent a "four" or perhaps even a "five."[52] We must now consider the variations in the sizes of the sockets to see if gradations exist that might represent differences in ship classes.

d. A Tentative Sequence of Ship Classes

The evidence currently at our disposal reveals that the ship classes corresponding to the preserved sockets should range from "tens" to "fives." We leave the determination of ship sizes from the dimensions of these sockets to naval architects. We believe, however, that one can appreciate certain obvious differences in size by comparing the shapes and exterior dimensions of the sockets depicted in Figures 20–22. Our attempt to form "groups" or clusters of similar sizes results in the following two sequences:

Sequence I		Sequence II	
10:	[1], [2], [4]	10:	[1], [2], [4]
9:	[3], [5], [6]	9:	[3], [5], [6]
8:	[7], [8], [9], [10]	8:	[7], [8], [9], [10]
7:	[11], [12], [17], [B], [C]	7:	[11], [12], [17], [B], [C]
6:	[13], [14], [15]	6:	[13], [14], [15], [16],
5:	[16], [18], [A], [D]		[18], [A], [D]
4:	Athlit ram (Fig. 22, Ram 1)	5:	Athlit ram? (Fig. 22, Ram 1)
3:	suspended rams of the *Anaglypha*	4:	Athlit ram? (Fig. 22, Ram 1)
	Traiani (cf. Fig. 22, Ram 2	3:	suspended rams of the
	from the trireme replica)		*Anaglypha Traiani* (cf. Fig.
2:	?		22, Ram 2 from the trireme
1:	Bremerhaven ram? (Fig. 22, Ram 3)		replica)
		2:	?
		1:	Bremerhaven ram? (Fig. 22,
			Ram 3)

By presenting these two sequences we do not mean to imply that the precise classes of the sockets have been determined within these two limits. Each reader may arrive at his own conclusions by comparing the relative sizes of the individual sockets. The true importance of such an exercise, however, lies in the *number* of gradations in size identified in the surviving sockets. Regardless of their precise identifications, we feel

[52] It should be noted that the ram of the trireme replica weighs 200 kg. and is visibly smaller than the Athlit ram. Its cross-section where it would have been mounted on the Campsite Memorial is shown in Fig. 22 (as Ram 2) for the purpose of comparison.

that *at least* five gradations in size can be discerned (sequence II). Whether or not there are six, as suggested by sequence I, we are less able to determine, much less prove. A truly defensible sequence awaits the analysis of the sockets' dimensions by expert naval architects, which we are not. From the evidence presently available, the Athlit ram should come from a "five" or a "four." Even though we suspect that it belongs to a "four," we cannot prove it conclusively at this time.

The class of the Bremerhaven ram (Fig. 58) cannot be determined with any certainty from these two sequences because of its very small size. The ram is clearly smaller than a "three," but whether it belongs to a "two," a *hemiolia,* or some type of "one" is impossible to deduce from the evidence of these larger sizes. Its very light weight (53 kg.), however, inclines us to believe it comes from a very small warship. In the absence of additional evidence, we favor assigning it to some type of *monokrotos,* or "one."[53]

Finally, even the most casual inspection reveals that the sockets are not arranged in a strict sequence of sizes from large to small. This mixing of sizes hints that whoever placed the rams along the monument's facade either found it difficult to distinguish between the ship classes of the rams once the weapons were removed from their ships, or that some other factor no longer discernible (such as the length of each weapon's driving center or the weight of each weapon) helped to determine their placement along the wall. It is best to admit that much remains uncertain about the rams once displayed at Octavian's campsite.

One observation, however, emerges clearly from this analysis of the bow dimensions of ancient warships, and that concerns the massive sizes of the examples chosen for display on the Campsite Memorial. These rams were taken from classes much larger than those regularly employed in the navies of the period following the Battle of Actium. Certainly, this was one message that Octavian intended to convey through this memorial. But were there other, more subtle messages that lay behind the seemingly odd design of the Campsite Memorial?

---

[53] We doubt that this ram could withstand the impact of a blow driven by a moderately heavy ship powered by 50–100 oarsmen. For this reason, we believe it must come from a very small ship, and this would correspond best to some type of "one."

IV: The Significance of the Campsite Memorial's Design

Official memorials of successful wars or victories are designed to inspire patriotism, pride and gratitude for the victor's accomplishments, which the Campsite Memorial clearly does. The intent of this monument, as we might have expected from one built by Augustus, goes beyond these limited ends. In order to understand the monument fully as a statement of propaganda, one first needs to appreciate the traditions behind its seemingly odd design. Many years ago, Gagé observed that Octavian had combined in this memorial "the Roman traditions of a trophy with those of the great commemorative monuments of the Greek world."[1] Although our reconstruction of the monument is somewhat different from Gagé's, we agree fully with his observation that the design mixes both Roman and Greek elements. The separation of these strains is necessary to determine the full scope of the message the memorial was intended to convey.

Greek dedications following important naval victories usually consisted of captured naval gear: detached rams, figureheads, anchors and ropes, etc.[2] On exceptional occasions, however, whole ships were offered in thanksgiving, usually at sanctuaries near the battle site. For example, a Phoenician trireme was dedicated to Poseidon at the Isthmus, to Athena at Sounion and to Ajax at Salamis after Xerxes' defeat in 480 B.C.[3] The Peloponnesians dedicated an Athenian trireme to Poseidon at Rhion in 429 B.C., and we know that at least one warship (and perhaps there were others) was dedicated to Apollo on Delos during the Hellenistic period. Here, in fact, the remains of a building suitable for a warship have been identified. Recently, another such building, with supports to hold a ship's hull still partly *in situ*, was discovered in the sanctuary of the Great Gods at Samothrace.[4]

---

[1] GAGÉ 1936, pp. 57–58.

[2] After a victory over the Samians ca. 520 B.C., the Aiginetans sawed off the boar's head prows from the enemy ships and dedicated them in the temple of "Aiginetan Athena," i.e., Aphaia (Hdt. 3.59.3); *akroteria* (ships' figureheads) taken from "the enemy" were dedicated in the stoa of the Athenians at Delphi ca. 478 B.C. (MEIGGS-LEWIS 1969, #25); and an *akrostolion* (an ornament which crowns either the stem or the stern post) is listed as a dedication to the *heros iatros* in 201/200 B.C. (*IG* II² 839, line 72). The inscriptions also record various dedications at Delos during the fourth to second centuries B.C.: *IG* II² 1641, lines 46 (a trireme ram), 49 (trireme gear); 1640, line 25 (3 trireme rams); 1648, line 8 (a trireme ram—identical with the one of 1641)j; 1649, line 11 (*hypozomata*, anchor lines); and DURRBACH 1929, No. 422 B, lines 167 (a ship ram), 168 and 171 (iron anchors).

[3] Hdt. 8.121.1.

[4] For the dedication at Rhion, see Thuc. 2.92.5; for that at Delos, see Paus. 1.29.1. TARN 1910 maintains that Antigonus Gonatas dedicated his flagship to Apollo on Delos. In his argument, Tarn identifies the "nine" of Paus. 1.29.1 with the statement of Moschion (quoted in Athenaeus 5.209e) that Antigonus Gonatas dedicated his ship after a naval

Inspired by this Greek tradition of offering whole ships, Octavian decided to dedicate a purely Greek-style monument at Apollo's sanctuary on Cape Actium.[5] Not to be outdone by anyone before his time, Octavian dedicated a full complement of ten ships—one from each ship class that had fought in the battle. Set inside shipsheds (called *neoria* by Strabo) attached to the sanctuary, these vessels constituted an offering unparalleled in size by any other whole warship dedication known to us from the Greek world. In making this offering, Octavian followed firmly in the traditions of the greatest and most powerful of the Hellenistic monarchs who had tried to outstrip one another in the size and complexity of their naval vessels.[6] Octavian built a monument at Actium appropriate to the grandeur of these ships—large and showy. It revealed a theme that was destined to become a central element in all subsequent accounts of the Actian War. The final battle on September 2 marked the last extensive use of these giant ships in the navies of the Mediterranean powers, and in the following generation, the standard ship of the line was once again the trireme.[7] As if to mark the passing of an era, the memorial at Apollo's sanctuary burned to the ground sometime during this same generation.[8]

For the major monument of his own personal foundation, his "Victory City" built on the site of his army's camp, a purely Greek-style memorial to the Actian War would not do. As it was built on the sacred site of Octavian's own tent, a particularly Roman image was desired for its outward appearance. For this purpose, Octavian approved a design which recalled the glorious days of the Roman Republic. And as was frequently the case, his reasons for this choice were complex and his intentions subtle. To understand what he was trying to accomplish, we must now consider the Roman traditions of naval dedications.

The Romans, like the Greeks, also dedicated parts of captured ships in the temples of their gods. And, as with the Greeks, rams seem to have been a favorite dedication.[9] Rams were also dedicated outside the confines of their temples in ways unique to the Romans. For example, C. Duillius (who was the first to win a naval triumph in 260 B.C.) was

---

victory at Kos (between 262 and 245 B.C.). For the building at Delos, see COUCHOUD-SVORONOS 1921. TARN 1930, p. 139, believes that this building originally housed a "fifteen" dedicated by Demetrius. BRUNEAU-DUCAT 1983, pp. 138–40, are more cautious. They believe that the late fourth century building may be identified with the *neorion* of Delian inscriptions, but consider the actual dedication contained within a matter of dispute. The discovery at Samothrace was made in the summer of 1986 and has not yet been fully published. For a picture of the ship's base, still *in situ*, see MCCREDIE 1986, p. 13.

[5] Cf. Chapter I, p. 6 with n. 29.

[6] For a discussion of the large polyremes in the Hellenistic navies, and of the largest ship produced by this naval arms race (a "forty" built by Ptolemy IV), see CASSON 1971, pp. 103–16, and 137–40.

[7] CASSON 1971, p. 141.

[8] Cf. Chapter I, n. 29.

[9] Much of the evidence for this assertion comes from depictions on coins. Parts of ships grouped around a column, or in a pile, or a trophy on the prow of a ship appear on coins after the time of Pompey; cf. REINACH 1919, p. 518.

awarded two *columnae rostratae*; the more famous of the pair stood on or near the Rostra and was surmounted by a bronze statue of the consul. This column, ornamented with a few of the captured rams suspended off the ground, bore an inscription on its base detailing the Carthaginian ships captured and sunk by the consul at Mylae.[10] Two other examples are known: one was granted to M. Aemilius Paulus, consul in 255 B.C., and was struck by lightning in 172 B.C.; the other was awarded to Octavian following his victory over Sextus Pompey at Naulochus in 36 B.C. (cf. Fig. 63).[11] The one of Duillius, being the first and placed conspicuously in the *Forum Romanum*, remains the best known.

The use of rams as ornaments on other kinds of monuments, both public and private, is also attested. For example, Pompey displayed in the foyer of his own house some of the 90 rams he captured during the Pirate War.[12] And from an image appearing on a coin minted in 12, it is possible (though we think it debatable) that the base of an equestrian statue of Agrippa was ornamented with warship rams (Fig. 64).[13] By far the most venerable and unique display of rams, however, was the Rostra or speaker's platform in the *Forum Romanum*. This was the monument that provided the inspiration for the two ram displays Octavian dedicated in 29 B.C. A brief consideration of the Rostra's history will help to explain the powerful associations it held for Octavian.[14]

1. The Successive Phases of the Rostra

The first true Rostra was created from the southernmost speaker's platform in the ancient Comitium some three centuries before Actium when C. Maenius affixed six warship rams to the front of its podium. While consul in 338 B.C., he had won a decisive victory over the Volscians who held Antium, a coastal city located to the west of Rome. As

[10] Cf. Servius Italicus *Punica* 6.663–667; Pliny *HN* 34.11; Quint. *Inst.* 1.7.12; and *CIL*, VI 31611 [= *ILS* 65 = WARMINGTON 1959, pp. 128–31]. According to the preserved inscription, Duillius captured 1 "seven," 30 "fives" and "threes," and sank 13 ships. Reconstructions of the column appear in CHIPIEZ 1887, p. 1351, Fig. 1787, and REINACH 1919, p. 518, Fig. 7133.

[11] For the rostrate column of Paulus, see Livy 42.20.1; for Octavian's column, depicted on a coin minted between 29 and 27 B.C. (= SUTHERLAND 1984, p. 60, #271), cf. PLATNER-ASHBY 1929, p. 134, and ZANKER 1988, pp. 41–42 with Fig. 32.

[12] Cic. *Phil.* 2.28 (68); the fact that 90 warships "with bronze rams" were captured by Pompey is recorded by Plutarch (*Pomp.* 28). It is interesting to note in this context that Petronius' character Trimalchio had bronze rams placed in some decorative manner at the entrance to his dining room (*Satiricon* 30.1). Do we have here a satirical reflection of Pompey's own ostentatious display?

[13] Cf. SUTHERLAND 1984, p. 73, #412. We believe it more likely that this coin depicts the equestrian statue of Octavian *in rostris*, rather than some statue base; cf. infra Section 2.

[14] For the traditional history of the Rostra in its various architectural stages, cf. THÉDENAT 1896, pp. 1297–99 with Figs. 3259–62; SCHNEIDER 1914, cols. 450–61; and PLATNER-ASHBY 1929, pp. 450–55. GJERSTAD 1941 further defined the different phases of the Comitium, and a full bibliography (up to 1968) is provided by NASH 1968, Vol. II, p. 276. The most recent attempt to reevaluate all the evidence is by COARELLI 1983 and 1985. Coarelli's views are clearly expressed and convincing, and have largely been adopted in the reconstruction appearing in the text.

a result of his success, the Antiate navy had been confiscated and their ships towed up the Tiber to Rome where some were presumably kept for use and the rest burned.[15] Rams removed from six of these ships were affixed in some way to the speaker's platform which henceforth took its name, "Rostra," from the naval spoils decorating its facade.[16] Archaeological remains of a good candidate for this platform have been located near the *Curia Iulia,* and according to the recent analysis of F. Coarelli (based on the work of E. Gjerstad) ought to correspond to a rectilinear podium ("platform C") of the Comitium's fourth paving phase.[17]

At some later time, the rectilinear platform corresponding to Maenius' Rostra was replaced with a new structure having a curved front and steps.[18] This phase (corresponding to pavement V) is not easy to date solely from its preserved remains but should fall sometime between 338 B.C. and the date of the seventh paving phase, around 50 B.C.[19] Gjerstad assigned this rounded platform to the period of Sulla's alteration of the Comitium, but according to Coarelli's revised chronology, it should correspond to a transformation of the Comitium into a circular theatral area during the first half of the third century B.C. (sometime between 290 and 263 B.C.).[20]

If Coarelli is correct, this rounded Rostra must have been the one embellished in 97 B.C. by the censor M. Antonius. The evidence for this act has curiously gone unnoticed by Coarelli, but is clearly presented by Cicero in his *De Oratore* (3.3.10): "Next M. Antonius, on the very platform on which as consul he had most resolutely championed the cause of the state and which as censor he had decorated with the trophies of his military command, laid down the life that had preserved the lives of many men . . . ."[21] If Cicero is correct, Antonius (the grandfather of the triumvir) must have decorated the Rostra from the spoils of his naval

---

[15] Cf. Livy 8.14.12; and Pliny HN 34.20.

[16] Florus (1.11) remarks that the six rams taken from the Antiates were still to be seen in his own day. I presume from this that the later rams added to the Rostra were recognizably different from the fourth century Antiate rams. Livy (8.14.12) tells us that the platform took its name from the rams decorating it. Nowhere are we told the precise placement of these original rams, but it seems likely they were placed on the front of the raised podium facing toward the audience in the Comitium. It should be noted that Roman authors such as Livy refer to this platform as the Rostra before it received the rams. In this discussion, the term is reserved only for the platform after 338 B.C.

[17] COARELLI 1982, pp. 119–38, presents a clear summary of the archaeological evidence revealed by GJERSTAD 1941 and offers a reevaluation of the chronological sequences involved in light of more recent excavations in the area.

[18] The "traditional" view holds that the Rostra took the form of a rounded structure in a phase corresponding to the fourth level of the Comitium (PLATNER-ASHBY 1929, p. 451), and that it is depicted on the coin of Lollius Palicanus (Fig. 65) minted in 45 B.C.; cf., for example, SCHNEIDER 1914, cols. 452–54.

[19] Cf. COARELLI 1983, pp. 126 and 133.

[20] COARELLI 1983, pp. 148–51.

[21] The text and translation are those of RACKHAM 1948: Iam M. Antonii, in eis ipsis rostris in quibus ille rempublicam constantissime consul defenderat quaeque censor imperatoriis manubiis ornarat, positum caput illud fuit a quo erant multorum civium capita servata. . . .

triumph over the Cilician pirates (around 100 B.C.).[22] And though Cicero says only that Antonius decorated the Rostra from his share of the "manubiae" (money resulting from the sale of booty), it is not difficult to imagine what he used to decorate the podium. Since he was awarded a naval triumph, and since we know of no statue or *columna rostrata* attributed to Antonius placed near or on the Rostra, there seems little reason not to conclude that he oversaw the embellishment or repair of the speaker's platform and affixed additional rams to its facade.[23] A dedicatory inscription describing his action in words such as "M. Antonius censor Rostra imperatoriis manubiis ornata refecit" could even have served as the source for Cicero's remark.[24] On the evidence given by Cicero, therefore, it seems reasonable to date some phase of the Republican Rostra to the period of M. Antonius, and archaeologically this would correspond to some phase of the rounded remains between the Comitium and the *Forum Romanum*.[25]

Some 53 years later, the Rostra was moved by Caesar to the location at the western end of the Forum where it remained during the Empire.[26] The monument here was first identified in the 1830s when a road was built through this area of the Forum, but it was not excavated until 1882 when the road built on top of it was removed. The structure of the monument is in two basic parts, which has caused a great deal of confusion. First, there is the western part, the so-called Hemicyclium—a concrete core with a flight of curved steps. The eastern part consists of a straight front wall on which the ships' rams were mounted, and two side walls, all of large rectangular blocks (*opus quadratum*); two or three rows of piers in the interior supported the rectangular platform. The standard interpretation of these remains is that a portion of this platform's north wall was removed and a segment of the concrete core was cut out to reveal the curved wall of the concrete core when the arch of Septimius Severus was built. This wall, the front of the Hemicyclium, was then faced with slabs of Porta Santa marble. A small triangular court

[22] On M. Antonius' career, cf. BROUGHTON 1952, Vol. I, pp. 568 (with n. 2., p. 569), 572 and 576; and Vol. II, pp. 6–7.

[23] For a list of the known statues on or near the Rostra, see SCHNEIDER 1914, col. 454.

[24] If the restored text of the Campsite Memorial is correct, the similarity between the words chosen by Octavian and the reference in Cicero's speech is striking: 1) "Imp. Caesa]r. . . c]astra. . . spoli]is [exornat]a c[onsacravit]"; and 2) "quaeque [Rostra] censor imperatoriis manubiis ornarat."

[25] Unfortunately, the archaeological remains of the Rostra are too scanty to allow for a detailed reconstruction of its chronological phases. The passage of Cicero, however, raises the unsettling possibility that the phases of the Rostra might not correspond in every instance to the different pavements determined in the Comitium. It is well known, for instance, that the focus of the speaker's platform changed from one side to the other during the mid-second century. At this time, the *comitia tributa* was transferred to the Forum and the speakers began to face toward the people gathered there, and not toward the Senate house; cf. Cic. *Amic.* 25 (96); Varro *Rust.* 1.2.9; and Plut. *C. Gracch.* 5.3. Antonius' embellishment of the Rostra may have had something to do with adjustments to the platform subsequent to its change in orientation; perhaps rams were placed for the first time on the Rostra's convex facade.

[26] Dio 43.49.1.

was thus formed from which steps led up to the rectangular platform. Later, a brick projection on the east was added in the fifth century to display rams taken from the Vandals.

Coarelli has also reevaluated the evidence for this structure, and has concluded that the original interpretation of the excavator, F.M. Nichols, should be followed.[27] Instead of being later in date, the so-called Hemicyclium is in fact the Rostra built in 45–44 B.C. He points out, therefore, that the denarius of Lollius Palicanus (Fig. 65), minted in the very same year this project was started, should depict the new Caesarian monument and not the rounded Rostra in the Comitium which was going out of use. In fact, it was probably minted to stress the continuity in appearance between the two platforms.[28]

What then of the rectangular platform? Dio (43.49.1) clearly states that the new monument was started in 45 and dedicated in 44. If we identify this monument with the Hemicyclium, then it must predate the "rectangular rostra" built around it; and this is what the remains tend to confirm. The full details are complicated, but the evidence from the north side of the monument might serve here to demonstrate the relationship between the two structures. The socle of the rectilinear Rostra clearly sits on top of the curving socle for the Hemicyclium and thus should postdate it. In addition, the rectangular structure must have been built before or at the same time as the pavement which respects its front face—a pavement thought to have been laid following the fire of 14, or perhaps the fire of 9 B.C.[29]

Whether or not one accepts this new interpretation of the evidence, Dio clearly states that Caesar allowed Antony the honor of putting his name on the finished monument.[30] If we remember that Antony's grandfather had embellished or rebuilt the previous monument, the project's supervision in 45–44 by the censor's grandson makes perfect sense, particularly if the censor's rams were to be reapplied to the new platform.[31] Thus, Caesar relocated a great Republican monument through a member of the same illustrious family that had previously rebuilt and decorated it.[32] Antony's direction of the project would have blunted any

---

[27] COARELLI 1985, pp. 237–57.

[28] COARELLI 1985, pp. 243–45. For the coin, see CRAWFORD 1974, Vol. I, pp. 482–83, #473/1.

[29] COARELLI 1985, pp. 245–55, argues that the Rostra predates the pavement. For the opinion that the pavement and the Rostra's socle were "constructed at the same time," see GIULIANI-VERDUCHI 1987, p. 47; see also infra n. 36.

[30] Dio 43.49.2.

[31] We know from Florus (1.11) that the six Antiate rams were still to be seen on the Rostra in his day, perhaps during the reign of Hadrian; cf. ROLFE 1951, pp. ix–x. If they had been repeatedly installed on the successive phases of the Rostra, it is likely that the rams of Antonius would have been treated in a similar manner.

[32] Caesar had done this before. The *Basilica Aemilia et Fulvia*, built originally by the censors M. Fulvius Nobilior and M. Aemilius Lepidus in 179 B.C., was reconstructed during the 50s B.C. by L. Aemilius Paulus with money received from Caesar. Henceforth, the building was called simply the *Basilica Aemilia*; cf. Plut. *Caes.* 29.3; Cic. *Att.* 4.16.14; Varro *Ling.* 6.4; and TORELLI 1982, pp. 93–94. On this building, see BAUER 1988.

conservative objections to moving such a sacred and venerable structure, while at the same time, being done by Caesar's close associate, the action would have remained firmly tied to the program of the dictator.[33] At any rate, Antony's hitherto underrated connection with the Rostra seems to have had a powerful effect on Caesar's heir.

2. *Octavian's Own Rostra Displays*

If we may conclude anything from the actions of Octavian's "adherents," Antony's dedication of the Rostra in 44 B.C. must have bothered the sensitivities of Caesar's heir. During the first few days of 43 B.C., less than a year after the monument's dedication, the Senate decreed (on the motion of Octavian's step-father Philippus) that a gilded equestrian statue of Octavian be placed *"in rostris"* (i.e., on or near the Rostra).[34] This was done to honor the young man for leading Caesar's veterans against Antony on behalf of the Senate.[35]

A similar motive may have also moved the Senate in early 29 B.C. to allow Octavian to decorate the podium of the Divus Iulius temple with rams captured at Actium. In effect, Octavian was allowed to build his own rostra across the Forum from Antony's platform and to decorate it with rams from Antony's fleet. The final outcome of Antony's "betrayal" was subtly stated to everyone who knew the history of these monuments. Observations made in a recent study of the Forum's central area allow us to say even more. Sometime between 14 and 12 B.C., when repairs were carried out following a fire, Antony's connection with the *Forum Romanum* was completely obliterated. At this time, the western "Antonian" Rostra was enlarged and rebuilt with a rectangular front, perhaps under the direction of L. Naevius Surdinus.[36] The offensive

[33] Dio (43.49.2) plainly states that Caesar received the praise both for the project and for allowing Antony the honor of inscribing his name on the finished product. Most scholars have followed Dio's lead and have minimized the role of Antony in this project. In this same vein, COARELLI 1985, pp. 238–39, implies that the monument was dedicated by Antony simply because he was consul in the year in which it was completed. We believe, however, that the previous connection between the Antonii and this monument explains why Antony was put in charge of its relocation.

[34] We should note here that although the phrase "in rostris" can mean both "on the Rostra" or "near the Rostra" (cf. LAHUSEN 1983, p. 16), a coin minted in 42 B.C. indicates that the statue was intended to be placed "on the Rostra"; cf. ZANKER 1988, pp. 37–38 with Fig. 29, a.

[35] App. BC. 3.51; Cic. ad Brut. 1.15.7; Vell. 2.61.3; Dio 46.29.2. For the time of the meeting, see HOLMES 1928, pp. 39–40. On the other hand, when Octavian learned in 35 B.C. that Antony had executed Sextus Pompey, he was so elated that he purposely honored his colleague in Rome. Among the honors he bestowed, it is interesting to note that he set up a chariot on Antony's behalf in front of the Rostra (Dio 49.18.6).

[36] According to COARELLI 1983, pp. 254–55, and 1985, pp. 211–33, the Augustan pavement corresponding to work following fires in 14 and in 9 B.C. postdates the rectilinear Rostra built around the Hemicyclium. The rebuilding of the Rostra, therefore, must follow Octavian's return to Rome in 29 and must antedate the fires of 14 to 9 B.C. The most recent study of the Forum's pavements (GIULIANI-VERDUCHI 1987), however, concludes that the Augustan pavement and the socle of the *Rostra Augusti* were built at the same time (p. 47). They conclude further (pp. 61 and 65) that this must have occurred following the fire

connections between this monument, Antony and the proscriptions were buried at last beneath the concrete of the new platform, hereafter called the *Rostra Augusti*.[37]

In light of this evidence, we believe it possible that a coin minted in 12 B.C. by Cossus Cornelius Lentulus (Fig. 64) depicts this new monument and thereby dates the completion of the project.[38] In the past, the statue on this coin has been assigned to Agrippa (who died in this year) because the rams on the base were thought to allude to his numerous naval victories.[39] Although the secure identification of the statue remains a problem, we believe that the rams are an attempt to depict the newly finished facade of the *Rostra Augusti*.[40] In an abbreviated side view of the speaker's platform, one sees the helmeted equestrian statue placed *in rostris* atop a high podium ornamented with rams suspended off the ground in two levels—an arrangement that corresponds perfectly with the surviving holes on the monument's facade. A trophy is placed over the shoulder of the seated rider, and alludes, perhaps, to the recent

---

of 14 B.C. and was perhaps included in the work of Surdinus attested by an inscription in the central part of the Forum.

[37] The term is used by the Roman jurist Pomponius (*Dig.* I.2.2); on its significance, see COARELLI 1985, pp. 242–43.

[38] For the coin, see SUTHERLAND 1984, p. 73, #412; its obverse depicts the head of Augustus facing right.

[39] For this coin, see SUTHERLAND 1984, p. 73, #412 with Pl. 7. The previous year, a coin minted by C. Sulpicius Platorinus depicted the general wearing a combined mural and rostral crown; cf. SUTHERLAND 1984, p. 73, #409 with Pl. 7; and ZANKER 1988, p. 216, Fig. 168a.

[40] We initially felt that the statue must be the equestrian one of Octavian, voted by the Senate in early 43 B.C., and described by Velleius (2.61.3) as standing on the Rostra in his own day (text and translation are those of SHIPLEY 1950): Eum senatus honoratum equestri statua, quae hodieque in rostris posita aetatem eius scriptura indicat. . . . "The Senate honored him with an equestrian statue, which is still standing upon the Rostra and testifies to his years by its inscription." There is a problem with this view, however, since the statue depicted on a coin of 42 B.C. (which must be the one voted by the Senate; it stands on a ledge above a ram signifying the Rostra) shows horse and rider in a slightly different pose and dress than appear on the coin of Cossus Cornelius Lentulus. The image is small and of poor quality, but the rider appears not to wear a helmet, and all four of the horse's legs appear planted on the ground; compare ZANKER 1988, p. 37, Fig. 29a with our Fig. 64. Zanker argues (pp. 37–38) that the image of 42 B.C. represents the intended pose of the statue only, and that when it was finally produced, the horse's pose had been changed from a standing to a galloping one, as is shown on coins of 41 and 31 B.C. The dress of Octavian has also changed; he now appears to be nude above the waist (although this is difficult to determine from the preserved tiny image). POLLINI (forthcoming) cautions that these two coin types (i.e., of 42 and 41/31 B.C) might well represent two different statues—one ordered by the Senate for placement on or near the Rostra, the other by the people (the legend reads POPVLI IVSSV on the 41 B.C. coin) for placement somewhere else. One thing is clear: on coins of this period depicting riders on horseback, only two show warship rams beneath the horse. Should we not conclude that these two images are the best candidates for the equestrian statue of Octavian placed *in rostris*? If we are willing to admit that the intended pose and dress of the proposed statue were changed before its execution in bronze, as Zanker argues, then our interpretation of the statue in 12 as that of Octavian is also defensible. If this seems unreasonable, however, then we must reject Zanker's view as well and conclude that the coin shows 1) a previously unattested statue on a base ornamented with rams, or 2) a statue *in rostris* of someone other than Octavian—perhaps Agrippa, or Tiberius, who received triumphal honors in this year; see infra n. 41.

victories won by Agrippa, or more likely by Tiberius, over the Pannon-ians.[41]

Another coin, minted a year earlier by C. Sulpicius Platorinus, ap-parently shows this new rectangular Rostra as well. In a very abbreviated view, Augustus and Agrippa sit atop a rectangular platform decorated with three rams suspended off the ground (Fig. 66).[42] Perhaps this coin marks the construction of the new podium's facade while the one minted by Lentulus marks the project's final completion a year later when the statue of Octavian was moved at last to its new position.[43]

Fig. 66.

---

[41] Dio (54.28.2) mentions Agrippa's success in quelling the Pannonian rebellion just before his death, although the continued unrest in the province shows that this success is overstated. Perhaps a better candidate than Agrippa for the allusion of a trophy is Tiberius. In the same year that Agrippa died, Dio tells us (54.31.3–4) that Tiberius soundly defeated the Pannonians. Although the Senate voted him a triumph during this year, Augustus did not allow him to celebrate it, but granted him triumphal honors instead (Vell. 2.96.3 says that Tiberius was granted an *ovatio*); on the precise meaning of the *ornamenta triumphalia*, cf. the literature cited by KIENAST 1982, p. 108 n. 165. We believe it likely, therefore, that this trophy refers to Tiberius' early victories in Pannonia. The intent of the symbol was to assure the public that the *Princeps*, through his relatives, was firmly in control of the situation.

[42] For this coin, see SUTHERLAND 1984, p. 73, #406–407.

[43] If one rejects the arguments posed in n. 40 supra, our interpretation of the Rostra's completion date remains largely unaffected. The coin of Platorinus clearly shows the rectangular facade of the Rostra, and logically seems to refer in some way to its construction or completion. Whether the project was completed in 13 or 12 B.C. is really unimportant for our argument.

Outside Italy, Octavian built a ram display at his former campsite which dwarfed the speaker's platform in Rome.[44] Unbound in Epirus by conservative sensitivities, Octavian clearly wanted to impress those who visited his former camp with the immense sizes of the ships that had composed the enemy fleet.[45] It was something he decided not to do in Rome, for he appears to have decorated the *Rostra Aedis Divi Iulii* with smaller rams, closer in scale to the Republican spoils on the speaker's platform.[46] Outside Rome, however, Octavian felt freer to emphasize his victory than to temper it with modest restraint, and thus the scale of the Nikopolis monument was more appropriate to a Hellenistic monarch, or to an Alexander.

Indeed, in all respects, Octavian's victory monument skillfully mixed Hellenistic with Roman forms and images. Like the Asklepieion at Kos, Octavian's campsite was framed between the wings of a Π-shaped stoa atop a lofty, stepped terrace. The upper terrace was supported by a long Roman rostra built on an appropriately large, Hellenistic scale. All the evidence from the preserved remains indicates that the sacred site atop the terrace was simple in design. We believe this simplicity was a personal touch of Octavian and reminds us of the modest living habits he displayed in later life.[47] The monument's massive scale, however, revealed the general's love for Hellenistic grandeur when it could be directed toward a suitable message. For the suburban site of his former camp, and for the primary monument of his Victory City, the monument's design skillfully and effectively delivered this message. It was a message of peace—peace won from strength and with the help of the gods.

An important memorial with an effective message demands recognition, and this is usually inaugurated by a special ceremony of dedication. From the sequence of events surrounding 29 B.C., the momentous year of this monument's dedication, it seems likely that as much care was lavished on staging the dedication as on its unique design. Since the intended effect of this monument (and thus its impact as propaganda) can best be appreciated in the context of these events, we must now turn to the period immediately following the battle.

---

[44] The front of the *Rostra Augusti* (the enlarged version of the Caesarian monument) measures about 24 meters; the front of the Campsite Memorial measures some 62 meters.

[45] The gigantic sizes of the warships brought out of the East by Antony and Cleopatra appear as a recurring theme in the surviving accounts of the battle; see Chapter VI, Section 2.c.

[46] This may explain the curious differences between the campsite ram display, and representations we have of the *Rostra Augusti* and of the *Rostra Aedis Divi Iulii*. On these two rostra, the rams are small, like the example in the Deutsches Schiffahrtsmuseum in Bremerhaven, and they are mounted halfway up the wall, suspended off the ground. Cf. supra Chapter III, Section 2.c.

[47] Cf. Suet. *Aug.* 72–73.

V: Nikopolis, the First *Aktia* and the Dedication of the Campsite Memorial

In the first few weeks after September 2, 31 B.C., it became increasingly apparent to Octavian and his advisers how complete a victory they had won. Antony's power at sea and on land was damaged beyond repair. In addition to the 330 to 350 warships that had been taken from the enemy, most of Antony's nineteen legions surrendered under terms after a week of negotiations.[1] Many of these men were incorporated into Octavian's army, but those beyond military age were discharged immediately and sent back to Italy.[2] Octavian now had more soldiers than he needed, and so Agrippa was dispatched to Italy to supervise the discharge of superfluous units. Meanwhile, Octavian traveled eastward through Macedonia and central Greece to reward and punish cities and rulers according to which side they had taken.[3] Presumably, men were left behind at the army's camp to gather the spoils and arrange for their protection until Octavian ordered them shipped elsewhere. The captured warships were probably gathered near the army's camp for inspection; those not wanted were stripped of all useful gear, including their rams, and then burned.[4] At least one of each type, however, was set aside for a large dedication planned for the sanctuary of Apollo Aktios. As these matters progressed in the camps near Actium, Octavian arrived in Athens and, around the first week of October, was initiated into the Eleusinian Mysteries.[5]

---

[1] Although there is some disagreement concerning the number of ships that fought on each side of the battle, we know from Augustus' own *Memoirs* (Plut. *Ant.* 68.1) that he captured 300 ships from Antony. Whether this number represents the total captured at Actium (as Plutarch clearly implies; cf. TARN 1931, pp. 178–79) or the total captured in the war including the engagements at Methone, Leukas, Patras and elsewhere (KROMAYER 1897, p. 462) is unimportant for our purposes. Octavian clearly had about 300 rams from which to choose examples for the Nikopolis monument. Dio 51.1.4–5 records the surrender of the army.

[2] Dio 51.3.1–2.

[3] Dio 51.2.1–2.

[4] The victor normally destroyed all captured warships that could not profitably be used. For example, some of the ships taken from the Antiates in 338 B.C. were laid up in the dockyards, but the rest were burned (cf. Livy 8.14.12). On another occasion, Scipio burned the Carthaginian fleet surrendered to him in accordance with the treaty concluding the Second Punic War (Livy 30.43.12). TARN 1931, pp. 178–79 and 183–84, suggests that the burning of ships before and during the battle derives from Octavian's burning of useless ships after the Battle of Actium. Although Tarn's view has not been generally accepted, he is clearly correct that a large portion of the captured ships would have been burned after the battle. Not all the ships were destroyed, however. Apart from the ten ship dedication, we know from Tacitus (*Ann.* 4.5.1) that at least one captured squadron was spared and stationed later at Forum Iulii (modern Fréjus, France).

[5] Dio 51.4.1; the Mysteries were held from 15 to 22 Boedromion, with a return to Athens

From Athens, Octavian crossed to Samos, where Suetonius specifically says he took up winter quarters, but was forced to return to Italy in "mid-winter" (i.e., December-January) to quiet further problems with the veterans.[6] The Senate as well as some veterans met him at Brundisium to discuss the grievances of those recently discharged.[7] Money was handed out to some, while land was given to those who had served with him the longest. According to Dio, this land was taken from communities in Italy which had sided with Antony.[8] Those dispossessed by this process either received payment, promises of payment, or a new plot of land in Dyrrachium, Philippi and elsewhere. Even after all this had been done, some veterans remained unrewarded except by promises of future benefactions. As a show of good faith, Octavian put his personal property up for auction, and when no one came forth as a buyer, it was clear his promises had been accepted and the crisis was over.[9]

After a stay at Brundisium of only 27 days, Octavian hastily returned to Asia.[10] The following summer, he marched through Syria to Egypt, took Pelusium and descended on Alexandria. Antony put up a brief resistance, and after an infantry defeat committed suicide. According to the *Fasti*, the date was August 1; Cleopatra's suicide followed some nine days later on August 10.[11] Sometime soon after these deaths, Octavian founded a city on the site of the final infantry battle. And, in a tradition reaching back to Alexander the Great, he also held athletic contests in honor of the victory. The words of Dio make it quite plain that the new city, called Nikopolis, was the second of that name; according to him, at least, the Nikopolis in Epirus had already been established.[12] Just when this previous settlement had occurred, however, is difficult to determine.

One wonders if plans for the Epirote Nikopolis were not first discussed at the winter meeting in Brundisium. Since it was not mentioned in connection with the resettlement plans devised there, we might assume the city was not yet in existence. But if we accept the clear statement of Dio as valid, Octavian must have initiated the synoecism that created Nikopolis during the winter or spring of 30 B.C. The execution of so energetic a plan—encouraging people to move from their paternal

---

on the 23rd of the month. Latecomers could arrive on the 18th and still receive the "standard initiation." Octavian might have joined the initiates on the 20th and 21st of the month to receive just the *telete*; cf. MYLONAS 1961, pp. 243–85, for the days of the initiation ritual. Boedromion corresponds to the latter half of September and the beginning of October.

[6] Dio 51.4.1; Suet. *Aug.* 17.3.

[7] Dio 51.4.5.

[8] Dio 51.4.6.

[9] The debts were eventually made good, according to Dio (51.4.8), from the spoils of Egypt.

[10] Suet. *Aug.* 17.3.

[11] DEGRASSI 1963, pp. 489–90; VOLKMANN 1958, pp. 198–206.

[12] Dio 51.18.1 (trans., CARY 1971): "After accomplishing the things just related Caesar founded a city there on the very site of the battle and gave to it the same name and same games as to the city he had founded previously."

homes, as well as from their ancestral tombs and shrines to a completely
new settlement—would have required management, manpower, money
and a degree of coercion, items in short supply until the capture of
Alexandria.[13] In sum, Epirote Nikopolis may have been "founded" prior
to its namesake in Egypt, but its true development could not have begun
until the wealth of Egypt was used to finance the plans of the victor.

During the rest of the year and into the winter months of 29 B.C.,
Octavian settled matters to his liking in the East, while the Senate in
Rome voted him honor after honor.[14] At some time during this period,
it was decreed that the podium of the Divus Iulius temple be decorated
with rams taken from the enemy fleet at Actium.[15] From this decree, it
seems possible that some of the battle spoils (like the bronze rams) had
finally arrived in Rome.[16] If this was the case, then the selection of rams
for the Campsite Memorial had already been made and the monument
was presumably under construction.

On this timetable, the builders would have had just under a year to
complete the project if it was ready when Octavian returned to Nikopolis
in early August 29 B.C. (see infra). This short construction schedule
explains why many blocks in the existing structure bear signs of reuse.
Obviously taken from abandoned structures in the nearby regions, many
blocks were hurriedly transported to the site and then recut to fit the
new memorial.[17] Even the massive blocks for the retaining walls look as
if they are reused (and recut) from some nearby fortification.[18]

By the winter of 29 B.C., Octavian had made his way back to Asia

---

[13] HOEPFNER 1987, pp. 131–32, argues that the city walls of surrounding communities
may even have been destroyed to discourage people from returning to their ancestral
homes. Evidence from Kassope shows that buildings were dismantled and cult images
removed from their bases in the process of enforcing the synoecism.

[14] For the arrangements made at this time, see, for example SYME 1939, pp. 300–302. The
honors voted him at this time are discussed by Dio 51.19.

[15] Dio 51.19.2

[16] Warship rams were valuable pieces of property and would not have been left lying
about unattended for long. We have no way of knowing what they cost at the time of
Augustus, but the bronze alone in the smaller Athlit ram (weighing 1028 pounds) was
worth 1116.2 drachmas of silver in the late fourth century; cf. MURRAY 1985, pp. 141–50.
If the daily wage for a skilled man is figured at 2 drachmas during this same period (cf.
ZIMMERMANN 1974, p. 100), the ram's bronze alone was worth almost 560 days of work.

[17] It should be remembered that Nikopolis was settled by an officially sponsored *synoikismos*. The *poleis* of the area had suffered greatly during the previous century, the
population of the region had declined and some cities lay partially abandoned; for the
evidence from western Akarnania, cf. MURRAY 1982, pp. 360–64. Since we know that statues
were transported to the new city from the surrounding communities (cf. Chapter I, n.
25), the reused blocks in the Campsite Memorial suggest that building materials were
taken from these abandoned communities as well. For evidence of this process from
Kassope in Epirus, see HOEPFNER 1987, pp. 131–32.

[18] If the blocks of the south wall were originally from some nearby fortification, it would
explain a few curious cuttings which seem to serve no purpose on the top of the third
course at the following places: a swallow-tail cutting exists in the block to the left of [4]
and in the block to the right of [5]; a rectangular cutting can be seen in the block forming
the left side of [D] and in the block to the right of [E].

where he learned to his great delight that the Senate, on January 11, had closed the temple of Janus Geminus with the pronouncement "after peace had been secured on land and sea."[19] At this time perhaps, or soon after, he must have composed or approved the text of the dedication for the Campsite Memorial containing the proud words PACE PARTA TERRA MARIQUE, which was then forwarded to Nikopolis for masons to carve into the frieze course of the wall. The disposition of the inscribed letters makes it clear that the frieze course was already in place on the monument before the text was carved.[20]

By now, Octavian's main concern was the orchestration of his arrival back to the shores of Italy and his triumphant entry into Rome. First, transport back to Rome had to be arranged for the immense amount of booty he had captured.[21] And second, he needed performers, wild animals and athletes for the extravagant celebration he staged following the three triumphs awarded him by the Senate, and the dedication of the temple to Divus Iulius.[22] One can imagine the boat loads of participants that poured into Rome from the East in the weeks before August 13, the day Octavian entered the city.[23]

His route back home led past Actium and Nikopolis, which awaited his presence for its own dedication ceremonies.[24] From the date preserved in the text on the Campsite Memorial, it seems reasonable that

---

[19] The date of the temple's closing is preserved in the *Fasti Praenestini* (DEGRASSI 1963, pp. 112–13 = EHRENBERG-JONES 1976, p. 45), while the likely form of the pronouncement is discussed fully by GAGÉ 1936, pp. 70–82. For Octavian's route back through Asia, see Dio 51.20.6.

[20] From the surviving blocks of the inscription it is clear that single letters of the text whose positions fell at the joins between adjacent blocks were frequently cut across the surfaces of both blocks rather than spaced to fall in one block or the other; cf. blocks G6, G8, G19, G21, G20 and G2. It is difficult to see how partial letters could have been carved into two adjacent blocks unless they were already in place on the monument.

[21] Cf. Dio 51.21.3, 5, 7–8.

[22] Dio (51.22.4–5) says there were all kinds of contests held at the dedication of the temple of Divus Iulius, including animal hunts; "the whole spectacle lasted many days" (51.22.9). Octavian dedicated the temple on August 18, three days after the last day of his triple triumph; cf. DEGRASSI 1963, pp. 496–97.

[23] From Dio (51.21) and the entry in the *Fasti Antiates* (DEGRASSI 1963, p. 208 = EHRENBERG-JONES 1976, p. 50), the dates of Octavian's triple triumph can be restored as August 13–15, 29 B.C.; cf. DEGRASSI 1963, p. 496.

[24] The usual route between Greece and Italy for most travelers involved sailing up the western coast of Greece to Corcyra, then to Apollonia, and from there crossing to the heel of the Italian peninsula (cf. Thuc. 6.13.1). This coastal route was almost mandatory for military forces accompanied by warships (which hugged the coasts whenever feasible). For most travelers proceeding up the western coast to Greece, the entrance to the Ambracian Gulf served as a recognized port of call. When Cicero returned to Italy from the East in 51 B.C., he took exactly the same route. Letters written during the course of his journey trace his ports of call and Actium was one of those places at which his boat spent the night; see MURRAY 1982, pp. 410–16, for the evidence. For the likelihood that the present wind conditions (which demand such a route from Greece to Italy) reflect those of antiquity, see MURRAY 1987. Augustus, on this evidence, would have passed Nikopolis on his way back to Rome in 29 B.C.

Augustus was present at its dedication too. This event, logically, would have accompanied the dedication of the new city, and perhaps the first celebration of the Actian Games, a week or two before August 13.[25] Our sources are unclear on the year of the first *Aktia*, and the confusion may stem from the fact that in subsequent years the games were held on September 2, the anniversary of the battle.[26] But for this year, the presence of Octavian, the city's *oikistes* or "founder," was much more important than niceties of specific calendar dates. The date of the inscription ("imperator septimum"), the fact that three chronographers assign the official foundation of Nikopolis to the first year of the games (cf. n. 25), and the fact that Octavian sailed by Nikopolis just prior to his triumphal entry on August 13, attended by performers and athletes on their way to Rome, make it almost certain that Nikopolis, the *Aktia* and the two war memorials were dedicated within the span of a few days in early August 29 B.C. And since these events were to be greatly overshadowed by the festivities in Rome, they were not emphasized in the accounts of contemporary historians.

When Dio composed his account, he described these events immediately following the conclusion of the battle since it provided the *raison d'être* for the "Victory City" and war memorials. But in 31 B.C. Octavian did not have the same kind of leisure to settle cities and lay out monuments as he did following his final victory over Antony at Alexandria. In order to alert his audience to this fact, Dio (51.1.4) reminds us that as concerned Nikopolis "these things were done later." It appears, in fact, that the official dedication ceremony occurred almost two years after the victory at Actium.

And so, the monument was dedicated in 29 B.C. with Octavian most likely in attendance. The effect on those present who had participated in the war would have been undoubtedly powerful. Finally, after years of war, there seemed a real hope for peace. And this seems to have been an important part of the message conveyed by the monument in subsequent years. Tourists might gawk at the sizes of the rams, recreate the great battle in their minds along the lines of the "official" historians, or ponder the stories they had heard about "the barbarian woman" and how close she had come to conquering Rome, but in the end, the words

---

[25] Hieronymus (under the year 29 B.C.; HELM 1913, p. 163 = 245F, and 1926, p. 480 "f)"), Cassiodorus (under the consuls of the year 30 B.C.; MOMMSEN 1861, p. 628) and Syncellus (under the year 30 B.C.; DINDORF 1829, p. 583, lines 17–18 = P. 308 C) all couple the foundation of Nikopolis with the first celebration of the Actian Games.

[26] For the problem surrounding the date of the first *Aktia*, see SARIKAKIS 1965, pp. 147–48. GAGÉ 1936, pp. 92–97 and 1955, pp. 512–13, has argued that the first *Aktia* were celebrated a year later in 28 B.C. His evidence, however, is neither conclusive nor persuasive. He argues from coin evidence that games celebrated at Rome in 16 and 12 B.C. "pro valitudine Caesaris" were in reality *ludi Actiaci* and were parallel to those held at Nikopolis. Counting backwards in four year intervals, he arrives at 28 B.C. as the likely date of their inception. He offers no evidence, however, that these games in Rome had anything to do with the victory at Actium, much less that they paralleled the celebrations at Nikopolis.

pace parta terra marique had the biggest impact. This, at least, was what struck Philippus when he noticed that bees had built their hives inside the rams and mused, "He has taught the enemy's weapons to bear the fruits of peace instead."[27]

---

[27] Cf. the remarks of JOHNSON 1976, p. 97: "[Octavian] promised no impractical social programs or continued 'progress' but only relief from a foreign threat and a revival of the best of the past. His followers were not so likely to have their hopes frustrated. Victory, removal of the threat, the fall of Egypt, and peace were enough."

VI: New Light on the Battle of Actium

Although some like Philippus might appreciate the Campsite Memorial's message of peace, we must not forget that the monument's primary purpose was to glorify the Actian War and the victory gained over Antony's armada. Considering this fact, we are fully justified in looking for clues concerning the Battle of Actium and the nature of the fleets that determined its outcome. In so doing, we might even resolve disputes between conflicting ancient accounts or recover details that were eventually dropped from the surviving battle narratives. We begin first with the dominant interpretations of the battle's character that have emerged over the years, and then turn to the evidence of the Campsite Memorial.

1. The Kromayer-Tarn Debate

In 1899, J. Kromayer published what still remains the fundamental study of the battle.[1] The reconstruction he crafted relied heavily upon the secondary source tradition found in authors like Dio, Plutarch and the epitomators of Livy—Florus and Orosius. He argued that Antony intended to retreat from the Ambracian Gulf with as many ships as he could save and continue the war elsewhere. The battle was hard-fought and was won by Octavian after some four and one-half hours of combat. A. Ferrabino challenged this view in 1924 by arguing that Antony intended to fight for victory on September 2, not flee, and that he lost because a general of his refused to fight and returned to harbor.[2] His arguments were provocative but inconclusive and, although they were adopted by some scholars, did not receive widespread acceptance.[3] In 1931, the same year that Kromayer published a new defense of his views, W.W. Tarn published his own reconstruction of the battle, based in part on Ferrabino's earlier conclusions.[4]

Tarn, like Ferrabino, believed he could detect an alternate version of the battle in contemporary sources of information that were less contaminated by Augustan propaganda than were the standard historical narratives.[5] He started from Ferrabino's interpretation of Horace's *Epode* 9, which both men thought was composed just after the battle. He

---

[1] KROMAYER 1899.

[2] FERRABINO 1924 was the first to emphasize the importance of Horace's *Epode* 9 as a contemporary source which perserved an alternate version of the battle.

[3] Cf. for example, LEVI 1933, pp. 238–60, who accepted Ferrabino's conclusions, and HOLMES 1928, pp. 255–58, who did not.

[4] See KROMAYER 1931, pp. 662–71; and TARN 1931.

[5] TARN 1931, esp. p. 173; and 1938, p. 168.

concluded from two lines of the poem (lines 19–20; cf. note 11), which refer to some sort of naval maneuver, that a large portion of Antony's fleet returned to port without fighting and thus left Antony no other option but flight. Tarn maintained, therefore, that the actual battle was quite limited and unimpressive. The arguments he brought to bear were so seductively ingenious and so powerfully stated that he succeeded in forcing Kromayer and others to reconsider the validity of the secondary source tradition.

Two years after Tarn's article appeared in print, Kromayer responded in a paper which defended the validity of his original views. Though Tarn remained largely unconvinced, others came to Kromayer's defense. They argued that the contemporary evidence cited by Tarn was too limited in scope and required too high a degree of interpretation to provide a *substitute* for the clear (if sometimes over-embellished) secondary historical narratives. They also demonstrated that it was possible to interpret the contemporary evidence in a manner that was perfectly consistent with the secondary narratives of the battle.[6]

Understandably, this debate has produced two different versions of the battle. In order to decide which one corresponds better with the evidence from our memorial, we must first categorize the significant differences between the two versions. What follows is a brief discussion of five major issues that we feel differentiate the two versions resulting from the Kromayer-Tarn debate. They are discussed in the following order: the nature of Antony's battle-plan, the number of combatants, the use of fire in the battle, the degree of destruction suffered by the losers, and finally, the military significance of the battle.

a. Antony's Battle Strategy

On the day of the battle, did Antony primarily intend to flee, as only Dio (50.15.1) tells us, or to fight for victory? Was Cleopatra's and Antony's flight from the battlefield a planned maneuver or a shameful act of treachery (on Cleopatra's part) followed by a misplaced sense of allegiance (on the part of Antony)?

The nature of Antony's battle-plan lies at the core of the debate. Kromayer argued that by the end of summer 31 B.C., retreat was the only reasonable option left to Antony. As a result of Octavian's summer-long blockade, which had kept Antony's fleet bottled up inside the Ambracian Gulf, Antony's forces had suffered seriously. He had experienced a number of defeats on land and at sea, he was encamped in the malaria infested lowlands which formed Cape Actium, and as a result, many of his men had either died or deserted to the other side. By the beginning of September, Antony had no other choice but to burn those ships he

---

[6] This is the guiding principle behind KROMAYER 1933. For a selection of studies which have followed Kromayer's acceptance of the secondary tradition, cf. for example RICHARDSON 1937; PALADINI 1958; LEROUX 1968; CARTER 1970, pp. 200–27; JOHNSON 1976, pp. 48–56; and HARRINGTON 1984 (this last item, in fact, does little more than repeat some of Kromayer's and Richardson's arguments).

could no longer man and to lay plans for an escape from the gulf with as many ships as he could save.[7]

For those on the other side of the debate, Antony primarily fought for victory on September 2.[8] Ferrabino was the first to argue this position; Tarn agreed but added that Antony was also prepared to retreat toward Egypt if the battle went against him.[9] Subsequent opinion has largely sided with Kromayer on this particular point.[10]

As for Cleopatra's treacherous flight, both sides agreed that the queen fled the battlefield as part of a planned maneuver. For Tarn, Antony was forced to call for this retreat because a significant portion of his fleet (around 300 ships) deserted the line and returned to harbor, an event that he believed was recorded in Horace's *Epode* 9.[11] For those who accepted, with Kromayer, that the battle-plan primarily called for a "breakout," Cleopatra's successful escape showed her cool-headed use of the afternoon sea-breeze rather than an act of cowardly treachery.[12]

b. Numbers of Combatants

What were the numbers of ships that participated on both sides?

In order to determine the magnitude of the struggle at Actium, we need to establish the sizes of the forces that participated in the final battle. The evidence has been discussed extensively by Kromayer and Tarn, and their conclusions have been neatly summarized and discussed by G.W. Richardson, J. Leroux and J.R. Johnson.[13] From this extensive review of the matter, it seems reasonable to accept the numbers recorded by Florus and Orosius (which apparently go back to Livy's account) that

---

[7] KROMAYER 1899 (see especially pp. 33–34).

[8] FERRABINO 1924, pp. 470–71, argues that Antony fought for victory in order to regain his lost prestige and thus counter the disaffection that existed among his officers.

[9] TARN 1931, p. 188; 1934, p. 104; and 1938, p. 166.

[10] Cf. for example RICHARDSON 1937, pp. 158–59; LEROUX 1968, p. 30; CARTER 1970, p. 213; JOHNSON 1976, pp. 48–49; and KIENAST 1982, p. 62. HARRINGTON 1984, p. 62, rejects most of Tarn's views, but accepts that there were two plans. Perhaps J.R. Johnson says it best (p. 49): "[Antony] would take a victory if it developed, but he did not expect it nor plan for it."

[11] Lines 17–20 of Horace's *Epode* 9 refer to two setbacks for Antony: the defection to Octavian of 2,000 Gallic horsemen and the "leftward" movement of enemy ships to return to the safety of port. Both FERRABINO 1924, pp. 470–71, and TARN 1931, pp. 174–77 and 192–93, argue that the lines were written soon after the final battle and show that a portion of Antony's fleet refused to fight. KROMAYER 1933, p. 379, responded that the leftward movement in *Epode* 9 occurred most likely in one of the engagements prior to the final battle and thus had nothing to do with the decisive battle on September 2. For additional views concerning the date of *Epode* 9 and the interpretation of lines 17–20, see LEROUX 1968, pp. 37–47 and 57–60.

[12] KROMAYER 1899, pp. 45–48. For an excellent description of this breeze at Actium and Cleopatra's use of it, see CARTER 1970, pp. 218–20 and 223–24.

[13] The numbers adopted in the text are essentially those worked out by KROMAYER 1899, pp. 30–31; 1931, pp. 458–66; and 1933, pp. 362–73. TARN 1931, pp. 178–79, 191–92, argued that the fleets were roughly the same size, about 400 on each side. For the various reasons why Kromayer's opinion is preferable to Tarn's, see the summaries of RICHARDSON 1937, pp. 154–57; LEROUX 1968, pp. 31–36; and JOHNSON, pp. 36–39.

Antony manned about 170 vessels on the morning of the final battle. If we add to this number the 60 ship squadron of Cleopatra, the total Antonian fleet numbered around 230 vessels.[14] This means that out of the original fleet of some 500 vessels (Plut. *Ant.* 61.1), more than one-half of its strength had been lost to the enemy, burned before the battle (see below) or stationed elsewhere.[15] From this same tradition, although the numbers require some "interpretation," it seems reasonable that Octavian manned about 400 ships to oppose Antony's 230.[16]

c. The Use of Fire

How many ships (if any) did Antony burn before the battle? Did Octavian start a general conflagration among the enemy ships in order to terminate their stubborn resistance (as Dio 50.34.1 tells us), or was fire simply used by both sides during the course of the battle in the form of flaming projectiles?

According to Plutarch and Dio (Plut. *Ant.* 64.1; Dio 50.15.4), Antony burned an unspecified number of ships before the battle because he could not man them. Kromayer estimated the number as 80–90 ships, and concluded from the number of casualties he sustained (Plut. *Ant.* 68.1) that he lost an additional 40–50 ships during the battle, probably to fire.[17] Since Tarn believed there was no great battle on September 2, he argued that the references to fire in the surviving accounts referred solely to the burning of captured ships after the battle's conclusion.[18] His arguments were adequately answered by Kromayer in 1933, and now, most everyone accepts the reports in Plutarch and Dio that Antony burned some ships before the battle (the precise number remains unknown) and that fire was used as an offensive weapon, probably by both sides.[19] A problem still exists with Dio's battle narrative (50.34–35). He says that Octavian reluctantly called for fire from his camp to conclude the battle with a great conflagration that destroyed what remained

---

[14] Florus 2.21.5 (Antony commanded less than 200 ships); Orosius 6.19.9, 11 (Antony commanded 170 ships; Cleopatra's squadron numbered 60). The argument for Antony's 170 ship fleet is based on the statement of Plutarch (*Ant.* 61.1) that Antony boarded 20,000 legionaries and 2,000 archers on his ships. If one figures the average sized ship in Antony's fleet as a "five," and assigns 130 men to each ship, this yields a total number of approximately 170 ships.

[15] Although this number may seem inordinately large, see KROMAYER 1931, pp. 669–70; LEROUX 1968, pp. 31–36; and JOHNSON 1976, pp. 26–27.

[16] Florus (2.21.5) writes that Octavian had more than 400 vessels while Orosius (6.19.8) records the number as 230 rostrate ships plus 30 without rams. Since Orosius gives this same number (i.e., 230) as the strength of Octavian's fleet when he left Brundisium in the spring (6.19.6), we must presumably add to this number the ships under Agrippa's command; cf. RICHARDSON 1937, p. 155 n. 13., who argues that the same mistake must lie behind the total of 250 ships recorded by Plutarch (*Ant.* 61.2). There is no reason, therefore, to reject Florus' number.

[17] KROMAYER 1897, p. 465 (cf. p. 485); 1933, pp. 367–70.

[18] TARN 1931, p. 184.

[19] For Kromayer's defense of his earlier views, see KROMAYER 1933, pp. 366–70. For references to the use of fire during the battle, see Horace *Carm.* 1.37.12–13; Virgil *Aen.* 8.694–95, 710; Florus 2.21.6; Plut. *Ant.* 66.2; and Dio 50.34.1. Cf. as well, JOHNSON 1976, pp. 43–47.

of Antony's fleet. Few accept the strict truth of this version which may simply be an unfounded flourish developed by Dio to make the battle's conclusion appropriately impressive.[20] On the other hand, it might indicate that in some accounts now lost to us, fire played an important part in the final outcome of the battle.[21]

d. Degree of Destruction

How many of Antony's ships were captured? What were Antony's casualties and how many ships were destroyed?

Since the numbers of casualties and destroyed ships relate directly to the magnitude of the battle, these matters have received particular attention from both sides of the debate. All calculations must be based on two pieces of evidence: Plutarch *Ant.* 68.1 and Orosius 6.19.12. Plutarch (who claims to have taken the figure from Augustus' *Memoirs*) reports that less then 5,000 men were killed and that 300 ships were captured in the battle. Orosius, on the other hand, puts the numbers at 12,000 dead, plus 6,000 wounded (of which an additional 1,000 eventually died); he records no number for captured ships.

Kromayer argued that the casualty totals might roughly indicate the numbers of ships that were destroyed in the battle. If, according to standard Roman practice, the 5,000 dead mentioned by Plutarch represented fighting men only, and if the average ship class in Antony's fleet was a "five," then 5,000 men would correspond to the total loss of fighting men aboard about 40 "fives" (i.e., 40 × 120 men per "five").[22] Tarn, on the other hand, argued that the casualty figure might refer to everyone on board, rowers included (a total of 420 men on a "five"). Accordingly, he calculated the casualties as equal to the destruction of 11 to 12 "fives" with all hands lost (i.e., 12 × 420 men).[23] As concerns the 13,000 dead recorded by Orosius, J. Leroux has suggested that this number might correspond roughly to the comprehensive casualty total of which Tarn speaks.[24] If Orosius' source intended the figure to include

---

[20] Cf. JOHNSON 1976, p. 46. According to Johnson (pp. 44–46), PALADINI 1958, p. 12 n. 2, is mistaken in arguing that "the 'official' version maintained silence about such a decisive but inglorious use of fire." In fairness to Paladini, she argues only that Virgil refers to the use of fire during the battle and not as part of a grand finale to *win* the battle (cf. PALADINI 1958, p. 11). She does not deny that the use of fire is part of this "official" tradition; cf. PALADINI 1958, p. 47. On the other hand, MANUWALD 1979, p. 229 n. 390, argues that the use of fire should not be ascribed to the so-called Livian tradition, which seems not to mention it in spite of the reference to fire in Florus' account (2.21.6).

[21] Cf. LEROUX 1968, p. 53.

[22] KROMAYER 1933, pp. 168–69; for the numbers of rowers (300) and fighting men (120) placed on each "five" at Ecnomus in 256 B.C., see Polyb. 1.26.7 and KROMAYER 1897, p. 485.

[23] TARN 1931, p. 178: "if we call it 10 to 15, 15 is a very outside number." Tarn rightly observes that this type of calculation should not be pressed too hard; for the reasons, see text infra.

[24] LEROUX 1968, p. 54.

rowers, then it would correspond to the destruction of 30 "fives" with the loss of all hands.

Regardless of which total or calculation we follow, there are serious problems with using these totals to indicate destroyed ships. First, it is obvious that casualties would have occurred aboard ships that were not completely destroyed, particularly on the larger vessels that would have carried more men.[25] Second, because the shore of Cape Actium (held by Antony's army) was so near-by, an alert crewman might swim to safety even though his ship had been destroyed. In other words, it is conceivable that more ships were destroyed than a simple count of the dead might imply. And finally, there is a good chance that Plutarch (seemingly the better source since he claims to have used the *Memoirs* of Augustus) misunderstood Augustus and recorded a total that referred to losses sustained during the entire Actian campaign.[26] If we admit this possibility and conclude, therefore, that a destruction equal to the total loss of 30 ships occurred in the final battle (calculated from Orosius), we are left with a destruction equivalent to a loss of 10 ships for the events leading up the final battle (i.e., Plutarch's 40 minus Orosius' 30). This number seems a bit low, considering the known victories of Agrippa at Methone, Leukas and Patras, and considering that Antony's fleet at Actium was reduced to 170 ships from an original total of some 500 vessels.[27] Clearly, we can place no great trust in these calculations. Nevertheless, as a general means of gauging the minimum degree of destruction involved in the Actian War, the numbers seem roughly equivalent to the total loss of about 40 "fives." Whether or not this destruction occurred mainly on September 2 depends on how one interprets the fragment of Augustus' *Memoirs* preserved by Plutarch (see Section 2.a. infra).

e. Military Significance of the Battle

Did Octavian win a great victory after a long, hard-fought struggle, or was Actium a "shabby affair"—a small battle turned into a "grand and furious struggle" by the propaganda of the victors?

One's interpretation of the battle's character depends largely upon which side of the debate one chooses to stand. If we reject the validity

[25] TARN 1931, p. 178. It seems clear from the battle accounts that most of the large vessels were left behind when Cleopatra made her break. Orosius 6.19.11 refers to Cleopatra's squadron as "velocissimis navibus" (i.e., "very swift ships"); but on what authority he bases this observation, we do not know. And although Plutarch (*Ant.* 64.1) writes that all the Egyptian ships except the sixty largest and best were burned, he says (*Ant.* 66.3) that during the battle, Cleopatra's squadron had been posted "behind the large vessels." Perhaps most telling of all is the fact that Antony transferred from a larger ship (a "ten"?) to a "five" in order to flee after the departing Egyptian squadron (*Ant.* 66.5). If the larger vessels were left behind, then a large number of men might have died defending their ships without their vessels' eventual destruction. In other words, casualty totals do not necessarily relate directly to destroyed ships.

[26] LEROUX 1968, p. 54.

[27] See supra n. 15.

of the secondary narratives and accept Tarn's interpretation of Horace's
Epode 9, then most of Antony's fleet returned to harbor without offering
battle while Antony and Cleopatra managed to flee southward with 100
ships. At the most, Tarn thought that Antony lost 15 ships, although
he later conceded that the number could have been as high as 35 to 40
ships.[28] On the other hand, if we are willing to accept the validity of the
secondary narratives, then a consistent picture develops of a hard-fought
struggle lasting some four and one-half hours in which perhaps 40 to
50 ships from Antony's fleet were destroyed.[29]

2. The Evidence from the Campsite Memorial

Let us now reconsider some of these issues with the design and dedication text of Octavian's Campsite Memorial in mind. Obviously, the
monument tells us nothing about Antony's battle strategy, or about the
numbers of ships that fought on either side in the final naval battle. It
does provide us, however, with some interesting information concerning
the fragment of Augustus' *Memoirs* preserved by Plutarch. And this, in
turn, may have some important implications for the way we reconstruct
the numbers of casualties in the battle.

a. The Numbers of Captured and Destroyed Ships

Plut. *Ant.* 68.1: καὶ νεκροὶ μὲν οὐ πλείους ἐγένοντο πεντακισχιλίων, ἑάλωσεν δὲ
τριακόσιαι νῆες, ὡς αὐτὸς ἀνέγραψε Καῖσαρ.

There were not more than 5,000 dead, but 300 ships were captured, as Caesar
himself has written.[30]

If the fleet totals given by Orosius and Florus are correct for the battle
of Actium, then Octavian clearly could not have captured 300 ships
during the battle, as he apparently claimed in his *Memoirs*. Plutarch (or
Plutarch's source) must have misunderstood what Augustus had written. Kromayer saw, years ago, that the misunderstanding probably centered on the word "bellum," which can mean either "battle" or "war"
depending on the context in which it is used. Citing Augustus' use of
the word "bellum" in *Res. Gestae* 25.2 to refer to the entire Actian War,
he argued that the word probably had a similar meaning in the *Memoirs*,
and that Plutarch (or his source) simply misunderstood the sense in

[28] See supra n. 23; TARN 1931, pp. 195–96; and 1938, p. 167.
[29] Cf. KROMAYER 1897, p. 465; and 1899, p. 48. JOHNSON 1976, p. 43, remarks that when
TARN 1938, p. 167, finally conceded that Antony could have lost thirty-five to forty ships,
the battle "approaches the proportions of a 'real battle.' Once one allows for Dio's own
tendencies toward rhetoric and sensationalism, there is no reason to consider extant
accounts of the struggle, destruction, and loss of life at Actium as seriously distorted."
We need hardly mention that those authors who reject Tarn's views consider Actium to
have been a "real battle."
[30] Text and translation come from PERRIN 1920.

which it was utilized.[31] The 300 ship total, he argued, should represent the combined number of all ships captured from the time Octavian crossed to Epirus up until the fall of Alexandria.[32] Tarn criticized Kromayer's argument, but without any lasting effect; most subsequent accounts of the battle have adopted Kromayer's interpretation of the passage.[33]

The dedication text on the Campsite Memorial also uses the word "bellum" in a manner similar to the passage in Plutarch: *victoriam consecutus bello quod pro re publicae gessit in hac regione* ("following the victory in the war which he waged on behalf of the Republic in this region"). Octavian has chosen his words carefully: in the broadest sense, he pays honor to Neptune and Mars following the victory he won at Actium. Although the *battle* on September 2 may have decisively terminated Antony's resistance at Actium, it was only one event in a string of successful engagements. Each of these victories would have been important to Octavian and his men with each act of bravery and valor worthy of honor and remembrance. For this reason, we think it unlikely that Octavian would have built this monument simply to commemorate the final battle.

If Octavian had intended simply to give thanks for the naval battle fought on September 2, we also believe that he would have avoided using a general phrase like "in hac regione." Something like "ad Actium," "prope Actium," "iuxta Actium" or "extra Actium" would have implied more clearly that only the final battle and not the entire campaign was intended. This same impression is given by the phrase *pace parta terra marique* ("after peace had been secured on land and sea"). Since Octavian proudly implies that the final victory over the enemy was achieved through decisive victories on both land and at sea, it is unlikely that he considered the *bellum* fought in this region to consist simply of one naval engagement. The natural impression to be gained from the monument's text is that Octavian dedicated here naval spoils taken during the course of the summer's campaign in the entire region of Greece.[34]

If the text of the inscription is taken in conjunction with the size of the ram display, which we interpret as a tithe, we can see what the disputed reference to Augustus' *Memoirs* must have meant. Unless the 33 to 35 rams displayed on the monument is a lucky coincidence (and

---

[31] The following text and translation come from BRUNT-MOORE 1967, pp. 30–31: Iuravit in mea verba tota Italia sponte sua, et me belli quo vici ad Actium ducem depoposcit. . . "The whole of Italy of its own free will swore allegiance to me and demanded me as the leader in the war in which I was victorious at Actium."

[32] KROMAYER 1897, pp. 462–63 and 1933, pp. 364–66.

[33] TARN 1931, pp. 177–78; cf. for example RICHARDSON 1937, p. 155; LEROUX 1968, p. 35; JOHNSON 1976, pp. 29–30; HARRINGTON 1984, p. 62.

[34] For naval battles in addition to the one on September 2, cf. Livy (*Per.* 132) who speaks of "pugnae navales" before Actium, and Velleius (2.84.2) who says Agrippa had twice defeated the enemy fleet before September 2. In addition, Dio (50.13.5, 14.1., 30.1) implies actions in connection with the capture of Leukas and Patras, and Orosius (6.19.7) records a battle in connection with the capture of Corcyra.

thus not a tithe at all), the 300 ship total must refer to the ships taken in the entire Actian War. And that war must be interpreted as the one "fought in this region." In other words, the total should include ships taken in the battles leading up to and immediately following September 2. Aside from the few ships that may have fallen into Octavian's hands in the first few weeks following the battle, the 300 ship total should not include ships taken outside the region of Greece. These obviously belong to another *bellum*. This reasoning applies as well to the 5,000 dead reported from Augustus' *Memoirs;* these casualties would have been sustained largely in the events leading up to and including the final naval battle on September 2.[35]

This interpretation of Plutarch's text has an impact on how we might compute the minimum number of Antony's ships that were totally destroyed in battle during the Actian War. We have already referred to Plutarch's statement (*Ant.* 61.1) that Antony brought with him "no fewer than 500 fighting ships." The words of Plutarch's text reveal that he believed these vessels physically accompanied their commander to Greece.[36] If the monument preserves an accurate tithe, then Octavian captured between 330 and 350 of this 500 total.[37] When we add to the captured ships the 60 that fled with Cleopatra, we are left with at least 90 ships for which we have no record.[38]

This is a number which must accommodate the following possibilities. First, a small number of ships may still have been posted elsewhere, perhaps as escorts to protect transport vessels.[39] Others who may have remained in places which had not been captured by Agrippa may have fled southward to join Antony once they got news of the battle's outcome.[40] How many ships this involved is impossible to determine, but

---

[35] We stress this point because it differs from Kromayer's belief that the totals included all losses up to the fall of Alexandria (KROMAYER 1897, pp. 462–63 and 1933, p. 366).

[36] Plut. *Ant.* 61.1: συνιόντων δὲ πρὸς τὸν πόλεμον Ἀντονίω μὲν ἦσαν αἱ μάχιμοι νῆες οὐκ ἐλάττους πεντακοσίων . . . "When the forces came together for the war, Antony had no fewer than 500 fighting ships . . . . " The verb at the beginning of the passage clearly implies that Plutarch considered these 500 as coming along with Antony out of the Levant. KROMAYER 1897, p. 459, concludes that this total represents the ships that accompanied Antony to Greece.

[37] This number does not agree with Augustus' own count (i.e., 300) because he probably omitted classes smaller than the "three"; cf. *Res. Gestae* 3.4.

[38] We do not know whether Plutarch (or his source) intended this total to include classes smaller than triremes. For the purpose of discussion, however, we assume that he does include the smaller classes so long as they possessed rams (he calls them "fighting ships"). In so doing, we will achieve a minimum value for ships unaccounted for (and thus presumably sunk).

[39] From Plutarch (*Ant.* 67.5) we learn that some heavy transport ships gathered at Cape Tainaron following the battle, and these may have been protected by a small escort. Although our sources tell us that Antony's bases at Methone, Patras, Leukas, and Corinth were captured during the course of the summer (Vell. 2.84.2; Florus 2.21.4; Dio 50.13.5, 30.1), others may have existed on the offshore islands. Nevertheless, aside from a possible escort associated with the heavy transports, we hear of no warships coming to join Antony at Tainaron.

[40] If, on the other hand, some of these ships eventually went over to Octavian, they would have been included among the 300 ships listed as captured during the Actian War.

the number cannot have been very large, or some mention of them would have appeared in the surviving record.[41] Second, these 90 vessels must include those who managed to flee from the battle with Antony. Tarn first argued that some 40 ships escaped with Antony. He may be correct, but there is no real evidence to support or reject this view, and he eventually conceded the number might have been as low as 15 to 20.[42] Third, these 90 ships must include all those destroyed in battles during the course of the summer at Methone, Leukas, Patras and at Actium prior to September 2.[43] Here, too, the number must remain unknown, but we suspect that it cannot have been very large. The complete destruction of a vessel so that it cannot be recovered for salvage is a rare occurrence outside the realm of major battles and storms. No doubt, some vessels were completely destroyed before the final battle, but we should expect some mention of decisive battles in the surviving narratives had the number been large.[44]

Should we include among this 90 ship total the vessels that were burned by Antony before the battle? Most scholars who have considered this question would argue that we should.[45] In other words, they think it unlikely that Octavian would have claimed Antony's burned hulls among his total of captured ships. Although this view seems at first glance to make sense, we feel, however, that Octavian would have claimed these burned hulls, with their fire-warped fittings and scorched rams as "captured ships." Our conclusion is based on the likelihood that the majority of warships seized during the Actian War were eventually burned, thereby insuring that Antony could never use them again.[46] Is it reasonable to expect that Octavian would have made such

[41] Antony's initial occupation of Greece seems not to have required an extensive use of garrisons and the fleet was wintered in numerous places for logistical reasons of supply. It was not until a large force was concentrated at Actium and not until Agrippa had cut off the lines of supply by sea that we hear of communities being coerced to provide food and other material for Antony's army (cf. Plut. *Ant.* 68.4–5).

[42] Plutarch (*Ant.* 66.5) records that Antony fled on a "five" before transferring to Cleopatra's flagship, so we know that at least one ship beyond Cleopatra's squadron managed to escape. For the suggestion of "about 40," see TARN 1931, p. 195; for the lower estimate see TARN 1938, p. 167.

[43] See supra note 34.

[44] Nowhere do we hear of a naval conflict which involved great destruction before the battle on September 2. According to Dio (50.13.5) Leukas was captured with its ships as the result of a sudden raid, and although Patras was captured as the result of a naval battle, no details are given. Nor are any ships mentioned in conjunction with the capture of Corinth. The only engagement described in any detail is the one which occurred between L. Tarius Rufus and C. Sosius (Dio 50.14.1–2). RICHARDSON 1937, p. 155 n. 10, concludes from this brief notice that Sosius sustained "fairly heavy losses," although this is really far from certain. We should also note that every damaged ship recovered by Antony's forces would have eventually fallen to Octavian after September 2, and thus, would have been counted among the total of 300 captured ships.

[45] See for example KROMAYER 1933, p. 366; and RICHARDSON 1937, pp. 155–56. LEROUX 1968, pp. 33–34, argues that the 300 total captured by Octavian should refer only to those ships taken in battle at sea; and JOHNSON 1976, p. 29, implies that the 300 total represents complete ships only.

[46] Although we reject Tarn's view that fire was not used as a weapon during the battle, his argument that most of the captured ships would have been burned after the battle accords perfectly well with standard Roman practice. See supra Chapter V, n. 4.

a fine distinction between the ships destroyed by Antony and those destroyed by himself? Most everyone agrees that Octavian wished to make Actium into a greater battle than it had, in fact, actually been. The real issue centers on the degree of distortion that Octavian brought to bear to achieve his goal. If we admit that Octavian actively promoted the glory of his victory, how can we object to the possibility that he added the burned hulls to his total of captured vessels? In a valid sense, he had captured these vessels when he took over the camps once occupied by Antony's fleet and army. Since both the whole and burned ships would have provided Octavian with tangible spoils, what did it matter who had actually applied the torch? The significant fact was simply that Antony's ships had fallen into Octavian's hands, and what may have mattered most in the final tally was the total number of rams that remained, whether they were fire-warped or not.

If we are correct in this assumption, then the 90 ship total must represent vessels that either managed to escape with Antony or were lost in the battles leading up to and including the one on September 2. The degree of destruction involved during the war, therefore, depends largely upon how many ships one believes fled with Antony. If we accept Tarn's guess of 40 ships (and the number may have been a good deal less than this, as Tarn himself admitted), we are still left with a total of 50 ships that were so badly destroyed that they were unavailable for salvage.[47] This number, admittedly a guess, does correspond well to the casualty totals given by Plutarch and Orosius (i.e., 5,000 fighting men or 13,000 men if we include the rowers).

At this point, we might do well to consider what action would be required to damage a ship so completely that it could not be salvaged. There are two possibilities, and both involve the ship's sinking so that it cannot be towed back to shore. A ship can be burned to the waterline and thus sunk, or it can be sunk by ramming.[48] Though we cannot be sure how many ships were sunk in the naval battles prior to September 2, the most likely occasion for such a high degree of destruction by fire and ramming would have occurred during the final battle on September 2. As J.R. Johnson remarks, "the battle of Actium approaches the proportions of a 'real battle' " when one contemplates the total destruction of so many ships.[49] The Campsite Memorial is in full agreement with this conclusion.

---

[47] TARN 1931, pp. 190–191, is probably correct that Antony's fleet was composed of squadrons of about sixty ships each. Had more ships escaped with Antony, i.e., almost an entire squadron, we should have heard of it. There is no need, therefore, to rely on the elaborate reconstruction of numbers presented by TARN 1931, p. 193 n. 1.

[48] Many examples could be cited to demonstrate this generalization; cf. for example the casualties incurred by the Syrian fleet at the battle of Myonnesus in 190 B.C.: of 42 ships lost, 13 were captured, and 29 were destroyed by fire or sunk (Livy 37.30.7); cf. THIEL 1946, pp. 352–57. Additional examples can be found in KROMAYER 1897.

[49] JOHNSON 1976, p. 43.

b. The Composition of Antony's and Cleopatra's Fleet

Can the monument tell us anything truthful about the composition of Antony's and Cleopatra's fleet? Perhaps, but only if we limit our inquiries to the larger classes. We can see clearly from the sockets on the monument that Antony and Cleopatra possessed multiple numbers of their largest warships. If we remember the relatively limited numbers of the large classes in the fleet of Ptolemy II, the totals for the large ships on the Campsite Memorial may correspond closely to the actual numbers existing in Antony's fleet at the beginning of the war.[50] This reasoning assumes that Octavian composed his tithe exclusively from the biggest rams he had captured. In other words, if he had captured four "tens," and five "nines" we believe he chose to display them all, rather than to select a token number from each class and thereby present a selection from every class. Only in this way can we explain the irregular totals for the constituent rams of different sizes on the monument. If we are correct in this assumption, the Campsite Memorial preserves the total number, minus one (one example from each class was exhibited in the *dekanaia* on the Actian promontory), for each of the larger classes in the enemy fleet.

Following either Sequence I or II (Chapter III, Section 2.d.), the fleet of Antony and Cleopatra probably contained at least four and perhaps five "tens" (i.e., the three attested on the Campsite Memorial plus Cleopatra's flagship plus the one in the Actian *dekanaia*), four "nines," and perhaps five "eights" and six "sevens." And even though the smaller sizes may not represent as closely the original totals in the fleet, we can presume that there were at least eight "sixes" (Sequence II) or perhaps four "sixes" and five "fives" (Sequence I). Admittedly, this attempt to reconstruct the composition of Antony's and Cleopatra's fleet is speculative. We do not know, for example, how many large ships were completely destroyed (and thus not salvaged), nor how many comprised the squadron of 60 vessels that managed to escape from the gulf.[51] Nevertheless, our conclusions, if not precisely accurate, reveal that the fleet contained multiple numbers of large ships which correspond roughly to the totals we have for the large ships in the fleet of Ptolemy II. Though Octavian might wish us to believe otherwise, the enemy fleet seems to have been less a monstrous collection of immovable "eights" and "tens" than a moderately large Ptolemaic fleet of the late Hellenistic Age.[52]

---

[50] According to Athenaeus 5.203d, the fleet of Ptolemy II contained 2 "thirties," 1 "twenty," 4 "thirteens," 2 "twelves," 14 "elevens," 30 "nines,"37 "sevens," 5 "sixes," 17 "fives," and 224 "fours" to "triemioliai." CASSON 1971, p. 140, calls this fleet "the mightiest the ancient world was to know."

[51] On the composition of this squadron, see supra n. 25.

[52] Surprisingly, this fact has been overlooked by some scholars who have argued for Orosius' and Florus' total for Antony's fleet at Actium; cf. supra nn. 13 and 14. This argument holds that if we reckon the average sized ship in Antony's fleet as a "five," then we can nicely place on 170 ships the 22,000 men that Plutarch (*Ant.* 64.1) tells us

c. The "Heavy Fleet vs. Light Fleet" Tradition of the Battle

At first glance, the Campsite Memorial appears to support fully the secondary narratives which stress the massive sizes of Antony's ships in comparison to those used by Octavian. No one can question the impressive sizes of the rams that were originally displayed at Octavian's campsite. If our interpretation of the monument is correct, however, we should reexamine this notion of the battle because it may be incorrect, or at the very least, misleading.

The secondary accounts are almost unanimous in stressing the unequal nature of the ships that fought against one another in the final battle. Although outnumbered by almost two to one, the immense sizes of Antony's ships more than made up for this apparent inequity. Despite this disadvantage in size, however, Octavian used his smaller ships more effectively and thus the superior seamanship of his crews was able to win the day. But is this what really happened? Did Octavian really win by using masses of smaller, more maneuverable ships against the larger, heavier, and less maneuverable vessels of the enemy? In other words, what is the validity of the "heavy fleet vs. light fleet" tradition that is preserved in most of the secondary battle narratives?

The Campsite Memorial's sockets preserve important information concerning some aspects of Antony's and Cleopatra's fleet. For example, if our arguments concerning the sockets' relative sizes are roughly correct, we know that over 75 percent of the monument's facade was covered with rams from ship classes of "fives" or greater. We also know that Octavian's Campsite Memorial displayed a larger and more massive array of warship rams than appeared on any other known rostral monument in the Mediterranean world. The weapons at his camp literally dwarfed the examples he sent to Rome for mounting in the *Forum Romanum*. As time passed and the standard warship of Roman fleets diminished in size to the "three," these massive weapons supported the dramatic story adopted by all later historians that Antony's Asiatic ships were of extraordinary size when compared to Octavian's Roman vessels. With this theme of Antony's "heavy fleet" versus Octavian's "light fleet," the monument may provide a "new" insight into the process by which the standard battle account developed.

The "heavy fleet vs. light fleet" tradition of the conflict seems to have been a basic element of the battle narrative as early as the end of Augustus' reign. Nevertheless, the tradition is doubtful as a meaningful statement of historical fact. The "light" fleet used by Octavian at Actium was the same one raised by Agrippa in 37 B.C. to defeat Sextus Pompey in Sicily.[53] Dio (50.19.3) reveals this fact in a speech supposedly delivered

---

Antony embarked for the battle. Once done, the average sized ship is forgotten, and Antony is assigned ships larger than the "fives" on which his men were hypothetically embarked; cf. for example LEROUX 1968, pp. 36–37.

[53] This observation has been made before by others; cf., for example, TARN 1931, p. 193, n. 8; 1938, p. 167; and STARR 1960, pp. 7–8.

by Antony before the battle. He also shows by his narrative of events in 36 B.C. (49.1.2, 3.2) that this fleet was composed of heavy ships. Appian concurs; he describes the fleet in 36 B.C. as composed of large, heavy vessels which could both give and receive crushing blows.[54] There is no cogent reason, therefore, why Octavian and Agrippa would have abandoned in 31 B.C. a strategy that had proved so effective in 36 B.C. against Pompey.[55]

Dio's inconsistent description of the same fleet as heavy in 36 B.C. and light in 31 B.C. must stem from his reliance on more than one source for these two events. Presuming that Dio was astute enough to recognize the inconsistency, the source which presented Octavian's fleet at Actium as "light" must have been authoritative enough to warrant its use. There is only one source we know of which would have carried such weight, and that is Augustus' own *Memoirs* (see infra). Additional evidence suggests that through this source, Augustus declared that his Liburnians defeated the heavier polyremes of his enemies. How far he exaggerated the overall difference in sizes between the two fleets is difficult to substantiate. But the massive display at his campsite suggests that he planned, soon after his victory, to emphasize one element of this version, namely, the enormous sizes of the enemy ships.

This observation is supported fully by the literary record beginning immediately after the Battle of Actium. Horace, who wrote a poetic version of the battle (*Epode* 9) soon after its conclusion, records no basic difference between the vessels of each fleet; nor is this hinted a year later in his poem celebrating the death of Cleopatra (*Carm.* 1.37).[56] Since the themes of these two poems would have been well served by the inclusion of this tradition, we can only presume that its absence signifies that the theme was not yet developed.[57] Virgil's description of the two

---

[54] Among the ships commanded by Octavian, one "six" was among a total of six "heavy" vessels destroyed in a storm before Mylae (App. *BC* 5.98–99); at Mylae, the fleet is described as larger and heavier than that of Sextus (5.106), whose flagship was apparently a "six" (Plut. *Ant.* 32.3); and although it was slower, Octavian's fleet was able to give and take stronger blows than were the ships of the enemy (App. *BC* 5.106).

[55] For this reason, we find the arguments of KIENAST 1966, pp. 15–16, totally unconvincing. He argues (p. 16 n. 35) from Dio's account that, after 36 B.C., Octavian adopted the tactics of Sex. Pompey in using smaller, more maneuverable ships. He further argues (p. 17) that between 36 and 31 B.C., Octavian's fleet had diligently practiced their manœuvers, an observation totally unrecorded in the preserved record. Kienast, in fact, never seems to address squarely the statement presented in our text (and first mentioned by Tarn; cf. supra n. 53). His main reason for preferring this tradition is to explain the later preference for smaller classes in the Imperial navy.

[56] The literature on *Epode* 9 is vast, but the arguments for its date and interpretation do not affect Horace's description of the two fleets. For the likely date of the poem, see PALADINI 1958, p. 14, with notes 1–3.

[57] Some scholars have seen in Horace's first Epode (lines 1–4) a reference to the "light fleet vs. heavy fleet" tradition, but this is unlikely (the text and translation are those of BENNETT 1927): Ibis Liburnis inter alta navium,/ amice, propugnacula,/ paratus omne Caesaris periculum/ subire, Maecenas, tuo. "On Liburnian galleys shalt thou go, my friend Maecenas, amid vessels with towering bulwarks, ready to encounter at thine own risk every peril that threatens Caesar." The context of the poem would place its composition during the late winter or early spring of 31 B.C., before Maecenas left Rome for Brundisium.

fleets (*Aen.* 8.671–713), written between 29 and 19 B.C., also fails to distinguish between their sizes.[58] For him, the ships of both sides were massive: the enormous battleships made one think that the Cyclades had been uprooted to float on the sea, or that lofty mountains rushed one against the other (lines 691–92). Those who attempt to see in these lines a reflection of the "heavy fleet vs. light fleet" tradition (i.e., a comparison between Antony's large ships and Octavian's smaller ships) are simply reading too much into Virgil's general description of *both* fleets.[59]

Propertius' eleventh poem in Book 3 of his Elegies (published perhaps in 22 or 21 B.C.) is the first to hint, ever so slightly, that its author knows of the "heavy fleet vs. light fleet" version of the battle.[60] In a brief allusion to the conflict in the straits, the poet characterizes the two fleets by the vessels most identified with each commander: Liburnian galleys are pursued by the queen's barge (line 44). The image is certainly not historical, but it is striking, and reveals the kernel of the later, more fully developed tradition.[61] Another of his poems (4.6), written a few years later, presents a similar subtle allusion to the size differential between the fleets.[62] Cleopatra's ships are each rowed by "a hundred oars" (we are clearly supposed to be impressed by the number) and decked out

---

Some translators have taken the first four lines of the poem to refer to the lofty fighting towers of Antony's warships: "While you, Maecenas, dearest friend,/ Would Caesar's person with your own defend;/ And Antony's high-tower'd fleet,/ With light Liburnian galleys fearless meet . . . " (translation by Phillip Francis in WHICHER 1947, p. 30). But if the date of the poem is correct, these lines cannot refer to any specific feature of the actual battle, but rather to reports, then current in Rome, of the lofty towers and enormous sizes of Antony's ships (cf. FORDYCE 1977, p. 282). It may also be that these lines refer to something else. STARR 1960, p. 8, notes that "these may well be taken as a reference to the fact that Octavian customarily cruised about in a Liburnian while Agrippa commanded the fleet . . . " (for this particular use of a Liburnian, see App. *BC* 5.111). At Actium, we are told by Plutarch (*Ant.* 65.2, 4) that each commander reviewed his fleet's deployment from a small boat before taking up his position in the line. If this is the intended image (as we believe it must be), then Horace's passage merely refers in a graphic manner to the dangers of accompanying one's commander-in-chief on a sea campaign.

[58] For the date of the *Aeneid*, see WILLIAMS 1982, pp. 333–46. It is likely (although impossible to prove) that Virgil's views of the battle and of the fleets that participated in it were based on first-hand accounts which circulated in Rome soon after the battle's conclusion. From *Georgics* 3.8–48, composed soon after Cleopatra's final defeat, we know that he was impressed enough with Octavian's victory over the East to begin contemplating a great Roman epic as a way of honoring the victor.

[59] The comments of FORDYCE 1977, p. 281, are instructive. Although he realizes that the tradition is suspect, he nevertheless compares line 692 with Dio 50.33.8, where the size difference between the fleets is clearly stated. This passage is also compared by Bennett (BENNETT 1934, p. 417) with the first four lines of Horace *Epode* 1 to illustrate the "heavy fleet vs. light fleet" tradition. According to our argument, such a comparison is misleading and does not stem from the tradition (which is nearly, but not quite, contemporary) that pits Octavian's Liburnians against Antony's heavy fleet.

[60] See HUBBARD 1975, pp. 41–44, for the evidence behind dating Book 3 to the late 20s B.C.; she suggests 22 or 21 B.C. (p. 44).

[61] One should note here the reference to Liburnian galleys. As stated previously, the Liburnian galley may be identified with Octavian because he used it to shuttle from one section of his fleet to another; cf. supra n. 57; Veg. 4.33; and infra n. 67.

[62] HUBBARD 1975, p. 117, dates this poem to "the quadrennial festival celebrating Augustus' rule that was held by Agrippa during the emperor's absence in 16 B.C."

with elaborate figureheads and painted bows (lines 47–50). Although no direct comparison between the two fleets is drawn, the passage begs for one and leads the reader to conclude that Octavian's ships were not rowed by hundreds of oars nor were they so elaborately decorated.

The first author (after Augustus published his *Memoirs*) to state the "heavy fleet vs. light fleet" theme in unambiguous terms may have been the historian Livy, whose account of Actium was composed toward the end of Augustus' reign.[63] Although our evidence is limited to the brief synopsis of Livy's 132nd book, and although nothing is said specifically about the ship classes in Octavian's fleet, we are told that Antony collected for the war "a naval force as remarkably huge as was his land force" (ingentibus tam navalibus quam terrestribus copiis). This same theme is picked up a few years later by Velleius (writing in A.D. 30), whose account is the first surviving one to state specifically that Antony's ships were larger than Octavian's.[64] By the first quarter of the second century, the further elaborations of Florus and Plutarch establish this theme fully as an integral part of the battle narrative.[65]

Dio's account, composed a century later in the first three decades of the third century, reveals the theme at its fullest extent.[66] He tells us that Antony purposefully built larger ships than existed in Octavian's navy in order to beat him (50.23.2–3). As a result, his naval architects constructed only a few "threes" (the standard warship during Dio's lifetime) and focused their efforts on building ships from "fours" to "tens." Shortly before describing the final battle, Dio presents speeches ostensibly delivered by both generals to rouse their troops. And while Antony urged his men to rely on the gigantic timbers of their superior fleet, Octavian explained in detail how the enemy's large ships would actually bring about their own destruction (50.29.1–4).

By time of Vegetius in the late fourth century, the theme was inseparable from the rest of the battle narrative. According to him (4.33), Antony was defeated chiefly by means of the Liburnian galleys attached to Octavian's fleet ("cum Liburnorum auxiliis praecipue victus fuisset Antonius"). Alone, this statement might arouse little curiosity, especially

---

[63] For the date of the later books of Livy, cf. for example MCDONALD 1970, p. 614.

[64] According to Velleius (2.84.1), although Antony's ships were larger than Octavian's, they were formidable only in their appearance. This idea seems to be the logical extension of the theme first expressed by Propertius (4.6 lines 47–50), who stopped short of saying that the fleets differed in size. Velleius' book was dedicated to M. Vinicius when the latter man was consul in A.D. 30. One of the last events mentioned in the work is the death of Tiberius' mother, Livia Drusilla, in A.D. 29 (2.130.5).

[65] According to Florus (2.21.5–7), the massive sizes of Antony's ships proved fatal to the fleet. Octavian's "twos" to "sixes" were much more maneuverable than Antony's "sixes" to "nines." Plutarch repeatedly stresses (*Ant*. 61–67) that Octavian's ships were smaller and more maneuverable. According to him, Antony used ships from "threes" to "tens" including numerous "eights" and "tens." Although these ships were taller and heavier than Octavian's, they were less effective in the battle because they were undermanned and too heavy to gain momentum.

[66] For the following discussion, cf. Dio. 50.18.4–19.5, 23.2–3, 29.1–4, and 32.1–35.6; for the date of Dio's history, see MILLAR 1964, pp. 28–32.

since Vegetius uses the term "Liburna" to signify all ships smaller than "sixes" (cf. Veg. 4.37). But taken in conjunction with the statements from Horace (*Epode* 1.1–4) and Propertius (3.11.44), we may see the origin of our theme. The accent on the Liburnian galleys, identified with Octavian both before and after the battle, helps to draw attention away from Agrippa and his polyremes and to emphasize the decisive role of Octavian, not Agrippa, as the victorious commander.[67]

The "heavy fleet vs. light fleet" tradition can be broken down into three significant elements: 1) the tradition is noticeably absent from the first poetic versions of the battle; 2) it first appears softly in the subtle allusions of Propertius during the late 20s and 'teens, and is developed more fully thereafter; and 3) the vessels credited with securing the victory are primarily the Liburnian galleys known to be favored by Octavian. All three elements can be neatly explained by the appearance in the mid-20s B.C. of Augustus' own version of the battle.

Published sometime between the end of the Cantabrian War in 25 B.C. and his departure for Asia in 22 B.C., the *Memoirs* (i.e., the *Commentarii de vita sua* or the *Autobiography* as some scholars refer to it) presented Augustus' own account of events up to the end of the recent war in Spain.[68] Although a mere 23 fragments of this work remain, we know

---

[67] The story of the Spartan Eurykles preserved by Plutarch (*Ant.* 67.2–3) presents a unique episode from a battle narrative otherwise devoid of specific exploits (for the career of Eurykles, Augustus' man in Sparta, see BOWERSOCK 1961). Its theme contains striking parallels to Octavian's own situation: during the height of the battle, Eurykles was so intent upon avenging his father (who was put to death by Antony) that he challenged Antony as he tried to escape on a much larger ship. Though only commanding a Liburnian, Eurykles managed, through a brash display of daring and courage, to capture one of Antony's flagships. Like Eurykles, Octavian had challenged Antony to fight at the beginning of the year (*Ant.* 62.2–3). Again like Eurykles, he fought to avenge the honor of his family—in this case, the honor of his sister (cf. Dio 50.3.2 and Plut. *Ant.* 57.3). And again like Eurykles, he prevailed chiefly through the courage and maneuverability of his Liburnian galleys. Such an heroic tale may or may not be accurate history, but it would have suited the purposes of the victor quite well. Though one cannot be certain, the story of Eurykles parallels that of Octavian so closely that we feel it may have originally appeared in his own *Memoirs*. In general, it seems that Octavian was personally fond of using Liburnians. In Sicily, he shuttled between sections of his fleet on such a vessel (App. *BC* 5.111); when he returned to Italy during the winter of 31–30 B.C., he apparently used a squadron of Liburnians as an escort (Suet. *Aug.* 17.3); to Horace (*Epode* 1.1–4; cf. supra n. 57), campaigning with Octavian was tantamount to cruising on a Liburnian; and for Propertius (3.11.44), a squadron of Liburnians brought to mind Octavian just as the queen's barge evoked images of Cleopatra. Finally, in Orosius' brief account of the battle written during the early fifth century, Liburnians are also mentioned, although no details of the actual battle are given. According to this last version (6.19.6–9), Octavian's fleet outnumbered Antony's (230 rostrate ships to 170), although the large sizes of Antony's vessels made up for his smaller total.

[68] Suetonius (*Aug.* 85) tells us that this work covered his life up to the end of the Cantabrian War (signified by the closing of the Janus Geminus gateway in 25 B.C.) in 13 books. PETER 1967, pp. LXXI-LXXII, argues that the work was probably completed before Augustus handed over his accounts to Cn. Calpurnius Piso in 23 B.C. For the view that Augustus composed the work in Spain (he returned to Rome in 24 B.C.) when he was incapacitated by illness from taking the field, see SYME 1939, p. 332. MALCOVATI 1969, p. XLVIII, accepts 22 B.C. (the date of Octavian's departure for Asia) as the likely *terminus ante quem* for the work's completion.

it was consulted by Plutarch and Dio, the earliest surviving authors to articulate fully the "heavy fleet vs. light fleet" tradition.[69] Since there are compelling reasons to doubt the strict validity of this tradition, and since it seems not to have been reflected in other authors' works before the oblique allusions of Propertius in the late 20s B.C., it seems plausible that this particular tradition stems from the *Memoirs* of Augustus.

If this suggestion is correct, it would imply that Dio composed Octavian's pre-battle speech by following the general lines of Octavian's own account, either from the *Memoirs* or from some intermediate source.[70] Although we cannot conclusively prove this to have been the case, the circumstantial evidence referred to above is impressive, particularly in light of the following observations. First, we have noted that the perceived authority of this version may help to explain the obvious inconsistency between Dio's descriptions of Octavian's fleet in 36 B.C. and in 31 B.C. This "authority" would also help to explain why Dio chose to embellish this particular theme as a key element in Octavian's speech. Second, Dio certainly knew of Augustus' *Memoirs*, which he refers to on at least one known occasion (cf. 44.35.3).[71] Third, Plutarch, who consulted the work for at least one aspect of his own battle account, says precisely the same thing as Dio concerning Octavian's strategy of using smaller ships.[72] And finally, if we accept the Campsite Memorial as proper evidence, Octavian officially began to stress an important element of the "heavy fleet vs. light fleet" tradition as soon as two years

[69] Twenty-three fragments are identified by MALCOVATI 1969, pp. 84–97.

[70] For the known fact that the *Memoirs* contained set speeches written by Augustus in the manner of Caesar's *Commentaries*, see MALCOVATI 1969, p. XLIX. For the problem concerning Dio's use of this work, cf. infra n. 71.

[71] The identification of the sources used by Dio is a difficult subject; see, for example, MILLAR 1964, pp. 34–38. More recently, MANUWALD 1979, pp. 182–85, follows the original opinion of HAUPT 1884, pp. 695–96, that Dio did not directly consult the *Memoirs* (on the subject of intermediate sources between many of the preserved fragments and the original work, see HAHN 1958). In spite of Dio's apparent reference to the work (44.35.3), his account of the star that appeared in 44 B.C. at the *ludi Veneris* (45.7.1) diverges from what is known to have come from the *Memoirs* (MALCOVATI 1969, pp. 86–87, #6); see MANUWALD 1979, p. 184 with nn. 80–84. It is possible, however, that Dio consulted the *Memoirs* selectively. In general, Dio is not known to have followed any one source slavishly. He does not, for example, seem to follow the Livian tradition for his account of the Actian War (MANUWALD 1979, pp. 228–31), which is thought by some to be a possible intermediate source (cf. HAHN 1958, p. 143). Since he recognized that much of what Octavian said and wrote about his enemies was exaggerated for effect (cf. Dio 50.1.1–2 and MANUWALD 1979, pp. 75–76), he may have chosen to avoid the *Memoirs* as a basic source for his narrative. But as concerns the actual battle, what better source would there have been than the account of the victorious commander himself, particularly if the text of the *Memoirs* preserved speeches (cf. supra n. 70) that he could further embellish? It should be noted, however, that if our arguments concerning the deities honored at the Campsite Memorial are correct (Chapter II, Section 5), then Dio apparently did not consult the *Memoirs* for this information. But whether Dio consulted the *Memoirs* directly or through some intermediate source is really unimportant for our argument. What is important is the likelihood that he made use of the "Augustan tradition" originally presented in the *Memoirs*.

[72] PETER 1906, pp. 54–64, lists the following five fragments of Augustus' *Memoirs* that derive from the works of Plutarch: #6, #7, #8, #10, #15 [= MALCOVATI 1969, pp. 84–97, #8, #9, #10, #12, #17]. The most important one (PETER 1906, p. 62, #15 = MALCOVATI 1969, p. 95 #17 = Plut. *Ant.* 68.1) shows that the *Memoirs* were consulted for Plutarch's account of the battle.

after the battle—even earlier when we consider that the rams were selected and the plans approved as much as a year before the monument's
dedication in August 29 B.C.

Exactly how Augustus worded his version of the battle is impossible
to determine, but we can make an educated guess at the general tenor
of his narrative if Dio's account (50.23.2–3) has any truth behind it.
Antony apparently tried to outbuild Octavian when he prepared his
own fleet. The composition of Octavian's Sicilian fleet had been no secret;
it was collected openly in 37 B.C. while the two men were still "friends."
Indeed, Antony had reluctantly contributed more than 100 ships to swell
its numbers, most of which (at least 70) were returned to him after
Octavian's defeat of Sex. Pompey.[73] Some of these men, recently discharged from Octavian's fleet, would have had first-hand knowledge of
Octavian's naval strength, the sizes of his ships and the numbers of
vessels in each class. From 34 B.C. onward, Antony used his newly
acquired Armenian wealth, plus help from Cleopatra, to build more
polyremes than he knew existed in Octavian's fleet.[74] Although he obviously did not build a fleet composed mainly of "eights" and "tens,"
it seems reasonable that he tried to surpass both the sizes and numbers
of the ships in Octavian's fleet.[75] It also seems reasonable that he sent
abroad exaggerated reports of his preparations; the stronger he appeared
before war was actually declared, the more willing Octavian should have
been to negotiate a settlement.[76]

Since Antony's attempt to outbuild his rival must have been part of
the propaganda passing between the hostile camps before the war, Octavian was free to utilize this ready-made theme to his own advantage
after the battle's conclusion. Because he did not personally invent the
report that Antony's fleet was unusually massive, his version would
have been accepted as valid by contemporaries who had heard Antony's
propaganda but who had not personally witnessed the battle. The crucial
help of the Liburnian galleys would also have neatly shifted the credit
for the final victory from Agrippa to Octavian, who was personally
identified with this type of vessel. The sailors and marines on the right
wing who had actually fought under his personal direction would have
been the version's strongest proponents (whether it was strictly true or
not) because it would have validated their own heroic role in the final
victory. And accounts like the heroic exploits of the Spartan Eurykles
(see supra n. 67) which circulated after the battle would have served to

[73] For the ships loaned to Octavian by Antony, see Plut. *Ant.* 35.4 and KROMAYER 1897,
pp. 454–55 with n. 161. Although Antony later complained that these ships were not
returned to him (Plut. *Ant.* 55.1), Appian's account (*BC* 5.139) indicates that this was not
strictly true.

[74] Such was the zeal behind this building program that trees were even cut from the
sacred grove of Asklepios on Kos (Dio 51.8.3).

[75] This is clearly the impression gained from Dio 50.23.2.

[76] The reports of Antony's preparations alarmed Octavian (Plut. *Ant.* 58.1), but the
defection of men like Titius and Plancus in 32 B.C. (Dio 50.3.1–3) provided Octavian with
excellent information about Antony's present actions and future plans.

bolster their claims to glory. We have no doubt that Octavian's smaller vessels had somehow proved effective against Antony's polyremes on September 2, 31 B.C. On the other hand, considering the nearly contemporary evidence of Horace, Virgil and Propertius, we can rest assured that the vessels of the two opposing fleets were more alike than they were different.

Is Octavian's account, therefore, a complete lie? Not likely; a lie is most believable when it cannot be distinguished from the truth. Although we still might argue over the precise details of the battle, we must concede that Octavian's self-serving view has some basis in fact. The truth must be that Antony's largest ships were larger than were Octavian's largest ships, and that these ships were packed with marines and put in the center of Antony's front battle line. But was the battle primarily a struggle between ships of unequal size, i.e., between Octavian's "sixes" and Antony's "tens"?[77] Did the Caesarean crews display their superior seamanship and maneuverability by breaking through the line and by carrying out the *diekplous* maneuver?[78] A careful reading of the sources closest in time to the battle does not bear this out.

Furthermore, if we are willing to accept that Antony embarked 22,000 men on 170 ships, then the class which predominated must have been the "five" or less, and this is precisely what the greater number of smaller sockets on the monument implies.[79] In general, it seems likely that the battle on September 2 was decided between ships of roughly the same size, except for the fact that Antony's largest ships were larger than were Octavian's. During the breakout of Antony and Cleopatra, the largest ships were unable to disentangle themselves and were mostly left behind to fight and be captured. In the end, the suspicion remains that the "heavy fleet vs. light fleet" tradition has more to do with Antony's propaganda before the war and with Octavian's role as the victorious commander than with the actual tactics of the battle.

Nevertheless, the design of the Campsite Memorial implies that as soon as one year following the battle, Octavian had already begun to formulate his preferred version of the struggle. A few years later, he expressed this version more fully in his *Memoirs*. Primarily through this "unimpeachable source," the theme was passed to subsequent historians, and in the absence of other authoritative accounts it was adopted and embellished as a standard element in all succeeding battle narratives of the conflict. Each fleet at Actium possessed both large and small ships.

---

[77] See, for example, CASSON 1971, p. 141.

[78] For this suggestion, see KIENAST 1966, p. 16, which is based on the pre-battle rhetoric found in Octavian's speech to his men! Although such a speech may have appeared in the *Memoirs*, it certainly does not prove that the *diekplous* was actually used in the final battle.

[79] If we conclude mathematically that the average sized ship was a "five," and accept that the advantage of the larger classes was their ability to carry disproportionately large numbers of men on their decks, then, *mathematically*, we must conclude that classes less than the "five" (the average sized ship, statistically speaking) predominated in actual fact.

But as time passed, two elements emerged to dominate the battle narrative: 1) the enormous sizes of Antony's vessels in comparison to those in Octavian's fleet, and 2) the decisive role of the Liburnian galleys. The moving force behind these distortions of the historical record was none other than Augustus himself. His object, no doubt, was to heroize the conflict and to glorify his own role in the final victory that was to become "the birth-legend in the mythology of the Principate."[80]

[80] The quote comes from SYME 1939, p. 297.

VII: Conclusion

During the many centuries that followed the Campsite Memorial's dedication, we lose sight of its subsequent history. Its final destruction and abandonment were no doubt connected somehow to the fate of Nikopolis which was probably attacked by Alarich in A.D. 397, occupied by Geiserich in 475 and sacked by Totilia in 551.[1] In response to these attacks, the city's fortifications were rebuilt along a shorter, more defensible line. When exactly this occurred is not securely known, although a piece of church decoration (in "late Theodosian style") incorporated into the new circuit at Tower 21 suggests that this part of the circuit dates to the late fifth century. By this time, if not sooner, the memorial's rams had probably been wrenched from their sockets for recycling into more modern weapons while its blocks were quarried for use in the new, smaller circuit wall.[2]

At the same time that the rams were removed (if not before) the statues of Eutychos and Nikon were probably removed to Constantinople, since we learn from Zonaras that in his day (the mid-twelfth century) the pair stood in the city's hippodrome.[3] If the monument had not been fully cannibalized for the city's Byzantine fortifications during the fifth or sixth century, this had certainly occurred by the year 1040 when the people of Nikopolis called in a Bulgarian force to help carry out a tax revolt.[4] The succeeding years saw the city's progressive abandonment as its inhabitants slowly drifted away to other communities.[5] In the meantime, earthquakes spilled the hillside down over the blocks of the southern retaining wall, a pine grove began to cloak the sides of Mt. Michalitsi, and everyone forgot the original glory of this pretty spot above the crumbling theater and overgrown stadium of the Actian Games.

Now, 75 years after its rediscovery, Octavian's memorial still awaits a complete study of its buried remains. Nevertheless, what has been exposed over the years reveals a surprising amount of new evidence

---

[1] SCHOBER 1936, cols. 517–18.

[2] For the Byzantine wall of Nikopolis, see HELLENKEMPER 1987. PHILADELPHEUS 1913, pp. 90–91, dates the new circuit to the period immediately following Alarich's raids. By the late fifth century, the monument may have already been in ruins. An earthquake had apparently racked the city in the second half of the fourth century; cf. SCHOBER 1936, col. 517.

[3] Zonaras 10.30 (p. I 526 D).

[4] SCHOBER 1936, col. 518. By this time the precious bronze on the hillside north of the city was certainly long gone.

[5] Nearby Preveza is not attested until the beginning of the fifteenth century when Albanians were settled at the entrance to the Ambracian Gulf; cf. KIRSTEN-KRAIKER 1967, p. 775.

concerning Augustus, the Battle of Actium and the massive ships that determined its outcome. We have tried to present all that is currently known about the memorial in order to correct the incomplete and often conflicting reports on the site that have appeared in the past. For the first time, we can explain the function of the monument's nose-shaped sockets and use them to recover the bow dimensions of the giant ships that fought in the Battle of Actium. The immense sizes of the rams revealed by these sockets astound and amaze us; we simply had no idea that Greeks and Romans were capable of producing such huge castings.

We have also examined the dedicatory inscription as an integral part of the monument's original design. Its surviving blocks have been illustrated, its text improved, and its original placement on the monument conclusively determined. The text of the inscription places the monument's dedication in 29 B.C. It seems reasonable that Octavian himself was present in early August at the ceremony which officially dedicated the city, the monument and the first Actian Games. Details of the stoa revealed by excavation atop the podium in 1974 have been presented along with the plan hurriedly completed after the project was suspended. This plan plus the photos taken in 1974 reveal the stylobate of the Π-shaped stoa originally surrounding Octavian's open-air campsite. This foundation helps to resolve the confusion concerning the monument's original appearance and (with help from the inscription's text) the gods to whom it was dedicated.

The monument's peculiar design supplements the text of the dedication and both together deliver a potent message. We see the simple camp of a pious Roman general whose just cause, virtue and support of the gods enabled him to defeat a force of vastly superior size. The "package" which delivers this message is both Roman and Greek in form, simple in design, yet executed on a grand scale. The dual character of its design—simple, yet somehow majestic—underscores the complex personality of the victor. He, too, displayed a mixture of Roman pragmatic simplicity and Hellenistic imperial grandeur.

Last, but not least, the monument's original number of sockets (ca. 33 to 35) has been interpreted as a tithe of the total of rams (and thus warships) captured during the Actian War. If this is so, the monument reveals that Octavian captured 330 to 350 ships from Antony's 500 ship fleet. Discounting the 60 vessels that fled with Cleopatra from the site of the battle, between 90 and 110 ships remain unaccounted for, which implies that the final battle may have been almost as hard fought and drawn out as the sources suggest.

As concerns our observations on the nature of the two fleets that fought in the battle, we have no illusions that they will go unchallenged. The "heavy fleet vs. light fleet" tradition of the conflict is too deeply rooted in Western literature for us to dislodge it without further discussion. Nevertheless, the new evidence from the Campsite Memorial should force us to rethink certain traditions concerning the battle, whatever our final conclusions may be. For three-quarters of a century, important evidence for an event which redirected the course of Western history has gone largely unnoticed. The time has now come for this evidence to be carefully considered and discussed.

We do not claim to have answered all the questions concerning Octavian's Campsite Memorial. We have tried to demonstrate, however, the importance of this monument for anyone hoping to understand the battle and the ships that determined its outcome. The side of a hill is certainly an odd place to look for naval vessels, and yet here lie excellent clues, amazingly preserved amid the thorns and thistles where bees still build their hives.

However inadequately we have described Octavian's Campsite Memorial in the preceding pages, we hope that its full historical importance will at last be recognized. Though difficult to interpret fully in unambiguous terms, the monument preserves important information about a man of great historical significance and about the fleet of the pair from whose clutches he claimed to have saved the Roman world. For these two reasons it ranks among the most important surviving monuments of the Augustan Age. Should our conclusions eventually be rejected or modified, we will have achieved our goal if the Campsite Memorial is finally included among the major monuments of the Augustan Age and if, henceforth, its evidence is considered by all who try to understand this important period of world history. One can only wonder what additional clues lie buried at Octavian's campsite. Hopefully, some day soon, we will return to the site to find out.

BIBLIOGRAPHY

[The journal abbreviations utilized in the bibliography are similar to the forms used in *L'Année Philologique*. In all other respects the forms utilized in the notes and text are those of the *Oxford Classical Dictionary*, 2nd ed. Unfortunately, we acquired a copy of L. Basch's exhaustive *Le museé imaginaire de la marine antique* (Athens 1987) too late for its use in this study.]

AMY 1962: R. Amy et al. *L'Arc d'Orange*. Supplement vol. 15 of *Gallia* (Centre National de la Recherche Scientifique). Paris
BASCH 1969: L. Basch. "Phoenician Oared Ships." *Mariner's Mirror* 55: 139–62, 227–45.
BASCH 1975: L. Basch. "Another Punic Wreck in Sicily: Its Ram. 1. A Typological Sketch." *IJNA* 4.2: 201–19.
BASCH 1980: L. Basch. "On the Reliability of Ancient Writers in Matters Maritime." *Mariner's Mirror* 66: 368.
BASCH 1982: L. Basch. "The Athlit Ram: A Preliminary Introduction and Report." *Mariner's Mirror* 68:3–7.
BAUER 1988: H. Bauer. "Basilica Aemilia." In Staatliche Museen Preussischer Kulturbesitz. *Kaiser Augustus und die verlorene Republik. Eine Ausstellung in Martin-Gropius-Bau, Berlin, 7. Juni—14. August 1988*. Berlin. Pp. 200–212.
BENNETT 1927: C.E. Bennett. *Horace The Odes and Epodes*. Rev. ed. Cambridge, Mass.
BENNETT 1934: C.E. Bennett, ed. *Horace Odes and Epodes*. Rev. ed. by J.C. Rolfe. New York.
BERLIN 1988: Staatliche Museen Preussischer Kulturbesitz. *Kaiser Augustus und die verlorene Republik. Eine Ausstellung in Martin-Gropius-Bau, Berlin, 7. Juni—14. August 1988*. Berlin.
BIERS 1987. W.R. Biers. *The Archaeology of Greece. An Introduction*. Rev. ed. Ithaca.
BLAKE 1947: M.E. Blake. *Ancient Roman Construction in Italy from the Prehistoric Period to Augustus*. Washington, D.C.
BOETHIUS-PERKINS 1970: A. Boëthius and J.B. Ward-Perkins. *Etruscan and Roman Architecture*. Harmondsworth, Middlesex.
BOWERSOCK 1961: G.W. Bowersock. "Eurycles of Sparta." *JRS* 51: 112–18.
BROUSKARI 1985: M. Brouskari. *The Paul and Alexandra Canellopoulos Museum. A Guide*. Athens.
BROUGHTON 1952: T.R.S. Broughton. *The Magistrates of the Roman Republic*. 2 vols. Cleveland.
BRUNEAU-DUCAT 1983: P. Bruneau and J. Ducat. *Guide de Délos*. 3rd ed. Paris.
BRUNT-MOORE 1967: P.A. Brunt and J.M. Moore. *Res Gestae Divi Augusti. The Achievements of the Divine Augustus*. Oxford.
CAGNAT 1911: R. Cagnat. "Spolia." *Dar. Sag.* IV.2: 1440–41.
CARTER 1970: J.M. Carter. *The Battle of Actium*. London.
CARTER 1977: J.M. Carter. "A New Fragment of Octavian's Inscription at Nicopolis." *ZPE* 24: 227–30.
CARY 1917: E. Cary. *Dio's Roman History*. Vol. VI. Cambridge, Mass.
CASSON 1971: L. Casson. *Ships and Seamanship in the Ancient World*. Princeton.
CHIPIEZ 1887: C. Chipiez. "Columna." *Dar. Sag.* I.2: 1338–55.
CHRONIQUE 1926: "Chroniques des fouilles et découvertes archéologiques dans l'Orient Hellénique (1926)." *BCH* 50: 561.
COARELLI 1983: F. Coarelli. *Il Foro Romano. Periodo Arcaico*. Rome.
COARELLI 1985: F. Coarelli. *Il Foro Romano. Periodo Repubblicano e Augusteo*. Rome.
COOK 1905: A. Cook. "Triremes." *CR* 19: 371–76.
COUCHOUD-SVORONOS 1921: P.L. Couchoud and J. Svoronos. "Le Monument dit 'des Taureaux' à Délos et le Culte du Navire Sacré." *BCH* 45: 270–94.
COULTON 1976: J.J. Coulton. *The Architectural Development of the Greek Stoa*. Oxford.

CRAWFORD 1974. M. Crawford. *Roman Republican Coinage*. 2 vols. Cambridge.
DEGRASSI 1963: A. Degrassi. *Fasti Anni Numani et Iuliani Accedunt Ferialia, Menologia Rustica, Parapegmata*. Vol. XIII. 2 of *Inscriptiones Italiae*. Rome.
DINDORF 1829: W. Dindorf, ed. *Georgius Syncellus et Nicephorus CP*. Vol. I, an unnumbered volume in the series *Corpus Scriptorum Historiae Byzantinae*. Bonn.
DURRBACH 1929: F. Durrbach, ed. *Inscriptions de Délos. Comptes des Hiéropes (Nos. 372–498). Lois ou Règlements, Contrats d'Entreprises et Devis (Nos. 499–509)*. Paris.
EHRENBERG-JONES 1976: V. Ehrenberg and A.H.M. Jones, eds. *Documents Illustrating the Reigns of Augustus and Tiberius*. 2nd ed. Oxford.
FERRABINO 1924: A. Ferrabino. "La battaglia d'Azio." *Rivista de Filologia e di Istruzione Classica* 52: 433–72.
FORDYCE 1977: C.J. Fordyce. *P. Vergili Maronis Aeneidos Libri VII–VIII*. Oxford.
FROST 1972: H. Frost. "The Discovery of a Punic Ship." *IJNA* 1: 113–17.
FROST 1974: H. Frost, et al. "The Punic Wreck in Sicily. Second Season of Excavation." *IJNA* 3: 35–54.
FROST 1975a: H. Frost. "The Ram from Marsala." *IJNA* 4: 219–28
FROST 1975b: H. Frost. "Discovery of a Punic Ram." *Mariner's Mirror* 61: 23–25.
FROST 1981a: H. Frost. "The Punic Ship Museum, Marsala, Its Presentation and Some Structural Observations." *Mariner's Mirror* 67: 65–75.
FROST 1981b: H. Frost, et al. *Lilybaeum (Marsala). The Punic Ship. Final Excavation Report*. Rome [= *Notizie degli Scavi di Antichità*. Supplement to vol. 30 (1976).]
FROST 1982: H. Frost. "The Athlit Ram." *IJNA* 11: 59–60.
GAGÉ 1936: J. Gagé. "Actiaca." *Mélanges d'archéologie et d'histoire* 53: 37–100.
GIULIANI-VERDUCHI 1987: C.F. Giuliani and P. Verduchi. *L'Area Centrale del Foro Romano*. Vol. I of *Il Linguaggio dell' Architettura Romana* of the Università degli Studi di Roma la Sapienza. Firenze.
GJERSTAD 1941: E. Gjerstad. "Il comizio romano dell' età repubblicana," *Opuscula Arch.* II. 2: 97–158.
GOW-PAGE 1968: A.S.F. Gow and D.L. Page, eds. *The Greek Anthology. The Garland of Philip and Some Contemporary Epigrams*. 2 vols. Cambridge.
GROS 1976: P. Gros. *Aurea Templa: recherches sur l'architecture religieuse de Rome à l'époque d'Auguste*. Rome. [= Fasc. 231 of Bibliothèque des Écoles Françaises d'Athènes et de Rome].
HABICHT 1957: C. Habicht. "Eine Urkunde des Akarnanischen Bundes." *Hermes* 85: 102–109.
HAGY 1986: J.W. Hagy. "800 Years of Etruscan Ships." *IJNA* 15: 221–50.
HAHN 1958: H. Hahn. "Neue Untersuchungen zur Autobiographie des Kaisars Augustus." *NouvClio* 10: 137–48.
HARDIE 1970: C.H. Hardie. "Virgil." In *OCD*. 2nd ed. Oxford. Pp. 1123–28.
HARRINGTON 1984: D. Harrington. "The Battle of Actium—A Study in Historiography." *The Ancient World* 9: 59–64.
HAUPT 1884: H. Haupt. "Jahresberichte 49. Dio Cassius." *Philologus* 43: 678–701.
HEILMEYER 1970: W-D. Heilmeyer. *Korinthische Normalkapitelle. Studien zur Geschichte der römischen Architekturdekoration*. Heidelberg. [= Ergänzungsheft 16 of *Mitteilungen des Deutschen Archäologischen Instituts. Römische Abteilung*].
HELLENKEMPER 1987: H. Hellenkemper. "Die byzantinische Stadtmauer von Nikopolis in Epeiros. Ein kaiserlicher Bauauftrag des 5. oder 6. Jahrhunderts?" In E. Chrysos, ed. *Nicopolis I. Proceedings of the First International Symposium on Nicopolis (23–29 September 1984)*. Preveza. Pp. 143–51.
HELM 1913: R. Helm, ed. *Die Chronik des Hieronymus*. Vol. VII.1 ("Text") of *Eusebius Werke* in the series *Die Griechischen Christlichen Schriftsteller der Ersten Drei Jahrhunderte*. Leipzig.
HELM 1926: R. Helm, ed. *Die Chronik des Hieronymus*. Vol. VII.2 ("Lesearten der Hand schriften und Quellen—Kritischer Apparat zur Chronik") of *Eusebius Werke* in the series *Die Griechischen Christlichen Schriftsteller der Ersten Drei Jahrhunderte*. Leipzig.
HÖLSCHER 1984: T. Hölscher. "Actium und Salamis." *JDAI* 99: 187–214.
HÖLSCHER 1985: T. Hölscher. "Denkmäler der Schlacht von Actium" *Klio* 67: 81–102.
HOEPFNER 1987: W. Hoepfner. "Nikopolis—Zur Stadtgründung des Augustus." In E. Chrysos, ed. *Nicopolis I. Proceedings of the First International Symposium on Nicopolis (23–29 September 1984)*. Preveza. Pp. 129–33.
HOLMES 1928: T. Rice-Holmes. *The Architect of the Roman Empire*. Vol. I. Oxford.
HUBBARD 1975: M. Hubbard. *Propertius*. New York.
JOHNSON 1976: J.R. Johnson. "Augustan Propaganda: The Battle of Actium, Mark An-

tony's Will, the Fasti Capitolini Consulares, and Early Imperial Historiography." Diss., University of California at Los Angeles.

JONES 1924: H.L. Jones. *The Geography of Strabo*. Vol. III. New York.

JONES 1931: H.L. Jones. *The Geography of Strabo*. Rev. ed, vol. I. Cambridge, Mass.

JONES 1987: J.E. Jones. "Cities of Victory—Patterns and Parallels." In E. Chrysos, ed. *Nicopolis I. Proceedings of the First International Symposium on Nicopolis (23–29 September 1984)*. Preveza. Pp. 99–108.

JUCKER 1982: H. Jucker. "Apollo Palatinus und Apollo Actius auf augusteischen Münzen." *Museum Helveticum* 39: 82–100 with Plates 1–18.

KIENAST 1966: D. Kienast. *Untersuchungen zu den Kreigsflotten der römischen Kaiserzeit*. Bonn.

KIENAST 1982: D. Kienast. *Augustus: Prinzeps und Monarch*. Darmstadt.

KIRSTEN-KRAIKER 1967: E. Kristen and W. Kraiker. *Griechenlandkunde*. 5th ed., 2 vols. Heidelberg.

KIRSTEN 1987: E. Kristen. "The Origins of the First Inhabitants of Nikopolis." In E. Chrysos, ed. *Nicopolis I. Proceedings of the First International Symposium on Nicopolis (23–29 September 1984)*. Preveza. Pp. 91–98.

KLEINER 1988: F.S. Kleiner. "The Arch in Honor of C. Octavius and the Fathers of Augustus." *Historia* 37: 347–57.

KOS 1979: M.S. Kos. *Inscriptiones Latinae in Graecia repertae. Additamenta ad CIL III*. Vol. 5 of *Epigrafia e Antichità*. Studi a cura dell' Istituto di Storia Antica dell' Università di Bologna. Faenza.

KRAAY 1976: C. Kraay. "The Coinage of Nikopolis." *Numismatic Chronicle* 16, Series 7 [Vol. 136, continuous series]: 235–47.

KROMAYER 1897: J. Kromayer. "Die Entwicklung der römischen Flotte vom Seeräuberkriege des Pompeius bis zur Schlacht von Actium." *Philologus* 56: 426–91.

KROMAYER 1899: J. Kromayer. "Kleine Forschungen zur Geschichte des zweiten Triumvirats, VII. Der Feldzug von Actium und der sogenannte Verath der Cleopatra." *Hermes* 34: 1–54.

KROMAYER 1931: J. Kromayer. "Zur Schlacht von Actium." Vol. 4, Part 4 of *Antike Schlachtfelder: Bausteine zur einer antiken Kriegsgeschichte*. Berlin. Pp. 662–71.

KROMAYER 1933: J. Kromayer. "Actium: ein Epilog." *Hermes* 68: 361–83.

LAHUSEN 1983: G. Lahusen. *Untersuchungen zur Ehrenstatue in Rom*. Rome.

LAMBRECHTS 1953: P. Lambrechts. "La politique 'apollinienne' d'Auguste et le culte impérial." *NouvClio* 5: 65–82.

LAMMERT 1929: F. Lammert. "Spolia opima." *RE* 3.A: 1845–46.

LEAKE 1835: W.M. Leake. *Travels in Northern Greece*. Vol. I. London.

LEHMANN 1962: K. Lehmann. *The Hall of the Votive Gifts*. Vol. 4.2 of *Samothrace. Excavations Conducted by the Institute of Fine Arts of New York University*. New York.

LEROUX 1968: J. Leroux. "Les problèmes stratégiques de la bataille d'Actium." *Recherches de Philologie et de Linguistique* 2: 29–61.

LEVI 1933: M.A. Levi. *Ottaviano Capoparte: Storia Politica di Roma Durante le Ultime Lotte di Supremazia*. Vol. II. Firenze.

LINDER 1988: E. Linder. "The Ram of Athlit: Summary and Conclusions of a Multidisciplinary Study." *Sefunim* 7: 61–67.

LINDER-RAMON 1981: E. Linder and Y. Ramon. "A Bronze Ram from the Sea off Athlit, Israel." *Archaeology* 34.6: 62–64.

LLOYD 1972: A.B. Lloyd. "Triremes and the Saite Navy." *JEA* 58: 268–79.

MACKENDRICK 1983: P. MacKendrick. *The Mute Stones Speak. The Story of Archaeology in Italy*. 2nd ed. New York.

MALCOVATI 1969: H. Malcovati, ed. *Imperatoris Caesaris Augusti Operum Fragmenta*. 5th ed. Torino.

MANNSPERGER 1982: D. Mannsperger. "Annos undeviginti natus: Das Münzsymbol für Octavians Eintritt in die Politik." In *Praestat Interna, Festschrift für Ulrich Hausmann*. Tübingen. Pp. 331–37.

MANUWALD 1979: B. Manuwald. *Cassius Dio und Augustus: Philologische Untersuchungen zu den Büchern 45–46 des Dionischen Geschichteswerkes*. Wiesbaden. [= Vol. 14 of *Palingenesia. Monographien und Texte zur Klassischen Altertumswissenschaft*].

MCCREDIE 1986: J.R. McCredie. "A Ship for the Great Gods: Excavations Resume in Samothrace." *ASCSA Newsletter*, Fall: 13.

MCDONALD 1970: A.H. McDonald. "Livius." In *OCD*. 2nd ed. Oxford. Pp. 614–16.

MATTINGLY 1936: H. Mattingly. *Nerva to Hadrian*. Vol. 3 of *Coins of the Roman Empire in the British Museum*. London.

MEIGGS-LEWIS 1969: R. Meiggs and D. Lewis, eds. *A Selection of Greek Historical Inscriptions to the End of the Fifth Century B.C.* Oxford.

MILLAR 1964: F. Millar. *A Study of Cassius Dio.* Oxford.

MOMMSEN 1861: Th. Mommsen. "Die Chronik des Cassiodorus." *Abhandl. der königl. Sächs. Gesell. der Wissensch.* 8: 628.

MOMMSEN 1887: Th. Mommsen. *The Provinces of the Roman Empire from Caesar to Diocletian.* Trans., W.P. Dickson. Vol. I. New York.

MORRISON-WILLIAMS 1968: J.S. Morrison and R.T. Williams. *Greek Oared Ships 900–322 B.C.* Cambridge.

MORRISON 1979: J.S. Morrison. "The First Triremes." *Mariner's Mirror* 65: 53–63.

MORRISON 1984: J.S. Morrison. "Some Problems of Trireme Reconstruction." *IJNA* 13.3: 217.

MORRISON-COATES 1986: J.S. Morrison and J.F. Coates. *The Athenian Trireme. The History and Reconstruction of an Ancient Greek Warship.* Cambridge.

MURRAY 1982: W.M. Murray. "The Coastal Sites of Western Akarnania: A Topographical-Historical Survey." Diss., University of Pennsylvania.

MURRAY 1985: W.M Murray. "The Weight of Trireme Rams and the Price of Bronze in Fourth Century Athens." *GRBS* 26: 141–50.

MURRAY 1987: W.M. Murray. "Do Modern Winds Equal Ancient Winds?" *Mediterranean Historical Review* 2: 139–67.

MURRAY (forthcoming): W.M. Murray. "The Provenience and Date of the Athlit Ram: The Evidence of the Symbols." In *The Athlit Ram.* J.R. Steffy and L. Casson, eds. Collegeville, TX.

MYLONAS 1961: G.E. Mylonas. *Eleusis and the Eleusinian Mysteries.* Princeton.

NASH 1968: E. Nash. *Pictorial Dictionary of Ancient Rome.* 2nd ed., rev., 2 vols. New York.

NICOPOLIS 1987: E. Chrysos, ed. *Nicopolis I. Proceedings of the First International Symposium on Nicopolis (23–29 September 1984).* Preveza.

OBERHUMMER 1887: E. Oberhummer. *Akarnanien, Ambrakia, Amphilochien, Leukas im Altertum.* München.

OIKONOMIDOU 1975: M. Karamesine-Oikinomidou. *He Nomismatokopia tes Nikopoleos.* Vol. 79 of the *Bibliotheke tes en Athenais Archaiolkogikes Etaireias.* Athens.

OLIVER 1969: J.H. Oliver. "Octavian's Inscription at Nicopolis." *AJP* 90: 178–82.

ORMEROD 1924: H.A. Ormerod. *Ancient Piracy.* London.

PALADINI 1958: M.L. Paladini. *A proposito della tradizione poetica sulla battaglia di Azio.* Vol. 35 of *Collection Latomus.* Bruxelles.

PERRIN 1920: B. Perrin. *Plutarch's Lives.* Vol. IX. Cambridge, Mass.

PETER 1906: H. Peter. *Historicorum romanorum reliquiae.* Vol. II. Lipsiae.

PETSAS 1974a: Ph. Petsas. "Anaskaphe Romaikes Nikopoleos." *Praktika:* 79–88 with plates 60–70.

PETSAS 1974b: Ph. Petsas. *Ergon:* 50–53.

PHILADELPHEUS 1913: A. Philadelpheus. "Anaskaphai Nikopoleos." *Praktika:* 83–112.

PHILADELPHEUS 1921: A. Philadelpheus. "Anaskaphai Nikopoleos." *Praktika:* 42–44.

PHILADELPHEUS 1927: A. Philadelpheus. "Les fouilles de Nicopolis." *Acropole* 2: 222–29.

PHILADELPHEUS 1938: A. Philadelpheus. *Les Fouilles de Nicopolis, 1913–1926.* Athens.

PICARD 1928: Ch. Picard in the "Chronique de la sculpture étrusco-latine." *REL:* 213–33.

PICARD 1957: G. Ch. Picard. *Les trophées romaines: Contribution à l'histoire de la Religion et de l'Art triomphal de Rome.* Páris. [= Fasc. 187 of Bibliothèque des Écoles françaises d'Athènes et de Rome].

PLATNER-ASHBY 1929: S.B. Platner and T. Ashby. *A Topographical Dictionary of Ancient Rome.* London.

POMEY 1983: P. Pomey. "Remarques à propos de l'épiron d'Athlit." *Mariner's Mirror* 69: 247–48.

POLLINI (forthcoming): J. Pollini. "Man or God: Divine Assimilation in the Late Republic and Early Principate." In a collection of essays on Augustus (title undetermined). Berkeley.

PRITCHETT 1979: W.K. Pritchett. *The Greek State at War. Part III: Religion.* Berkeley.

PURCELL 1987: N. Purcell. "The Nicopolitan Synoecism and Roman Urban Policy." In E. Chrysos, ed. *Nicopolis I. Proceedings of the First International Symposium on Nicopolis (23–29 September 1984).* Preveza. Pp. 71–90.

RABAN 1981: A. Raban. "Recent Maritime Archaeological Research in Israel." *IJNA* 10: 287–308.

RABAN 1985: A. Raban. *Harbour Archaeology.* Vol. 257 of *British Archaeological Reports. International Series.*
RACKHAM 1948: H. Rackman. *Cicero. De Oratore.* Vol. II, rev. ed. Cambridge, Mass.
REINACH 1919: A. Reinach. "Tropaeum." *Dar. Sag.* V: 497–518.
REISCH 1893: Reisch. "Aktia." *RE* 1.2: 1213–14.
RHOMAIOS 1922: K. Rhomaios in *BCH* 46: 515.
RHOMAIOS 1925: K. Rhomaios. "Parartema 1922–25" to *Deltion* 9: 1–4.
RICHARDSON 1937: G.W. Richardson. "Actium." *JRS* 27: 153–64.
ROLFE 1951: J.C. Rolfe. *Suetonius.* Vol. I, rev. ed. Cambridge, Mass.
ROSSITER 1967: S. Rossiter, ed. *Blue Guide, Greece.* London.
ROSSITER 1981: S. Rossiter, ed. *Blue Guide, Greece.* 3rd ed. London.
SARIKAKIS 1965: Th. Sarakakis. "Aktia ta en Nikopolei." *Arch. Eph.*: 145–62.
SCHATZMAN 1932: P. Schatzman. *Kos.* Vol. I. Berlin.
SCHNEIDER 1914: K. Schneider. "Rednerbühne." *RE* I A: 450–61.
SCHOBER 1936: F. Schober. "Nikopolis." *RE* 17 A: 511–18.
SEAR 1982: F. Sear. *Roman Architecture.* Ithaca.
SHEAR 1937: T.L. Shear. *Hesperia* 6: 346–48.
SHERK 1984: R.K. Sherk. *Rome and the Greek East to the Death of Augustus.* Cambridge.
SHIPLEY 1950: F.W. Shipley. *Velleius Paterculus Compendium of Roman History. Res Gestae Divi Augusti.* Cambridge, Mass.
SOULE 1987: Ch. Tzouvara-Soule. "Latreies ste Nikopole." In E. Chrysos, ed. *Nicopolis I. Proceedings of the First International Symposium on Nicopolis (23–29 September 1984).* Preveza. Pp. 169–96.
STARR 1960: C.G. Starr. *The Roman Imperial Navy 31 B.C.–A.D. 324.* 2nd ed. New York.
STEFFY 1983: J.R. Steffy. "The Athlit Ram. A Preliminary Investigation of its Structure." *Mariner's Mirror* 69: 229–47.
SUTHERLAND 1984: C.H.V. Sutherland. *The Roman Imperial Coinage. From 31 B.C. to A.D. 69.* Vol. I, rev. ed. London.
SYME 1939: R. Syme. *The Roman Revolution.* Oxford.
TARN 1905: W.W. Tarn. "The Greek Warship." *JHS* 25: 139–56 and 175–224.
TARN 1910: W.W. Tarn. "The Dedicated Ship of Antigonus Gonatas." *JHS* 30: 189–208.
TARN 1930: W.W. Tarn. *Hellenistic Military & Naval Developments.* Cambridge.
TARN 1931: W.W. Tarn. "The Battle of Actium." *JRS* 21: 173–99.
TARN 1934: W.W. Tarn. "The Actium Campaign." In *The Augustan Empire. 44 B.C.–A.D. 70.* Vol. X of the *Cambridge Ancient History.* S.A. Cook, F.E. Adcock, and M.P. Charlesworth, eds. Cambridge. Pp. 100–106.
TARN 1938: W.W. Tarn. "Actium: A Note." *JRS* 28: 165–68.
THÉDENAT 1896: H. Thédenat. "Forum." *Dar. Sag.* II.2: 1277–1320.
THIEL 1946: J.H. Thiel. *Studies on the History of Roman Sea-Power in Republican Times.* Amsterdam.
THOMPSON-WYCHERLY 1972: H.A. Thompson and R.F. Wycherly. *The Agora of Athens.* Vol. XIV of *The Athenian Agora,* Princeton.
TORELLI 1982: M. Torelli. *Typology & Structure of Roman Historical Reliefs.* Ann Arbor.
TORR 1964: C. Torr. *Ancient Ships.* 2nd ed. Chicago.
TRILLMICH. 1988: W. Trillmich. "Münzpropaganda." In Staatliche Museen Preussischer Kulturbesitz. *Kaiser Augustus und die verlorene Republik. Eine Ausstellung in Martin-Gropius-Bau, Berlin, 7. Juni—14. August 1988.* Berlin. Pp. 474–528.
VOLKMANN 1958: H. Volkmann. *Cleopatra. A Study in Politics and Propaganda.* Trans., T.J. Cadoux. New York.
WARMINGTON 1959: E. Warmington, ed. *Remains of Old Latin.* Vol. IV. Cambridge, Mass.
WEIS 1976: A. Weis. "Nikopolis." In R. Stillwell, ed. *Princeton Encyclopedia of Classical Sites.* Princeton. Pp. 625–26.
WHICHER 1947: G.F. Whicher. *Selected Poems of Horace.* New York.
WILLIAMS 1982: R.D. Williams. "The Aeneid." In *Latin Literature.* Vol. II of E.J. Kinney and W.V. Clausen, eds. *The Cambridge History of Classical Literature.* Cambridge. Pp. 333–69.
ZANKER 1988: P. Zanker. *The Power of Images in the Age of Augustus.* Trans., A. Shapiro. Ann Arbor.
ZIMMERMANN 1974: H.-D. Zimmermann. "Freie Arbeit, Preise und Löhne." In E.C. Welskopf, ed. *Hellenische Poleis.* Vol. I. Berlin. Pp. 92–107.

INDEX OF MODERN AUTHORS

R. Amy: 101
P. Anastasi: ix

L. Basch: 21, 95, 99, 103, 104
H. Bauer: 120
C.E. Bennett: 144, 145
W.R. Biers: 86
M.E. Blake: 29, 58
A. Boëthius and J.B. Ward-Perkins: 86
G.W. Bowersock: 147
T.R.S. Broughton: 119
M. Brouskari: 103
P. Bruneau and J. Ducat 1: 8
P.A. Brunt and J.M. Moore: 138

R. Cagnat: 92
J.M. Carter: 2, 12, 18, 19, 62, 64, 72,
    73–74, 76, 77, 132, 133
E. Cary: 126
L. Casson (see also J.R. Steffy): 95, 96, 97,
    98, 100, 103, 109, 111, 116, 142, 150
C. Chipiez: 117
F. Coarelli: 117, 118, 120, 121, 122
A. Cook: 97
P.L. Couchoud and J. Svoronos: 116
M. Crawford: 120

A. Degrassi: 126, 128

V. Ehrenberg, and A.H.M. Jones: 6, 77,
    111, 128

A. Ferrabino: 2, 131, 133
C.J. Fordyce: 145
H. Frost: 21, 95, 103

J. Gagé: 2, 5, 11, 12, 14, 15, 16, 17, 62, 86,
    87, 115, 128, 129
C.F. Giuliani and P. Verduchi: 105, 120,
    121
E. Gjerstad: 117, 118
A.S.F. Gow and D.L. Page: 10

C. Habicht: 5
J.W. Hagy: 103
H. Hahn: 148

D. Harrington: 2, 132, 133, 138
H. Haupt: 148
W-D. Heilmeyer: 78
H. Hellenkemper: 153
T. Hölscher: 1, 93, 101
W. Hoepfner: 4, 12, 78, 127
T. Rice-Holmes: 121, 131
M. Hubbard: 145

J.R. Johnson: 1, 2, 130, 132, 133, 134, 135,
    137, 138, 140, 141
H.L. Jones: 5, 6, 10
J.E. Jones: 4, 5
H. Jucker: 18, 19, 84, 91

D. Kienast: 1, 123, 133, 144, 150
E. Kirsten and W. Kraiker: 11, 12, 14, 18,
    153
F.S. Kleiner: 87
M.S. Kos: 62
C. Kraay: 4
J. Kromayer: 2, 125, 131, 132, 133, 134,
    135, 137, 138, 139, 140, 141, 149

G. Lahusen: 121
P. Lambrechts: 85
F. Lammert: 92
W.M. Leake: 12–14
K. Lehmann: 92
J. Leroux: 2, 132, 133, 134, 135, 136, 138,
    140, 143
M.A. Levi: 131
E. Linder: 21, 95, 100
E. Linder and Y. Ramon: 21
A.B. Lloyd: 95

H. Malcovati: 1–2, 147, 148
B. Manuwald: 135, 148
J.R. McCredie: 116
A.H. McDonald: 146
R. Meiggs and D. Lewis: 92
F. Millar: 146, 148
Th. Mommsen: 4, 5
J.S. Morrison: 95, 104
J.S. Morrison and J.F. Coates: 95, 96, 97
J.S. Morrison and R.T. Williams: 96

W.M. Murray: 11, 21, 85, 100, 103, 104, 105, 127, 128
G.E. Mylonas: 126

E. Nash: 105, 117

M. Karamesine-Oikonomidou: 4, 12, 19, 78
J.H. Oliver: 18, 62, 76
H.A. Ormerod: 109

M.L. Paladini: 2, 132, 135, 144
B. Perrin: 10, 99, 137
H. Peter: 1, 147
Ph. Petsas: 19, 62, 64
A. Philadelpheus: 14, 15, 23, 62, 153
Ch. Picard: 11, 14
G. Ch. Picard: 17, 21, 91, 92, 101
S.B. Platner and T. Ashby: 117, 118
P. Pomey: 104
J. Pollini: 122
W.K. Pritchett: 92
N. Purcell: 5

A. Raban: 21
H. Rackham: 118
A. Reinach: 117
Reisch: 5
K. Rhomaios: 15, 62, 64, 72, 75, 78
G.W. Richardson: 2, 132, 133, 134, 138, 140
J.C. Rolfe: 10, 120
S. Rossiter: 18

Th. Sarikakis: 5, 12, 129
K. Schneider: 117, 118, 119
F. Schober: 5, 15, 16, 153
T.L. Shear: 92
F.W. Shipley: 122
Ch. Tzouvara-Soule: 6, 12
C.G. Starr: 143, 145
J.R. Steffy: 21, 95
J.R. Steffy and L. Casson: 95
C.H.V. Sutherland: 111, 117, 122, 123
R. Syme: 2, 127, 147, 151

W.W. Tarn: 2, 97, 99, 115, 116, 125, 131, 133, 134, 135, 136, 137, 138, 140, 141, 143
H. Thédenat: 117, 123
J.H. Thiel: 141
H.A. Thompson and R.E. Wycherly: 92
M. Torelli: 105, 120
C. Torr: 97, 103
W. Trillmich: 2, 91

H. Volkmann: 1, 18, 126

E. Warmington: 117
A. Weis: 12
G.F. Whicher: 145
R.D. Williams: 145

P. Zanker: 1, 2, 91, 93, 101, 111, 117, 121, 122
H.-D. Zimmermann: 127

GENERAL INDEX

Actian Games (see *Aktia*)
Actian straits: 3
Actian War: ix, 1, 4, 6, 10, 16, 56, 62, 77,
  90, 99, 116, 131, 136, 137, 138, 139,
  140, 148, 154
Actium: 93, 100, 101, 105, 116, 117, 121,
  125, 127, 128, 129, 136, 137, 140,
  142, 143, 144, 145, 146, 150
  a) Battle of: ix, x, 2, 15, 18, 40, 86, 90,
    99, 100, 101, 114, 125, 129, 131–51,
    154
  b) Cape: ix, 1, 5, 11, 99, 116, 132, 136
Aemilius Lepidus, M.: 120
Aemilius Paulus, L.: 120
Aemilius Paulus, M.: 117
Aetolia: 5, 85
after-end (of a ram): 34, 41, 44, 51, 55
after cowl curvature (of a ram): 34
Agrippa, M. Vipsanius: 2, 3, 72, 117, 122,
  123, 125, 134, 136, 138, 139, 140,
  143, 145, 147, 149
Aiginetans: 115
Ajax (at Salamis): 115
Akarnania: 5, 85, 127
akrostolion: 115
akroteria: 92, 115
Aktia (Actian Games): 5, 6, 12, 90, 125,
  129, 153, 154
Alarich: 153
Alexander III (of Macedonia): 96, 124, 126
Alexandria: 126, 127, 129, 138, 139
Ali Pasha: 11
Ambracian Gulf: ix, 3, 128, 131, 132, 153
Anaglypha Traiani: 105, 110, 111, 113
Antiate rams: 109, 118, 120
Antigonus Gonatas: 115
Antistius Vetus, C.: 17, 19, 91
Antium: 109, 110, 117
Antonius, M. (censor in 97 B.C.): 109,
  118, 119, 120
Antony (M. Antonius, the triumvir): ix, 1,
  2, 3, 4, 34, 56, 99, 109, 120, 121,
  122, 124, 125, 126, 129, 131, 132,
  133, 134, 135, 136, 137, 139, 140,
  141, 142, 143, 144, 145, 146, 147,
  149, 150, 151, 154

Aphaia (see Athena, Aiginetan)
Apollo: 87, 90, 116
  a) Aktios: 5, 6, 9, 11, 12, 91, 99, 125
  b) Delian: 115
  c) sacred hill at Nikopolis: 6, 11, 12, 16,
    90
  d) statue at Campsite Memorial: 11, 17,
    91
Apollonia: 128
Arausio (Orange): 93, 101
Asklepieion at Kos: 86, 124
Asklepios (at Kos): 149
Athena
  a) Aiginetan: 115
  b) at Sounion: 115
Athens: 4, 78, 92, 96, 109, 125, 126
Athlit ram: 21, 34, 41, 44, 87, 95, 100, 101,
  103, 104, 105, 111, 113, 114, 127
Augustan foot (at the Campsite
  Memorial): 78, 84
Augustus: x, 1, 4, 56, 77, 99, 101, 110,
  111, 115, 122, 123, 127, 129, 136,
  137, 139, 143, 144, 145, 146, 147,
  148, 149, 151, 154
Augustus' *Memoirs*: 56, 71, 99, 125, 135,
  136, 137, 138, 139, 144, 146, 147,
  148, 150

baseline (BL): 42, 44, 45–49, 61
Basilica Aemilia et Fulvia: 120
bellum: 137, 138, 139
bireme (also *dikrotos*): 96
bottom plate (of a ram): 34, 41, 101
Bremerhaven ram: 56, 103, 104, 105, 111,
  113, 114, 124
Brundisium: 126, 134, 144
burned (war)ships (see ships)
Byzantion (Constantinople): 10, 72, 153

caementum/caementa: 29, 57, 58, 74
Caesar, C. Julius: 119, 120, 121
Calpurnius Piso, Cn.: 147
camp(site) (Octavian's): ix, 2, 6, 9, 10, 11,
  12, 14, 34, 57, 71, 72, 84, 90, 91, 99,
  114, 124, 134, 143, 144, 154, 155
Campsite Memorial: passim

Campus Martius: 90
Cannae: 93
Cantabrian War: 147
Cape Tainaron: 139
capital (at the Campsite Memorial): 84, 90
  a) Corinthian: 14, 22, 78
  b) Doric: 74
Carthaginian(s): 96, 98, 117
Cicero, M. Tullius: 109, 119, 128
Cilician pirates: 109, 119
clamp cuttings (at the Campsite
    Memorial)
  a) double T: 29, 57, 58
  b) rectangular: 127
  c) swallow-tail(ed): 85, 127
  d) wooden: 85
class (ship class): 40, 93, 95–104, 105, 111,
    113, 114, 135, 139, 142, 143, 144,
    146, 149, 150
Cleopatra: ix, 1, 3, 4, 56, 124, 126, 132,
    133, 136, 137, 140, 142, 144, 145,
    147, 149, 150
Cleopatra's squadron: 3, 134, 136, 139,
    140, 142, 154
Coates, J.: 86, 95, 104
column base (at the Campsite Memorial):
    74, 78, 84, 90
columns (at the Campsite Memorial): 15,
    22, 64, 74, 78, 80, 84, 85, 90
columna rostrata: 111, 117, 119
Comitium: 117, 118, 119
Constantinople (see Byzantion)
Corcyra: 3, 128
core
  a) concrete (of the podium at the
      Campsite Memorial): 23, 29, 57, 58,
      59, 74
  b) socket or cutting: 34, 41, 43, 45–49,
      50, 58, 99
Corinth: 4, 95, 139, 140
Cornelius Lentulus, Cossus: 122, 123
cowl (of a ram): 41, 43, 58, 101
Curators in charge of the Athenian
    shipyards: 105
Curia Iulia: 118

Dalmatia: 93
dekanaia (the "ten ship dedication" at
    Actium): 6, 99, 116, 125, 142
dekeres (see also "ten"): 99
Delion: 92
Delos: 115, 116
Delphi: 4, 92, 115
Demetrius Poliorcetes: 97, 116
dikrotos (see bireme)
Dionysius II (of Syracuse): 96
Divus Iulius
  a) temple: 29, 105, 121, 127, 128
dowel cutting (at the Campsite Memorial):
    59, 84

driving center (of a ram): 101, 114
Duillius, C.: 111, 116, 117
Dyrrachium: 126

Ecnomus, Battle of: 135
Egypt: 72, 126, 127, 130, 133
Egyptian ships: 136
"eight": 96, 142, 146, 149
eikosoros: 96
"eleven": 96, 99, 142
Epirus: 3, 4, 12, 85, 124, 138
Eurykles: 147, 149
Eutychos and Nikon (statues at the
    Campsite Memorial): 10, 16, 72, 93,
    153

facing blocks (on a concrete core): 23, 29,
    57, 58
Fasti Antiates: 128
Fasti Arvalium: 90
Fasti Praenestini: 128
"fifteen": 96, 116
"five": 96, 97, 98, 99, 104, 105, 109, 111,
    113, 114, 117, 134, 135, 136, 140,
    142, 143, 150
"forty": 97, 98, 116
Forum Romanum: 92, 105, 109, 110, 111,
    117, 119, 121, 122, 143
Forum Iulii (Fréjus, France): 125
"four": 96, 97, 98, 104, 105, 109, 111, 113,
    114, 142, 146
Fulvius Nobilior, M.: 120

Gabinius, A.: 93
galeasses: 98
Geiserich: 153
Goths: 23

Hadrian (Publius Aelius Hadrianus): 105,
    109, 110, 120
Hannibal: 93
Hannibalic War: 93
hedos ti. . . hypaithrion: 11, 19, 85, 90
Hemicyclium (Antonian Rostra, 45/44
    B.C.): 119, 120, 121
hemiolia: 109, 114
hopla: 92

Illyrians: 93
inscription (on the Campsite Memorial): 6,
    15, 16, 18, 19, 22, 55, 59, 62–77,
    85–86, 128, 129, 138, 154
Isthmus: 115

Janus Geminus: 127, 147
Jupiter Feretrius: 92
Justinian: 23

Kanellopoulos Museum: 103
Kassope (Epirus): 127

keel: 100
keelson: 100
Kos: 86, 116

Lake Trasimenus: 93
Leukas: 5, 125, 136, 138, 139, 140
Liburna: 147
Liburnian(s) (galleys): 95, 144, 145, 146,
    147, 149, 151
Lollius Palicanus: 118, 120
ludi Veneris: 148

"MD" (measuring device): 42, 43, 44, 55
Macedonia: 4, 125
Maecenas, C.: 144
Maenius, C.: 117, 118
manubiae: 109, 119
marble (at the Campsite Memorial)
    a) moldings: 80, 85
    b) revetment slab: 80, 85
    c) sculpture: 80
Mars: 10, 11, 12, 15, 17, 71, 85, 86, 87, 90,
    91, 92
Marsala (Sicily): 95, 103
Mausoleum of Augustus: 29
Methone: 125, 136, 139, 140
Michalitsi (Mt.): 11, 12, 13, 14, 153
Miliadis, I.: 16, 62, 64, 75
monokrotos (see also "one"): 99, 114
Mylae: 117, 144
Myonnesus, Battle of (190 B.C.): 141
myoparo: 109

Naevius Surdinus, L.: 121, 122
natalis Caesaris: 90
Naulochus, Battle of: 72, 117
naval dedications (see also spoils): 91,
    115, 116, 125
    a) anchors: 21, 91, 92, 93, 115
    b) figureheads: 93, 115, 146
    c) in stoas (and porticos): 91, 92–93
    d) in temples: 92–93, 115, 116
    e) misc. naval gear: 93, 115
    f) rams (see also the entries at Rostra,
        etc.): 115, 116
    g) ropes: 93, 115
    h) ships: 115, 116
naval museum (the *neoria* at Actium): 5, 6,
    11, 116
neorion at Delos: 116
Neptune: 10, 11, 12, 15, 17, 71, 85, 86, 87,
    88, 90, 91, 115
Nikon (see Eutychos)
Nikopolis (Egypt): 126
Nikopolis (Epirus): 4, 5, 6, 9, 10, 11, 12,
    15, 18, 19, 21, 29, 77, 91, 124, 125,
    126, 127, 128, 129, 153

a) grove: 5, 11, 72, 85
b) gymnasium: 5, 9, 11
c) museum: 78, 80
d) stadium: 5, 11, 12, 153
e) theater: 9, 12, 153
"nine": 96, 98, 99, 104, 115, 142, 146

Octavian: ix, 1, 2, 3, 4, 5, 6, 9, 10, 17, 72,
    77, 84, 86, 90, 93, 98, 99, 101, 111,
    114, 115, 116, 117, 121, 122, 123,
    124, 125, 126, 127, 128, 130, 131,
    134, 136, 138, 139, 140, 141, 142,
    143, 144, 145, 146, 147, 148, 149,
    150, 151, 153, 154
Offset: 44, 45–49
oikistes: 129
Olympias (trireme replica): 95, 98, 99, 104,
    105, 113
"one": 99, 100, 114
ornamenta triumphalia: 123

pace parta terra marique ("after peace had
    been secured on land and sea"):
    128, 130, 138
Pannonia: 123
Papirius, L.: 92
Patras: 4, 125, 136, 138, 139, 140
Pelusium: 126
penteconter (*pentekontoros*): 96
Philip V (of Macedonia): 92
Philippi: 126
Philippus, L. Marcius: 121
Phoenicia: 95
Piraeus: 96
Pirate War: 117
Plancus, L. Munatius: 149
Platorinus (see Sulpicius)
podium (at the Campsite Memorial): 15,
    16, 18, 19, 21, 22, 23, 29, 57, 58, 60,
    74, 77, 78, 80, 85, 91, 93, 154
polyreme: 40, 97, 98, 116, 144, 149, 150
Pompey (Cn. Pompeius Magnus): 110,
    116, 117
portico (see also stoa): 16, 77, 84, 86, 92
Porticus Octavia: 93
Poseidon (see Neptune)
Praeneste, sanctuary of Fortuna
    Primagenia: 86
Preveza: x, 2, 12, 18, 153
proembolion: 103
propaganda: 1, 3, 6, 115, 124, 131, 136,
    149, 150
Ptolemy II Philadelphos: 97, 142
Ptolemy IV Philopator: 97
Ptolemy V Epiphanes: 100, 116
Ptolemy VI Philometor: 100

Quirinus: 92

ram (see also Turin ram, Bremerhaven
    ram, Athlit ram)
  a) display: 15, 17, 19, 57, 84, 93, 117,
    124, 144
  b) in the Fitzwilliam Museum: 103
Ramon, Y.: 21
Rhion: 115
Rome: 29, 77, 93, 101, 118, 121, 124, 127,
    128, 129, 143, 144, 145, 147
rooftiles (see tiles)
rostra (rams): 86, 93, 109
rostra (used to refer to ram displays other
    than the Republican speaker's
    platform in its various phases): 105,
    110, 121, 122, 123, 124
  a) *Rostra Aedis Divi Iulii*: 105, 110, 111,
    124
  b) *Rostra Augusti*: 29, 105, 109, 121, 122,
    124
    1) rectangular/rectilinear Rostra (built
      in front of the Hemicyclium): 110,
      119, 120, 121, 123
  c) Republican Rostra (or Rostra): 109,
    117, 118, 119
    1) rectilinear platform (corresponding
      to Maenius' Rostra): 118
    2) rounded Rostra: 118, 120
rostral column (see *columna rostrata*)
rowing unit: 97, 98, 99

Samians: 115
Samnites: 92
Samothrace: 116
  a) Hall of Votive Gifts: 92
  b) Sanctuary of the Great Gods: 92, 115
Scipio Africanus, P. Cornelius: 125
"seven": 96, 99, 111, 117, 142
Severus, L. Septimius: 12, 19, 80, 90, 119
Sextus Pompey (Sextus Pompeius Magnus
    Pius): 117, 121, 143, 144, 149
ships (at the Battle of Actium)
  a) burned: 132–35, 134, 140, 141
  b) captured: 56, 72, 111, 125, 134, 135,
    137–41, 142
  c) destroyed: 135, 136, 137–41, 142
shipsheds: 96
Sidon: 96
"six": 96, 98, 99, 111, 142, 144, 146, 147,
    150
"sixteen": 96–97, 98
Smyrtoula: 2
socket profile: 51, 55, 100, 101
socket (at the Campsite Memorial): 19, 21,
    23, 29, 34, 40, 41, 42, 43, 44, 45–51,
    55, 56, 57, 58, 59, 64, 73, 74, 75, 77,
    78, 86, 91, 99, 100, 103, 111, 113,
    114, 142, 143, 150, 153, 154
  a) flare: 43, 58, 59
Sosius, C.: 140
Sounion: 115

Spain: 147
Sparta: 4
spoils
  a) battle: 10, 15, 72, 92, 101, 125, 126,
    127
  b) naval: 10, 11, 71, 72, 86, 91, 93, 101,
    109, 118, 125, 138, 141
spolia opima: 92
Steffy, J.R.: 100, 101
Stoa Poikile (in Athens): 92
Stoa of the Athenians at Delphi: 92, 115
stoa (at the Campsite Memorial): 16, 23,
    74, 77–85, 86, 90, 91, 93, 154
stylobate (of the stoa at the Campsite
    Memorial): 14, 19, 22, 74, 85, 154
Sulla (L. Cornelius Sulla Felix): 118
Sulpicius Platorinus, C.: 122, 123
Surdinus (see Naevius)
synoecism (*synoikismos*): 5, 126, 127
Syracuse: 96, 104
Syria: 126

tailpiece (of a ram): 41, 55, 100, 101, 103
Tarius Rufus, L.: 140
temenos: 5, 11, 15, 16, 17, 90
Temple (of Apollo and/or Neptune) at the
    Campsite Memorial: 14–15, 16, 18,
    22, 23, 80, 87, 90
templum: 11, 16
"ten": 96, 98, 99, 104, 113, 136, 142, 146,
    149, 150
Theater of Pompey: 93
Thebes: 92
Thermon: 92
"thirteen": 96, 99, 142
"thirty": 97, 98, 99, 142
"three" (*trieres, triremis* or trireme): 95, 96,
    97, 100, 103, 104, 109, 110, 111, 113,
    114, 115, 116, 117, 139, 143, 146
Tiberius (Ti. Julius Caesar Augustus): 123,
    146
tiles (rooftiles at the Campsite Memorial):
    84
  a) Corinthian: 15, 80, 85
  b) Laconian: 15, 80, 85
tithe (at the Campsite Memorial). 56, 138,
    139, 142, 154
Titius, M.: 149
Tivoli, sanctuary of Hercules Victor: 86
Totila: 153
triaconter (*triakontoros*): 96
triemiolia: 142
triple triumph: 128
trireme, *trieres, triremis* (see "three")
triumph (naval): 109, 116, 118–19
trophy: 16, 122
  a) naval: 116
  b) St. Bertrand: 17, 91
trough (of a ram): 29, 34, 41, 43, 55
Turin ram: 103

"twelve": 99, 142
"twenty": 97, 98, 99, 142
"twenty-four": 98
"two" (see also bireme, *dikrotos*): 98, 109,
    114, 146
Tyre: 96

Vandals: 120
Vanderpool, E.: 18
Victory City/Cities: 4, 9, 116, 124, 129
Volscians: 117

warships (dedicated): 6, 9, 99, 115
waterspout (at the Campsite Memorial):
    80, 84

"x" line: 41, 44, 55
Xerxes: 115

"y" line (or axis): 41, 42, 44, 49, 50, 51
"y–y" interval: 56, 57

Zea: 96

INDEX OF ANCIENT CITATIONS

ANCIENT AUTHORS:

Ael. *VH* 6.12	96	Dio 43.49.1	119
Antipatros in *Anth. Pal.* 9.553	5	Dio 43.49.2	120, 121
App. *BC.* 3.51	121	Dio 44.35.3	148
App. *BC.* 5.98–99	144	Dio 45.7.1	148
App. *BC.* 5.106	144	Dio 46.29.2	121
App. *BC.* 5.111	145, 147	Dio 49.18.6	121
App. *BC.* 5.139	149	Dio 50.1.1–2	148
App. *Hann.* 7.11	93	Dio 50.3.1–3	149
App. *Illyr.* 28	93	Dio 50.3.2	147
App. *Mith.* 92	109	Dio 50.9.2–3	2
Arr. *Anab.* 2.22.3–5	96	Dio 50.11.1–51.15.5	2
Ath. 5.203d	99, 142	Dio 50.11.3	2
Ath. 5.203e–204c	97	Dio 50.12	3
Augustus *Memoirs* [= *Commentarii de vita*		Dio 50.13	3, 138, 139, 140
sua or the *Autobiography*]		Dio 50.14.1–2	138, 140
MALCOVATI 1969, pp. 84–97:		Dio 50.15	3, 132, 134
#6	148	Dio 50.18.4–19.5	146
#8	148	Dio 50.19.3	143
#9	148	Dio 50.23.2–3	146, 149
#10	148	Dio 50.29.1–4	146
#12	148	Dio 50.30.1	3, 138, 139
#17	2, 148	Dio 50.31.4–6	3
PETER 1906, pp. 54–64:		Dio 50.32.1–35.6	146
#2	71	Dio 50.32	3, 98
#4	71	Dio 50.33.1–3	3
#5	71	Dio 50.33.8	145
#6	148	Dio 50.34–35	4, 134
#7	148	Dio 50.34.1	134
#8	148	Dio 51.1.1–2	1, 99
#10	148	Dio 51.1.3	5, 9, 19, 85, 87
#15	2, 148	Dio 51.1.4–5	4, 125, 129
#20	71	Dio 51.2.1–2	125
Augustus *Res Gestae* 3.4	56, 99,	Dio 51.3.1–4	4, 125
	101, 111, 139	Dio 51.4.1	125, 126
Augustus *Res Gestae* 8.1; 15.1,3; 21.3	77	Dio 51.4.2–5.1	4
Augustus *Res Gestae* 25.2	137	Dio 51.4.5	126
Cassiodorus [under the consuls		Dio 51.4.6	126
of the year 30 B.C.]:		Dio 51.4.8	126
MOMMSEN 1861, p. 628	129	Dio 51.8.3	149
Cic. *Amic.* 25 (96)	119	Dio 51.18.1	126
Cic. *Att.* 4.16.14	120	Dio 51.19	127
Cic. *ad Brut.* 1.15.7	121	Dio 51.20.6	128
Cic. *Phil.* 2.28 (68)	117	Dio 51.21	128
Cic. *de Orat.* 3.3.10	109, 118	Dio 51.22	128

Dio 54.28.2	123	Plut. *Ant.* 55.1	149
Dio 54.31.3–4	123	Plut. *Ant.* 57.1	2
Diod. 12.70.5	92	Plut. *Ant.* 57.3	147
Diod. 16.44.6	96	Plut. *Ant.* 58	2, 149
Florus 1.11	110, 118, 120	Plut. *Ant.* 61–68	2, 146
Florus 2.21	2	Plut. *Ant.* 61.1	99, 134, 139
Florus 2.21.4	139	Plut. *Ant.* 61.2	134
Florus 2.21.5	99, 134	Plut. *Ant.* 64.1–2	3, 99, 136, 142
Florus 2.21.5–7	146	Plut. *Ant.* 65.2	145
Florus 2.21.6	134, 135	Plut. *Ant.* 65.3	10
Florus 2.21.7–8	4	Plut. *Ant.* 65.3–5	3
Hdt. 3.59.3	115	Plut. *Ant.* 65.4	145
Hdt. 8.121.1	115	Plut. *Ant.* 65.4–66.2	98
Hieronymus [under the year 29 B.C.]:		Plut. *Ant.* 66	3
HELM 1913, p. 163 = 245F, and		Plut. *Ant.* 66.2	134, 147
1926, p. 480 f)	129	Plut. *Ant.* 66.3	136, 147
Hor. *Carm.* 1.37	2, 134, 144	Plut. *Ant.* 66.5	136, 140
Hor. *Epod.* 1	144	Plut. *Ant.* 67.2–3	147
Hor. *Epod.* 1.1–4	145, 147	Plut. *Ant.* 67.5	139
Hor. *Epod.* 9	1–2, 131, 133, 137, 144	Plut. *Ant.* 68.1	2, 56, 99, 125,
Hor. *Epod.* 9 (lines 17–20)	132, 133		134, 135, 137, 148
Timaeus Grammaticus *Lexicon*	11	Plut. *Ant.* 68.3	4
Livy 8.14.12	118, 125	Plut. *Caes.* 29.3	120
Livy 10.7.9	92	Plut. *C. Gracch.* 5.3	119
Livy 10.46.7–8	92	Plut. *Dem.* 43.5	97
Livy 22.57.10	93	Plut. *Pomp.* 28	117
Livy 23.23.6	92	Polyb. 1.20.10	109
Livy 28.30.5	98	Polyb. 1.26.7	135
Livy 30.25.5–7	98	Polyb. 5.8.9	92
Livy 30.43.12	125	Pomponius (in *Dig.* I.2.2)	122
Livy 37.30.7	141	Prop. 2.1	101
Livy 38.43.11	92	Prop. 3.11	2, 145
Livy 42.20.1	117	Prop. 3.11.44	145, 147
Livy *Per.* 132	138, 146	Prop. 4.6	2, 145
Mamertinus in *Paneg. Lat.* 11.9	5	Prop. 4.6.47–50 ·	145–46
Moschion (quoted in Ath. 5.209e)	115	Quint. *Inst.* 1.7.12	117
Orosius 6.19.5–12	2, 3, 147	Servius Italicus *Punica* 6.663–667	117
Orosius 6.19.6	2, 134	Servius (*ad. Georg.* 3.29)	72
Orosius 6.19.7	3, 138	Servius *Verg. Aen.* 3.276	5
Orosius 6.19.8	134	Strabo 7.7.6	5, 6, 10, 87, 99
Orosius 6.19.9	134	Strabo 10.2.2	5
Orosius 6.19.10	3	Suet. *Aug.* 2	71
Orosius 6.19.11	134, 136	Suet. *Aug.* 17.3	4, 126, 147
Orosius 6.19.12	135	Suet. *Aug.* 18.2	5, 6, 9, 71, 87, 91
Paus. 1.15.4	92	Suet. *Aug.* 27	71
Paus. 1.29.1	115	Suet. *Aug.* 42	71
Paus. 5.23.3	5	Suet. *Aug.* 62	71
Paus. 7.18.8–9	5	Suet. *Aug.* 72–73	124
Paus. 8.24.11	5	Suet. *Aug.* 74	71
Paus. 10.38.4	5	Suet. *Aug.* 85	147
Petron. *Sat.* 30.1	117	Suet. *Aug.* 96.2	10
Philippus in *Anth. Pal.* 6.236	10	Suet. *Caes.* 55	71
Pliny *HN* 4.5	4	Suet. *Nero* 38	92
Pliny *HN* 7.207	96	Suet. *de Grammaticis* 16	71
Pliny *HN* 34.11	117	Syncellus [under the year 30 B.C.]:	
Pliny *HN* 34.13	72	DINDORF 1829, p. 583, lines	
Pliny *HN* 34.20	118	17–18 = p. 308 C	129
Pliny *HN* 35.2.7	92	Tac. *Ann.* 4.5.1	125
Plut. *Ant.* 32.3	144	Tac. *Ann.* 5.10	4
Plut. *Ant.* 35.4	149	Thuc. 1.13.2–3	95

Thuc. 2.92.5	115	Vell. 2.84–85	2
Thuc. 6.13.1	128	Vell. 2.85.3	3
Thuc. 7.70	104	Vell. 2.96.3	123
Varro *Ling.* 6.4	120	Vell. 2.130.5	146
Varro *Rust.* 1.2.9	119	Verg. *G.* 3.8–48	145
Veg. 4.33	145, 146	Verg. *Aen.* 8.694–695, 710	134
Veg. 4.37	147	Verg. *Aen.* 8.671–713	2, 144–45
Vell. 2.61.3	121, 122	Zonaras 10.30 (p. I 526 D)	5, 10, 72, 153
Vell. 2.84.1–2	2, 3, 138, 139, 146	Zosimus 2.22.1–2, 24.1	95

INSCRIPTIONS:

CIL VI 701 and 702 [= *ILS*³ 91]	77	DEGRASSI 1963, pp. 496–97	128
CIL VI 31611 [= *ILS*³ 65, =		DURRBACH 1929, No. 442 B	115
WARMINGTON 1959,		*IG* II² 839, line 72	115
pp. 128–31]	117	*IG* II² 1629, lines 808–11	96
DEGRASSI 1963, pp. 112–13		*IG* II² 1640; 1641; 1648; 1649	115
[= EHRENBERG-JONES 1976, p. 45]		*ILS*³ 65, see *CIL* VI 31611	
(*Fasti Praenestini*)	128	*ILS*³ 81 [= EHRENBERG-JONES 1976,	
DEGRASSI 1963, p. 208		p. 57, #17]	77
[= EHRENBERG-JONES 1976,		*ILS*³ 91, see *CIL* 701 and 702	
p. 50] (*Fasti Antiates*)	128	MEIGGS-LEWIS 1969, #25	115

PUBLICATIONS

OF

The American Philosophical Society

The publications of the American Philosophical Society consist of PROCEEDINGS, TRANSACTIONS, MEMOIRS, and YEAR BOOK.

THE PROCEEDINGS contains papers which have been read before the Society in addition to other papers which have been accepted for publication by the Committee on Publications. In accordance with the present policy one volume is issued each year, consisting of four quarterly numbers, and the price is $24.00 net per volume. Individual copies may be purchased at $10.00 per copy.

THE TRANSACTIONS, the oldest scholarly journal in America, was started in 1769. In accordance with the present policy each annual volume is a collection of monographs, each issued as a part. The current annual subscription price is $70.00 net per volume. Individual copies of the TRANSACTIONS are offered for sale.

Each volume of the MEMOIRS is published as a book. The titles cover the various fields of learning; most of the recent volumes have been historical. The price of each volume is determined by its size and character, but subscribers are offered a 20 per cent discount.

The YEAR BOOK is of considerable interest to scholars because of the reports on grants for research and to libraries for this reason and because of the section dealing with the acquisitions of the Library. In addition it contains the Charter and Laws, and lists of members, and reports of committees and meetings. The YEAR BOOK is published about April 1 for the preceding calendar year. The current price is $12.00. A separate volume of GRANTEES' REPORTS is published annually. The listed price is $10.00.

An author desiring to submit a manuscript for publication should send it to the Editor, American Philosophical Society, 104 South Fifth Street, Philadelphia, Pa. 19106.

www.ingramcontent.com/pod-product-compliance
Lightning Source LLC
Chambersburg PA
CBHW080925100426
42812CB00007B/2378